ALLIGATORS IN B-FLAT

Florida History and Culture

UNIVERSITY PRESS OF FLORIDA

Florida A&M University, Tallahassee
Florida Atlantic University, Boca Raton
Florida Gulf Coast University, Ft. Myers
Florida International University, Miami
Florida State University, Tallahassee
New College of Florida, Sarasota
University of Central Florida, Orlando
University of Florida, Gainesville
University of North Florida, Jacksonville
University of South Florida, Tampa
University of West Florida, Pensacola

University Press of Florida | Gainesville · Tallahassee · Tampa · Boca Raton
Pensacola · Orlando · Miami · Jacksonville · Ft. Myers · Sarasota

For the astonishing
Gator Gal —
the one + only
Angie DeLeón.

ALLIGATORS
IN
B-FLAT

Improbable Tales from the Files of Real Florida

Thanks for your
great j-school work

Jeff Klinkenberg

Foreword by Raymond Arsenault and Gary R. Mormino

Jeff Klinkenberg

St. Pete 2015

VIVA FLORIDA 500
1513–2013

A Florida Quincentennial Book

Many of the photographs in this book are reproduced courtesy of the *St. Petersburg Times*, in which they first appeared. Unless otherwise specified, the photographer is Jeff Klinkenberg.

18   17   16   15   14   13   6   5   4   3   2   1

Library of Congress Cataloging-in-Publication Data
Klinkenberg, Jeff.
Alligators in b-flat : improbable tales from the files of real Florida / Jeff Klinkenberg ; foreword by Raymond Arsenault and Gary R. Mormino.
p. cm. — (The Florida History and Culture Series)
ISBN 978-0-8130-4450-7 (alk. paper)
1. Florida—History—Anecdotes. 2. Florida—Biography—Anecdotes. 3. Florida—
Social life and customs—Anecdotes. I. Arsenault, Raymond. II. Mormino, Gary Ross, 1947– III. Title. IV. Series: Florida history and culture series.
F311.6.K55 2013
975.9—dc23
2012046691

The University Press of Florida is the scholarly publishing agency for the State University System of Florida, comprising Florida A&M University, Florida Atlantic University, Florida Gulf Coast University, Florida International University, Florida State University, New College of Florida, University of Central Florida, University of Florida, University of North Florida, University of South Florida, and University of West Florida.

University Press of Florida
15 Northwest 15th Street
Gainesville, FL 32611-2079
http://www.upf.com

For Eugene C. Patterson

Contents

Foreword

Alligators in B-Flat: Improbable Tales from the Files of Real Florida is the latest volume of a series devoted to the study of Florida history and culture. During the past half-century, the burgeoning population and increased national and international visibility of Florida have sparked a great deal of popular interest in the state's past, present, and future. As a favorite destination of countless tourists and as the new home for millions of retirees and transplants, modern Florida has become a demographic, political, and cultural bellwether. Florida has also emerged as a popular subject and setting for scholars and writers. The Florida History and Culture Series provides an attractive and accessible format for Florida-related books. From avenging hurricanes to disputed elections, from tales of the Everglades to profiles of Sunbelt cities, Florida is simply irresistible.

The University Press of Florida is committed to the creation of an eclectic but carefully crafted set of books that will provide the field of Florida studies with a new focus to prompt Florida writers to consider the broader implications and context of their works. The series includes standard academic monographs, as well as works of synthesis, memoirs, and anthologies. And while the series features books of historical interest, authors researching Florida's environment, politics, literature, and popular or material culture are encouraged to submit their manuscripts as well. Each book offers a distinct personality and voice, but the ultimate goal of the series is to foster a broad sense of community and collaboration among Florida scholars.

Alligators in B-Flat reintroduces readers to the lyrical prose of Jeff Klinkenberg. Floridians who appreciate great writing will recognize Klinkenberg, who for three and a half decades has labored in Florida's vineyards for the *St. Petersburg Times*, now the *Tampa Bay Times*. His newspaper columns introduce natives and newcomers to some of the oddest, most eccentric, and interesting characters found between the Perdido River and Key West docks. If Thomas Wolfe could never go home again and searched in vain for the "lost, wind grieved, ghost," Klinkenberg reminds us that home in Florida is never far away. Magically, he takes us to 1965 Miami, to his Miami elementary school, along the paper route where he flung the *Miami News* each afternoon, and to the ornate Fontainebleau Hotel where his father worked and found his son an honest job scrubbing pots and pans. He also takes us to Ravine Gardens in Palatka and introduces us to the Fort Gates ferryman and to the "honey man" selling tupelo honey and mayhaw jelly on a roadside south of Tallahassee.

Alligators in B-Flat features a cast of characters who will bring smiles and an occasional tear. Reading about the musical appreciation of alligators is worth the price of the book. We get to know Joanie, she of Joanie's Blue Crab Café, located in the Big Cypress, where patrons can sample frog legs and lima bean stew, gawk at photographs of nude women in the men's restroom, and occasionally encounter a black bear. "A half century ago," writes Jeff, "there were plenty of places like Joanie's scattered about our state, little mom-and-pop joints with personality." He also introduces Floridians to Miss Beverly Hanson, Steinhatchee's fastest scallop shucker, to worm grunters who ply their trade in the Apalachicola National Forest, and to the irrepressibly private model Bunny Yeager. That moss weavers, bouzouki players, and Bradley's General Store are disappearing is a powerful theme in Klinkenberg's writings. He warns us that we are losing something precious but reminds us to slow down and cast down our buckets where we are, for such characters and places still exist.

Alligators in B-Flat represents Klinkenberg's third book in our UPF series. Alas, it is also the last book in our series. In fifteen years, the Florida History and Culture Series has proudly introduced sixty books to readers. In fitting symmetry, the first book in our series was *Al Burt's Florida: Snowbirds, Sand Castles, and Self-Rising Crackers*. Al Burt was Jeff Klinkenberg's role model, writing columns for the *Miami Herald* that helped Floridians better understand this amazing and baffling state. From the vantage point of 2012, we can appreciate Al Burt even more, for he brought us insights and a great deal of joy. In this new era of fiscal austerity and newspaper downsizing, Jeff Klinkenberg remains one of the last Florida journalists who has the creativity and good fortune to stand in Al Burt's sandy footsteps.

Raymond Arsenault and Gary R. Mormino
Series Editors

Preface

Yes, I'm still here, a cantankerous gray-haired bastard who can't stop exploring, can't stop asking personal questions, can't stop telling tales tall and small about Florida, the Real Florida, where they put cane syrup on homemade biscuits, eat their oysters raw, and wade once-in-a-blue-moon swamps to look for ghost orchids while acting kind of scaredy-cat about those snaggle-toothed alligators. My God, it's been fun. I only wish I had some mayhaw jelly to spread on a cracker as I type up this snarky preface.

"Civilization is a stream with banks," the historian-philosopher–big shot Will Durant wrote a long time ago. "The stream is sometimes filled with blood from people killing, stealing, shouting and doing the things historians usually record, while on the banks, unnoticed, people build homes, make love, raise children, sing songs, write poetry and even whittle statues. The story of civilization is the story of what happened on the banks."

Well, as a writer of Florida culture I like that quotation a whole lot. Sometimes my stories do include a little shouting and the occasional bloodshed as I drift down the middle of the Florida stream thinking about history. More often than not, though, you'll find me stalking the stream's endlessly interesting bank for stories about our culture. One of these days I'll find somebody to whittle me a statue of Ponce de Leon.

I believe the story of real Florida is found in the quieter voices, the art, the music, the food, the critters, the ways people choose to make a life in a unique place, a crowded place if you look at the numbers (19 million people) but also a place where bears and panthers still roam and where a gator might bite you on the butt. As I often tell my bride, the astonishingly smart, beautiful, and sophisticated New York–born Princess Susan: "You can be mugged in Manhattan, but you will never be bitten on the butt by a dinosaur." See, Florida is special. Doctor, let me tell you why I need stitches.

I hope you enjoy these stories. I wrote them originally for the *St. Petersburg Times*, which is now called the *Tampa Bay Times*, and then gussied them up for this book. I traveled from the Florida Panhandle to the Keys to get these stories, talked to a lot of nice people, ate a lot of good food, and chewed on some delicious scenery. I wish you could have been with me.

Acknowledgments

First, let me thank everybody at the *Tampa Bay Times* who has made my work possible and usually a pleasure. And thank you always to readers in Florida and elsewhere—your encouragement keeps me going.

Tip of my "Mack's Fish Camp" ballcap to Paul Tash, Neil Brown, Mike Foley, Tom French, Kelley Benham, William McKeen, Lane DeGregory, Leonora LaPeter, Michael Kruse, John Barry, Bill Duryea, Dawn Cate, Bruce Moyer, Ben Montgomery, Roy Peter Clark, Dalia Colon, Paul Shea, Rick Bragg, Bill Cooke, Joann Biondi, and my amazing photographer/videographer pal with the even more amazing name, Maurice "Mo" Rivenbark.

A hug and kiss for Gary Mormino and Ray Arsenault of the Florida Studies Department at the University of South Florida in St. Petersburg. Back when I feared that nobody cared about my Florida stories they convinced me otherwise.

For my wife, Susan King, my kids, Kristin, Peter, Kate, and Lindsay, and my talented journalist brother, Marty, I want to say thanks for the love even when I've been a self-centered jerk.

I bow toward the legendary "Boys Without Dates Club"—the notorious friends from my misspent youth who were so wild about Florida and Florida critters, especially the fish and the snakes that grossed out the snobby members of the fair sex. Hey! Girls! You know who you are! Your loss!

Finally, I genuflect at the feet of my terrific editor, Mike Wilson. You made every one of these stories better, brother. Now please quit bossing me around.

1

An Incomplete History of a Florida Boyhood

Snake

I was the first one to see the snake draped across the poinsettias.

"Daddy," I cried.

"My God!" he bellowed. "Bea! We have a snake in our yard."

"Kill it, Ernie!" my mother shrieked through the screen door. "Or I'll never go outside again!"

When I was a toddler in 1951, we moved from Chicago to Miami. Now I was about 7. Now everything was both amazing and scary. We had coconut trees in our yard and softball-sized crabs scuttling into holes under the croton bushes. Barred owls hooted from the poinciana tree at midnight. Manatees—everyone called them sea cows—lazed in the canal at the end of the block. We never saw alligators—they'd been hunted for generations—but Domingo, an older boy, and therefore an authority on everything, claimed they were common.

To my parents, to the countless Yankees who had moved south after World War II, Miami seemed both an Eden and the jungle from *King Kong*. Trembling in horror, my dad grabbed his shovel and took a panicked swing at the snake, which dropped off the branch and slithered toward the hibiscus shrubs—between his legs. Adrenalin flowing, dad flew off the ground like a rocket ship and fell onto his butt. Behind the screen door, Mom exploded with laughter, which only made him more determined to rid our yard, and our neighborhood, and our state, and our world, of the terrifying serpent.

When the Spaniards clanked ashore in 1513, they must have been scared, too. What kind of a terrifying place had they discovered? Yes, there were pretty flowers. But what manner of beasts?

Danny, the chain-smoking Bostonian from across the street, trotted over to investigate the excitement. Herb, who had moved his family to Florida from Youngstown a few weeks earlier, arrived next. They heard the word "snake" and ran home to get their shovels.

Jeff Klinkenberg
and his dad, 1954.
(Photo by Beatrice
Klinkenberg.)

A kid, I was no smarter than the grown-ups. They were alarmed, so I
was alarmed. As I watched and screamed in excitement, the three hunters chased the snake through the bushes and across the lawn as if it were
a tiger that had recently eaten a villager.

Thud, thud, thud.

That was the sound of shovel slaying snake.

My dad and his panting friends shook hands, stood on the sidewalk
in the gloaming, and congratulated themselves again and again for being
men who could protect their families from a loathsome Florida menace.

I picked up the limp reptile by the tail and studied it in front of my
face. It was 18 inches or so, a harmless green snake I later learned. I dug
a little hole in the black earth under Mrs. Crespo's banana trees and conducted a quiet funeral.

Winter 2011.

Summer of 1965

Whenever I visit South Florida as a gray-haired man, I like to drive past the places I knew as a dark-haired boy. I drive past my elementary school, the Little League baseball field, and even the old fishing holes where I caught snook and let the memories wash over me. Sometimes I drive past the Fontainebleau Hotel, the Miami Beach resort where my dad worked for decades. Not long ago, when I slowed for a long look, the sentimental part of me wanted to stop and ask for a tour. The adult part of me broke into a cold sweat while I remembered the worst summer of my life.

I was a teenage loser. In 1965, when I was 16, I was what the cool kids called a "fink." Being cool was beyond me. I had no car and no access to a car, which meant I was a fink who rode a bus—or even more damning in the hot-rod era—a bicycle. Girls liked dangerous boys who burned rubber, smoked Pall Malls, and got in rumbles. I read Tarzan novels in my room and built Popsicle stick rafts under the bridge on Sixth Avenue. I liked to fish and catch snakes and study my pimples in the reflection of the tea-colored water.

In the Miami of my youth, the cool kids wore Madras shirts and Bass Weejuns. As a fink, as the founding member of what should have been called the "Boys Without Dates Club," I matched stripes with plaids and danced in cardboard Thom McAns. Yes, I was quite a dancer—alone in my room. Strumming a badminton racket and lip-synching *I Want To Hold Your Hand*, I elbowed Paul McCartney aside while winking at the front-row fantasy girls. At the Sunday night CYO galas I'd wait until the very last song—usually Jesse Belvin's romantic recording of "Goodnight, My Love"—before seeking a warm-blooded partner for my lone excursion onto the dance floor. Yes, I was rejected by even the girl with the face of a stuffed cabbage.

In 1965, Florida boys often had summer jobs. Rich kids parked cars at the fancy restaurants or toted golf clubs at the ritzy country clubs. I mowed lawns. On a good Saturday, I mowed half a dozen with our terrible, always-on-the-fritz Briggs & Stratton that stalled the instant it approached Mrs. Crespo's jungle of intimidating St. Augustine grass. Then I'd edge, rake, and sweep for $1.50 a yard, hardly enough long green to pay for a roll or two at the bowling alley. Yes, finks liked to bowl, often alone.

That summer, I also toiled as a paper boy, throwing the *Miami Herald* on doorsteps before dawn from my fat-tired bicycle; in the afternoon I flung the *Miami News* at far fewer stoops. Lonely old Mrs. Posner demanded that I knock on her door and hand her the paper. She just wanted to talk, even if her listener was the neighborhood fink. Her house smelled of poodle urine. I had a weak stomach and tried not to heave.

Finished with my route, I engaged in a game of Wiffle Ball with my younger brother—in the front yard, for all the world to see. I don't know how many times I got caught in flagrante Wiffle Ball delicto by a cool kid driving past my house in his own GTO, the prettiest girl in the neighborhood at his side.

Sixteen years old!

One night after work, as he ate from a jar of Limburger cheese, which he washed down with a stein of beer, my dad cleared his throat. "I need someone to help at the Fontainebleau tomorrow," he whispered. "Want a real job?"

It was as if Brian Epstein had called and asked if I wanted to strum my badminton racket onstage with the Beatles. The Fontainebleau was the coolest hotel on earth in 1965. My dad managed the kitchens but always talked about the celebrities. James Bond made a movie there called *Goldfinger*. Dad saw hotel guests Mick Jagger and Keith Richards cavorting in the pool. "Bea," he told my mother that night as she adjusted her bobby pins, "I wanted to give them a bath."

At the Fontainebleau, perhaps I might be invited for a swim by Mick and Keith. Perhaps sex kitten Ann-Margret would ask for me—by name—to visit her cabana and apply lotion to her nude back. If nothing else, Frank Sinatra, who often stayed at the hotel, might invite me up to the VIP suite to help plan the next *Ocean's 11* caper. "How'd you like to go fishing with me and the rest of the Rat Pack?" he'd ask.

Jeff Klinkenberg, 16, proud of the morning's catch, a pair of snook. (Photo by Dennis Domingo.)

Thanks to my job at the Fontainebleau, I'd finally have serious cash. First off, I'd replace the Huck Finn wardrobe with rich-boy threads. But more than anything I wanted a car. I knew I wouldn't be able to buy the Corvette right away, but maybe Ed ("Mark 'Em Down") Lane—Miami's celebrity car monger—might find me a fire-engine red 1957 Chevrolet Bel Air Sports Sedan with low mileage.

Before dawn the next morning, my dad led his fink son into the cavernous kitchen of the Fontainebleau Hotel and explained the task at hand. "There was a banquet last night. We fed lots of people. The busboys are real sloppy after a big banquet. When they dump the food, valuable things get tossed away by accident. Recover them."

For the next eight hours I sifted through heaping cans of last night's mackerel for the hotel's expensive cutlery. Between dry heaves I located missing knives, forks, and spoons by the gross. The next morning, he dragged me out of bed before sunrise. "You're a working man now," he said as I grabbed the doorway.

In the hotel kitchen he led me to a sink full of greasy water. "Today," he said, "you're going to be scrubbing pots." I needed a chisel to chip away the dried mashed potatoes and something red and mysterious. Bouillabaisse! Fish soup! Dry heaves!

"You did well yesterday," Dad said the next morning, Limburger on his breath. "So we have a special challenge waiting for you in the vegetable room."

In the summer of 1965, onions became my life. For week after week, I peeled six bags a day, about 300 pounds, weeping from the first onion to the last. "My abuela always say you must put stick of carrot in your mouth when you peel the onions," a Cuban cook told me. "The carrot, it will take away the tears." I lipped the carrot like Bogey smoking a butt in *The Big Sleep* while adding drooling to the weepy fink repertoire.

Every night, as I traveled home by bus, I tried to find a lonely seat far away from other passengers, especially if they were pretty girls. My hands stank of onions. As the summer drew to a close, they were stained yellow. I was sure they matched my teeth.

Sixteen years old! Just thinking about it gives me the dry heaves.

Summer 2010.

Bunny Yeager

My courtship of Bunny Yeager began when I punched her number into my phone and felt like a nerdy kid asking Madonna out on a date. I had rehearsed what I was going to say: "Miss Yeager, we grew up in the same neighborhood. I remember the glory days of Miami and have always appreciated your contributions to Florida culture. I wonder, Miss Yeager, how you might feel about the possibility of me visiting you at home and writing a story." But when she answered I felt 13 again though I was past 60.

"HELLO! HELLO!" I heard myself braying into the phone like it was a Dixie cup connected to Bunny's house by a waxed string. "Uh, am I talking to Bunny Yeager? REALLY? COOL! CAN I CALL YOU BUNNY?"

Silence on her end of the line.

"Who is this?" Bunny asked. I took a deep breath and told her.

"Honey, who do you work for?" she asked.

In the middle of the twentieth century, when I was a boy and a teen, Bunny Yeager was the queen of glamorous Miami, winning beauty contests and posing in sexy swimsuits for panting photographers who dispatched the glorious images all over the globe.

Eventually Bunny picked up a camera herself and became famous for her photos of gorgeous women who sometimes were naked. Then she became plain famous, her name in the gossip columns about her jet-set life. She dated Joe DiMaggio, sold her work to *Playboy*, and had a part in a Sinatra movie. She had once gotten me into hot water at Park Shore Pharmacy when Howard the druggist caught me peeking at one of Bunny's photos of an undressed redhead in *Cavalier* magazine.

"I'm going to tell your mother," Howard said, as my repressed Catholic boy bowels turned to water.

"Are you a freelancer?" Bunny asked, snapping me back into the present. Definitely not, I told her, sounding as if I had consumed a 12-pack of

Red Bulls. I've worked at the same paper for decades and decades, Bunny, a really big paper now, Bunny, we actually went to the same high school, Bunny!

"Honey," Bunny finally said. "I just don't have time right now. I have so much to do. I'm just kind of overwhelmed. Maybe some other time. Have a nice day."

She was born in 1930 or so—Bunny was always much more secretive about her age than her measurements—in a little town near Pittsburgh. Christened Linnea Eleanor Yeager, she took the name Bunny after watching a smoking-hot Lana Turner in a film. After moving to Miami, she was voted by Edison High classmates as "the girl with the sweetest smile." She was 5 feet 10 and a curvy 36-25-37, according to vulgarians who care about crass numbers.

She took modeling courses, posed on the beach for "Come on down" Chamber of Commerce photos, and was crowned Queen of Miami, Miss Trailer Coach of Dade County, Miss Personality of Miami Beach, and the Cheesecake Queen. Her image graced postcards, magazines and newspapers. Mechanics hung her photos in their work bays; teenage boys—let's not even talk about it.

Models earned less money than photographers, so Bunny bought a Kodak Reflex, mastered the camera, and beat the good old boys at their game. It was as if the Mona Lisa had picked up a paintbrush and given Leonardo a run for the money. Her breakthrough was a photo of a friend posed in a leopard-skin bikini at an animal park. *Eye* magazine paid $100.

Bunny continued to pose for other photographers, but eventually she figured out how to make self-portraits, sometimes using a string between camera and big toe. *U.S. Camera* magazine called Bunny "The World's Prettiest Photographer."

She thought the two-piece bathing suits sold at Burdines were a bore; using her sewing skills she created her own bikinis, frilly and revealing and tastefully risqué. She sold her most polished work to *Esquire*, *Cosmopolitan*, and *Life*. The grittier stuff went to girlie mags like *Swank*.

She didn't do dirty. She didn't do porn. Even her nudes had a girl-next-door quality.

In her own photos, Bunny posed as a brunette and a redhead, but she was most fetching as a Marilyn Monroe bombshell posing in one of those postage-stamp bikinis, or cavorting in a dark living room in a black nightie, or lounging in a tub behind a few suds.

Bunny Yeager as a blonde. (Photo by Bunny Yeager.)

In 1954, Bettie Page visited Miami. Famous for her fearlessness in front of cameras, Bettie never appeared in the pages of *Life* or in *Redbook*, probably because she sometimes posed with a leather whip while wearing a black garter. Yet Bunny somehow made even a naked Bettie look wholesome, posing her at the zoo and draped across a bumper car at the local amusement park.

For her most famous photograph, Bunny sat Bettie next to a Christmas tree in the only piece of clothing she apparently needed, a Santa cap. A new magazine, *Playboy*, bought the centerfold photo for a hundred bucks. Years later, Bunny's good friend Hugh Hefner bought her photos for $15,000 a pop and even published a pictorial of "The Queen of the Playboy Centerfolds"—Bunny Yeager.

A couple of months had passed since my incompetent telephone call. I worked up my nerve and tried once more. It was November now.

"Who are you again, honey?"

I reminded her. Reminded her I had mailed copies of my stories and even one of my books.

"Oh, that was from you," she said. "Thanks. Hey, do you know Carl Hiaasen?"

Her question about the best-selling Florida novelist caught me by surprise. Sure, I know him, Bunny. Alas, even Carl's famous name didn't open her door to me.

"You know, with the holidays coming, I just am so busy," she lamented. "It's kind of overwhelming around here right now. Call me in January."

I felt like an eighth-grader at St. Rose of Lima School again, the kid with a passion for fishing and snakes who was a nincompoop when it came to girls. I loved them, but they didn't love me back.

Of course, a lot of Americans were in love with Bunny back when. In Miami, where celebrities were as common as ripe grapefruits, she was on a first-name basis with Arthur Godfrey and Jackie Gleason. She was a guest on the TV game show *What's My Line?* and exchanged snappy patter on the *Tonight Show* with Johnny Carson.

There were Bunny sightings in Miami Shores, where I lived, usually by the hateful older boys who spotted her drinking a cherry Coke at Whalen's, skulking in the aspirin aisle at Hinst Pharmacy or sitting in the back of the Shores Theater at the opening of *Dr. No*. Bunny had taken the iconic movie-poster photograph of Ursula Andress bursting from her bikini from the surf.

Bunny Yeager (*right*) with Bettie Page. (Photo by Bunny Yeager.)

We clueless younger boys got our Bunny Yeager thrills wherever we could. Eddie, the buck-toothed geek with the giant Adam's apple, let us look at his dad's collection of girlie mags until we began fighting over them with our greasy hands. One desperate pal stole a *Playboy* that we studied daily in the croton bushes until it fell apart.

In January, I left a voice mail for Bunny. Bunny didn't call back. In March, I decided on another strategy, leaving a message announcing that I was going to see her at the end of the week. I had her address. I'd just knock on her door. See, I had questions I wanted to ask Bunny in person.

She had been married twice, divorced, widowed, raised two daughters on her own and excelled in a man's world, right? How had she managed? I wanted to know her thoughts about the sexual revolution, Internet porn, Kim Kardashian. How did a beauty queen cope with aging?

But Bunny Yeager, who in the exercise of her craft had persuaded countless young women to unsnap their bras, had no desire to share her privacy. "Don't come," she said, returning my call almost immediately. "I NEVER let anyone come to my house. I don't even like people to come to my office. And I'm so busy right now, I'm overwhelmed, in fact, so please don't come. I've got so much work to do getting ready for this show."

A show? My ears perked up. I'd have guessed those days were behind her.

"I'm putting together photographs for an art exhibit."

She told me where and when.

"See you there," I said.

"Okay," said Bunny Yeager.

In May I drove across the Everglades, past alligators and great blue herons, and into Miami, until I got to the Harold Golen Gallery in a blighted neighborhood where shadowy figures leaned in doorways. It was a Saturday afternoon. I went in to talk to Harold, who seemed even more nervous than I was about that night's event.

"My phone has been ringing off the hook," he said. "Everybody wants to know if Bunny's coming to the opening of her own show. I know she can't handle stress or a lot of attention anymore, but she told me she was going to try and come tonight. 'TRY AND COME.' God, I hope she does."

I returned at dusk. The streets had now been taken over by Miami's most colorful art denizens, tattooed bosomy women and gold-chained Latino men, straights, gays, and folks of indeterminate gender, a woman in go-go boots, a woman in a fur hat, a man wearing a homburg and a jacket draped across his shoulders like a cape. I saw Harold in the corner of his cozy studio preparing for a nervous breakdown.

"Bunny isn't coming," he was telling visitors. "I'm so sorry. She said she was going to try and come, but she won't be here. I'm so, so sorry."

BUNNY'S NOT COMING?

"She had every intention of being here," her manager, Ed Christin, explained smoothly from a sofa. "Bunny is not an extrovert, but she really wanted to come to this tonight. What happened was she had a procedure done on an eye earlier this week and the eye is bloodshot and uncomfortable. Bunny has a sore eye."

The 14 photos on the wall captured Bunny in her glory days—as a Marilyn Monroe blonde and a Jane Russell brunette, in a negligee, in a bathing suit, in a leotard, hands on her hips, standing on tippy toes, at the beach, looking young and happy to be alive.

"Things are happening for Bunny now," her agent continued. "For years, Bunny sold her photographs on eBay at prices that were terribly undervalued. But we're changing that. How much is her collection worth? I would say it's worth millions of dollars, but the exact number I can't say. I've never been to her house, but I went to her office, and she showed me boxes of photographs that have NEVER been seen. Amazing, erotic photographs, beautifully composed and shot. She's an artist."

A party broke out inside the gallery despite Bunny's absence. I saw Tara "Queen of the Night" Solomon, a raven-haired society gal dressed in leopard pattern dress, à la Bettie Page. I saw celebrity contemporary artist Carlos Betancourt, whose lush Caribbean-flavored mixed-media works are in the Smithsonian National Portrait Gallery in Washington and the Metropolitan Art Museum in New York. "Bunny captures a time and a place in her work," he told me. "That's exactly what every artist dreams of doing."

I saw Joann Biondi, glamorous author of *Miami Beach Memories: A Nostalgic Chronicle of Days Gone By*, a coffee table collection of photos and text with a picture of a fresh-faced Bunny on the cover. "It took about a year of trying before she was willing to see me," Biondi said. In 2007 Bunny attended Joann's book party and even posed for a picture. It reveals a striking woman with long blonde hair worn in a thick braid draped over a shoulder. It's one of the last-known photographs of Bunny Yeager in public.

Later in the evening came a disturbance near the door. A tiny brown-eyed woman shouted, "Bunny isn't here, Ferdie!" and her white-haired husband announced, "That's too bad. I really wanted to see her."

Ferdie Pacheco—garrulous author, painter, retired physician and former fight doctor to Muhammad Ali—was born in Ybor City but spent most of his adult life in Miami. After entering the gallery like a Roman emperor, he sat and held court, actually—and did his best to make up for the MIA main event. I asked if he knew her.

"Oh, yes," he whispered. "When I was a young physician, and I was single and a very eligible bachelor, she was the most eligible single woman in Miami," he said.

I wanted to know more.

"I yearned to call her and ask if she would do me the honor of spending an evening with me."

That's not an exact quote, of course. Ferdie actually explained in a more direct manner what he had hoped to do to enliven their evening together. Sadly for Ferdie, Bunny said no.

I got up early the next morning, packed, had breakfast and got ready to drive home. But I didn't go right away. I found a quiet corner in the hotel lobby and waited until 10 o'clock. She'd be up by then, drinking coffee, picking at a grapefruit, still looking like a million bucks even with a sore eye.

I punched in the telephone number.

The phone rang and rang. Then it rang some more.

Summer 2011.

Critters

Alligators in B-Flat

On the way to playing tuba for an audience of alligators, William Mickelsen felt cocky enough to talk about his musical chops. His taut jaw muscles, his lips and his tongue felt up to the task. His majestic lungs felt strong and elastic. He and his tuba were ready for whatever reptilian drama lay ahead.

The night before, he and his fellow artists in the Florida Orchestra had played at Clearwater's Ruth Eckerd Hall behind composer Marvin Hamlisch, the Oscar winner for *The Way We Were*. Everything had gone well. At Gatorland, the old tourist attraction near Kissimmee, Mickelsen was going to play a deep B-flat for a battle-scarred, amorous male alligator named Toxic.

During mating season, alligators are known to do astonishing things. They swim miles looking for mates, crawl over land to find new girlfriends, and scrap with other leathery Casanovas that get in their way. In the spring, feisty alligators, usually males, grunt and hiss. They roar like thunder.

My ambition was to find out whether Toxic and his gator colleagues might answer Mickelsen's tuba with earth-shaking roars of their own. If Toxic fell in love with the tuba, or even if he attacked it, we'd have a grand story to tell. Come to think of it, whatever happened would be interesting.

I had heard an intriguing report on National Public Radio about the musical note B-flat and its mysterious role in nature's soundtrack. Certain black holes in outer space, NPR reported, hum in the key of B-flat. Interesting, I thought. But not as interesting as the relationship between B-flat and alligators. Play a low B-flat just right, the reporter reported, and modern dinosaurs might reply with terrible mating bellows.

The radio story had been inspired by an obscure study, "Responses of Captive Alligators to Auditory Stimulation," conducted at the Museum

Bill Mickelsen gets ready to blow.

of Natural History in New York City in 1944. Researchers had discovered by accident that B-flat—and no other note—seemed to provoke alligator song. For whatever reason, that low B-flat was part of the alligator's vocabulary.

I called Kent Vliet, the University of Florida's alligator expert, and told him about my plans to bring the symphony to Gatorland. Vliet told me he had once tried to duplicate the B-flat experiment, but nothing had happened when his tuba guy started with the oom-pah-pah. "I suspect it's bunk," Vliet said.

I refused to be discouraged, seeing how I was headed to the reptile palace with a sweet-lipped ringer who could play tuba like Johnny B. Goode had played guitar. Chuck Berry wrote his rock 'n' roll anthem, by the way, in the key of B-flat.

William Mickelsen, who was born in Ohio in 1952, took up the tuba after seeing *The Music Man* at age 10. In high school he was known as "Mister Music." At Yale, thanks to his brains and his tuba, he received a master's degree. Mickelsen, who had played with the Florida Orchestra for three decades, knew something about difficult audiences. If he missed a note at the symphony, the temperamental conductor might scowl in his direction. If nothing else, sophisticated customers might tsk, tsk in disgust.

"It was worse when I was at Yale," Mickelsen told me. "I'd play my tuba in the cafés near campus for pocket change. Sometimes I'd play for an hour—and go home with just a quarter or two."

Of course, finger-snapping, coffee-swilling student bohemians never considered eating him. I couldn't vouch for the denizens of Gatorland. Alligators began performing their own singular music long before Homo sapiens crawled out of the muck. By the time the modern tuba was invented in 1835, the alligator had been around 30 million years.

Tim Williams, the legendary gator man, waited for us at the gate of the wonderfully kitschy theme park where reptiles, and only reptiles, are the stars. Williams, 57 that year, was probably the only alligator-wrestling teacher on the planet. When he appeared on Jay Leno or David Letterman to strut his stuff, he often toted something with fangs. His hands looked like they'd spent time in a meat grinder. I guess they had.

A few years before, a 9-foot alligator, Sassafras, had grabbed him as he straddled her during a performance. Gators bite with 2,000 pounds of pressure per tooth; one fang went through his right hand. "If you're a carpenter," Williams liked to tell anxious protégés, "you're gonna hit your thumb with a hammer. If you mess with alligators, you're gonna get bit. Get used to the idea."

The Alligator Maestro thought our B-flat experiment would end in disappointment, though probably without any biting of the orchestra. Williams had once allowed a high school musician to play tuba next to a pond. The alligators were not amused and the boy headed home in defeat.

"Sometimes we can get them to bellow by bringing an airboat close to their lake," Williams said. "We think the vibration of the loud engine stimulates them." Williams told us sometimes alligators bellowed at distant thunder. He told us he had heard them bellowing as the space shuttle descended over the park on its way to Cape Canaveral. "They'll start roaring—and then an instant later you hear the sonic boom when the shuttle breaks the sound barrier. They must feel it before we can hear it."

Bill Mickelsen unpacked his $20,000 weapon, a Walter Nirschl–built replica of the famous tuba Arnold Jacobs had played for four decades in the Chicago Symphony. "The Rolls-Royce of tubas," Mickelsen called it.

John Banther, a 20-year-old New England Conservatory pupil who studied with Mickelsen during the summer, unpacked his fine Meinl-Weston instrument. Tuba playing is hard work and Mickelsen wanted a backup.

On the boardwalk, we faced the breeding marsh. One hundred intimidating alligators drifted listlessly in a large lake. The one called Toxic stood out. At 13 feet, he was the alpha and the ugly; his head looked as if it had been gnawed on by wild beasts. It had. "Don't be reincarnated as a male alligator," Williams advised. "A lot of the big males here are missing eyes, legs, chunks of tail. Toxic has been in lots of fights."

Mickelsen and Banther, despite their reservations, aimed their tubas at the marsh and began honking. They did not play Johnny B. Goode, but a long sustained B-flat—a punishing, jet plane B-flat that must have echoed for miles. Mickelsen, it should be mentioned, plays with gusto. Some years ago, the contrabass player at the orchestra complained that Mickelsen's powerful notes had damaged his hearing during Berlioz's *Symphonie Fantastique*, ending their friendship.

The alligators failed to bellow, but they swam toward the sound. Within moments about a dozen faced the tuba players, looking interested, if bewildered. "This is harder work than playing for the Florida Orchestra," Mickelsen said, sweat streaming. During a concert he typically rests between short bursts of music. "I feel light-headed."

He and his partner began again, coached by an unlikely maestro, Gatorland's Mike Godwin, whose grandfather had founded the park in 1949. "Longer . . . drag that note out," Godwin recommended. They dragged it out. They even tried the theme from *Jaws*. Out on the pond, disturbed

A musically excited alligator.

bull alligators attacked each other in what Godwin called "territorial displays"—slashing with their tails and teeth, pounding the water with their jaws.

BLAAAA! Mickelsen hit B-flat so hard he crossed his eyes. The note got no bellow in return, but we started noticing some encouraging, R-rated action: a female alligator sashayed up to a larger male and nudged him with her nose. "Courtship behavior," Godwin whispered. Next the vixen climbed upon Lothario's back.

"She is trying to dunk him. If she can hold him under the water she will know he is not a suitable mate. She is looking for a strong, dominant male."

It was all pretty cool. But we wanted a bellow. We wanted to feel the earth move.

Mickelsen had a bad back, thanks to years of hauling his tuba from orchestra pit to alligator pit. He told us he could no longer stand and play the tuba, even for the sake of a majestic scientific experiment.

Bill Mickelsen eventually wrote a song to commemorate the occasion called "Song of the Alligator."

He suggested a change in strategy. He and his student assistant had been aiming tubas out at the alligators in the marsh. How about if they lay down and aimed their tubas down, at the wooden boardwalk and the water below? Perhaps the wood and the water might enhance the note.

"We want to hit the B-flat two octaves below middle C," Mickelsen reminded his young assistant. "At 57 hertz. That's what that old scientific report advised."

BLAAAA! The cheeks of the two musicians puffed out as if storing alligator eggs. Though only a few clouds scudded across the sky, we heard what sounded like thunder in the distance. It was a randy male alligator turned on by a tuba B-flat, telling the world that he was a magnificent stud.

Closer to us, Toxic disagreed with the stud wannabe, lifting his upper body out of the water, lowering his middle, and raising his tail. Though he barely moved, an explosion of water droplets flew off his back.

"The water dance!" Tim Williams cried. Toxic let loose a roar that shook the earth.

"Astonishing!" Mickelsen cried, taking a break. "I didn't think it would work!" Next we carried our experiment to the busiest section of the park, the main lake, filled with the attraction's largest alligators.

Once again, our intrepid musicians played their instruments through the boardwalk toward the water. They played all the notes on the scale for two octaves and then played the notes once more. Nothing happened until they hit the B-flat two octaves below middle C. All over the lake, male alligators bellowed back.

"It must be the vibrations caused by the note that's exciting them," Mickelsen shouted. John Banther knelt on the boardwalk about ten yards from the railing and peeked through the wood slats. He saw an alligator in the dim shadows below. As amused tourists detoured around him, the young musician lay on his side, adjusted the tuba and hit B-flat.

BLAAAA! Was Krakatoa erupting? The boardwalk shook. An instant later, the roar of the bull alligator beneath us was so loud and so deep we felt it in our chests.

I started running. Banther, young and nimble, leaped out of the way like a long-jump Olympian, abandoning his tuba. It sounded like T. Rex was coming after us through the wood.

He was only flirting.

Spring 2007.

Jarhead

Georgia Wilcox was first to see the bear cub known as Jarhead. Georgia lives in a double-wide in the Ocala National Forest outside of Umatilla. In the morning, before the bad heat arrives, she relaxes on her deck and looks for critters. She loves seeing deer and possums, raccoons and squirrels. She gets a kick out of watching the rattlers and coral snakes. She'd adopt them all if she could.

Once in while she sees a black bear, a special thrill. The day she spotted Jarhead she felt like crying. She heard something out by the clothesline: a mama bear was sniffing at the drying clothes while three cubs cavorted at her feet. Two looked adorably normal.

Georgia, 57, gasped. The last cub in line obviously had raided somebody's garbage. Somehow, and it must have taken some doing, the hungry little bear had jammed its head into a gallon jar for the last lick of mayonnaise or pickle juice. Now it wore the jar like a space helmet.

"How can it even breathe?" Georgia thought. "How can it eat and drink?" An Earth Mother with a long ponytail, Georgia knew the little bear was doomed unless she did something quickly. Inside her home she got on the phone.

"Garbage kills bears," Mike Orlando told me when we traveled together for the first time a few days later. He manages bears in the northeast part of the state for the Florida Fish and Wildlife Conservation Commission. More and more he manages people who live near bears. In his territory, which stretches from Orlando to the Osceola National Forest near Jacksonville, bears often share the suburbs with raccoons. Except that raccoons never weigh 600 pounds.

"Don't feed bears" was the gospel he preached to neighborhood groups, school principals, and city council members in a dozen counties. "Don't feed them on purpose and don't feed them by accident by leaving your garbage out. It's natural to enjoy seeing bears. But you don't want to tame them into coming onto your property. It won't end well for bears. And it might not end well for you either."

About 11,000 bears roamed Florida when the Spaniards arrived in 1513. In 1973, the year Mike Orlando was born, the state was down to about 300 bears. Florida finally listed bears as "threatened" about four decades ago and seriously began protecting their habitat. It also slowed down the carnage on roads and banned bear hunting. The population rebounded: in 2010 more than 3,000 bears tried to survive from the Everglades to the Florida Panhandle. Mike Orlando's jurisdiction was home to about a third.

For the most part Orlando's bears lived on public wilderness lands such as the Ocala National Forest. But bears, adventuresome creatures, had no problem exploring housing developments to hunt easy vittles. An odoriferous garbage can, percolating on the curb on an August night, is a delicatessen to a bear. In 1989, Floridians had called the state wildlife agency to complain about chummy bears 86 times. A decade later they filed more than 3,000 complaints.

"Here's the typical scenario," Orlando said as we traveled a suburban road near the St. Johns River. "A bear shows up one night in a backyard. The homeowner, you know, is a little scared at first. But he's also kind of thrilled. Maybe he feeds the bear to keep it around. Maybe the bear just knocks over the garbage can and eats the leftovers. The bear comes back the next night for more. The homeowner takes a bunch of pictures. The homeowner tells his neighbors about his nightly bear. The neighbors come over and get their photographs. Maybe they start feeding the bears, too.

"When the bears first showed up, maybe they were small and cute. But as months go by they get bigger and bolder. Pretty soon bears are showing up during the day. They're waiting at the front door. They're hanging around the carport and the driveway and sleeping in the bushes. You can't let your kids go outside to play.

"One day we get a call. It's somebody from the neighborhood telling us, 'Come catch your bear.'"

In his public talks, Orlando told people how to bear-proof their neighborhoods. He advised restaurants, state parks, and schools to replace plastic garbage bins with steel. He encouraged do-it-yourselfers to invent bear-resistant garbage cans. He lobbied city governments about making municipalities "bear safe." He coached North Florida law enforcement

Bear cubs, including one in trouble. (Photo courtesy of Florida Fish and Wildlife Conservation Commission.)

officials in the art of scaring bears out of suburbia. Shout at them. Shoot blanks over their heads. Ignite fireworks. Wallop them with paintballs and beanbags.

"Teach bears to stay wild."

Georgia Wilcox, the first to see Jarhead, hadn't been feeding bears. She knows better. So did most of her neighbors along the dirt roads in the forest. They took their bird feeders inside at dark. They remembered to bring in the cat food. Most of the time they stored their garbage behind closed doors. But not everyone was responsible. Some people left out their trash. Some dumped sofas, watermelon rinds, and pickle jars—illegally—along the deserted forest roads. Garbage may have been a bonanza for hungry bears, but it also was a deathtrap.

Mike Orlando sent a colleague, Cathy Connolly, to meet with Georgia to talk about Jarhead. The two women, animal lovers, hit it off. "We'll be on the lookout," Cathy said. "If he shows up again, please call."

Georgia promised. "That poor little bear with a jar on his head is going to die of thirst. You just got to catch him."

"I know it," Cathy said.

Bears are basically stomachs with legs. When Mike Orlando was courting his wife, Amy, a decade ago, they spent dates hunting for bear scat. Bears mostly eat nuts, berries, and leaves. They'll eat any small animal they can catch. They will endure a thousand bee stings for a taste of honey. A rotten fish on a river bank? Yum. They'll race a vulture to the most rancid dead armadillo steaming on the pavement. One time Orlando found a spent shotgun shell in a bear-scat pile.

Florida has no shortage of year-round food, including garbage. That's why our state boasts some of the largest bears east of the Mississippi. In 1991, near Naples, a car hit and killed a 621-pound male bear. The driver survived, but his car was totaled.

In Canada and in certain national parks in the United States, black bears attack and even devour hikers once in a while. For unknown reasons, the Florida black bear breed is less aggressive. Only three attacks on humans have ever been reported—but all three happened in Mike Orlando's Florida territory in 2009. All involved bears that had left nearby forests to feed in suburbia.

In Mount Dora, Mary E. Miller, 80, woke when she heard a commotion on her screened porch. At first she thought cats were fighting for the food she leaves out for Rusty, her tabby. Mrs. Miller padded across her mobile home, switched on the porch light, and opened the door. A large bear immediately burst through the porch screen to escape. As two cubs jumped on a table and bawled for Mama, Mrs. Miller slammed the door. When she opened it again, the cubs were gone.

Mrs. Miller was somehow feeling curious and fearless that night. She crept to the darkest section of the long porch and looked around. The two cubs, terrified, were huddled in a corner. Mrs. Miller decided to hold open the back porch door for them. When she opened it, Mama rushed in and bit her right thigh. Mrs. Miller fled inside and called police. At the hospital, doctors dressed her minor wounds and administered a tetanus shot.

Back at the Dora Pines Trailer Park, state biologists baited a trap with a favorite bear treat, doughnuts from Publix. They caught Mama and euthanized her with a drug. Fortunately, the cubs were large enough to survive on their own. The next morning Mrs. Miller cleaned the cat food from the porch and vowed to feed Rusty inside.

In the gated community of Heathrow near Orlando, bears had been raiding garbage cans. Mike Orlando and colleagues initiated a "store-your-garbage-can-inside" campaign to minimize bear encounters. Not everyone paid attention. One night David Amsler, 34, heard his garbage can falling over. "Raccoons," he thought. He grabbed a golf club, slipped out the back door, and prepared to frighten the brazen raccoons. A startled bear bowled him over as it fled. Years ago, Orlando routinely caught nuisance bears and moved them. Sometimes he still did—unless the bear had hurt someone or had completely lost its fear of humans. In a doughnut-baited trap that resembles a culvert, he caught Amsler's bear and euthanized it.

In a Seminole County neighborhood known as the Springs, Ernest Stamm, 49, opened his front door and was slapped across the face by a burly bear. Later, Stamm pleaded no contest to the charge of feeding bears, a misdemeanor in Florida. Orlando caught and euthanized the bear.

Not everyone in Steffanie Stimpson's Longwood neighborhood— which was around the corner from a Walgreens and a Chuck E. Cheese and a few minutes from bear-friendly Wekiva Springs State Park—secured their garbage. So the neighborhood suffered from chronic bear problems.

One spring night, Stimpson, 28, cooked a chicken dinner for herself and her 7-year-old daughter, Isabella. After Isabella nodded off, Steffanie settled on the couch to watch television. She'd left her front door ajar for her year-old dachshund, Sophie.

The door creaked open a few inches. "Sophie?" called Steffanie. But Sophie wasn't outside. Sophie was lying at Steffanie's feet. In the glow of the television, Steffanie watched the door creak open a little wider.

Steffanie was afraid, but she marched across the room and flung open the door. The head of an enormous bear was only inches from her feet. Maybe it had smelled the chicken dinner. Maybe it had smelled her. Steffanie slammed the door, screamed, and telephoned her dad next door.

Her dad, Dan Stimpson, was a chef. He was 52, a Florida boy who had lived in the neighborhood since 1970. He told me he'd never seen a bear until 2009. Now he took precautions that included scrubbing the barbecue grill every time he fixed a steak. Still the bears rambled through his neighborhood. He sprinted into his daughter's yard with a flashlight.

The bear was gone. In the flashlight beam Chef Dan saw that something large and heavy had crushed a chain-link fence upon entering the yard. Escaping the yard, that same something had barreled like a Mini Cooper through a 7-foot wood fence. "Holy smoke!" Chef Dan said to his daughter. "How big was that bear?"

In North Central Florida, black bears like the suburbs. (Photo courtesy of Dan Stimpson.)

"Huge." Three nights later the bear was lured into a doughnut-baited trap by a state wildlife biologist. The bear that tried to enter Steffanie Stimpson's house in the suburbs turned out to be a 590-pound male.

Rose West was next to spot Jarhead. She lived just down the dirt road from Georgia Wilcox. Rose saw the cub on the deck next to her mobile home. Jarhead was with his Mama, whose butt brushed up against the sliding glass doors. Rose, 20, lived in the forest with her boyfriend, Billy LeBree. They were used to bears. One night an enormous male bear chewed through their pig pen and killed a prized 90-pound Yorkshire. Another bear ate their chickens. Rose resented losing her livestock. But seeing that tiny, starving bear with a jar on its head took a bite out of her heart. After she saw Jarhead, Rose got on the phone.

Cathy Connolly arrived in a Chevy Blazer towing a culvert trap baited with doughnuts. "First we're going to catch Mama bear," Cathy explained. "Then we'll tranquilize her and let her sleep in the trap. We'll open the culvert trap door again. The cubs will go in to be with their Mama. Then we'll be able to get the jar off that poor little cub's head."

Minutes later Mike Orlando showed up, followed by another biologist, Brian Scheick. They set a second trap and waited in the 100-degree heat for the rest of the afternoon. "We know this little bear has gone at least two days without food and water," Scheick said.

"It's very sad," Orlando said. "This bear is the poster child for why bears and human garbage can't mix." They caught no bears that day. Or the day after. The future looked bad for Jarhead.

Born in Cape Coral, Orlando was one of those adventure-crazed boys who were becoming a vanishing species in modern Florida. His dad had been a fishing guide who taught him how to reel in giant tarpon. After graduating with a biology degree from the University of Florida, he served in the Peace Corps in Africa. Eventually he decided to go for his master's at the University of Kentucky. His project was studying Florida bears.

Everything about them fascinated him. He had a stuffed bear—it had been killed on a Florida road—standing on hind legs in his office. In his truck he kept the skull of another roadkill bear he used for natural history show-and-tells. "They hear well and have pretty good eyesight," he told me. "But their sense of smell is amazing. They can smell something good to eat miles away."

One time, after he had advised a beekeeper to protect hives behind an electric fence, guilt set in. To make himself feel better about shocking a bear he took the next opportunity to touch an electrified fence. "It was a pretty good jolt," Orlando said. "But it wasn't going to kill a bear." In Pennsylvania, where bear hunting was still allowed, he completed his ursine education by eating one. "Not bad at all. Maybe a little greasy."

He was a burly and bearded guy whose curiosity and sense of humor made him seem younger than 36. He liked Lady Gaga. He dabbled on Facebook. He tried to eat healthy but was a guilty regular at McDonald's. He knew how to sweet-talk the baker at Publix into donating yesterday's stale doughnuts to catch today's bears.

Bears had woofed at him. They had popped their jaws in a "back off" warning. Teeth bared, they charged him—only to stop at the last instant. "It's important you don't run from a bear," he said. "They have a chase reflex. Look down. Talk to them gently. Retreat." He had been bitten twice and had been scratched more times than he could remember.

One night, in Daytona Beach, only blocks from the ocean, he sat in his

Chevy pickup and watched a bear in a tree only a few feet from a packed biker bar. Perhaps the bear smelled food. Perhaps it was thirsty for a smooth lager. Orlando had no appetite for an encounter with an inebriated biker, much less dozens of them. He stepped reluctantly onto the sidewalk.

"What are you doing here?" a biker demanded, then followed Orlando's gaze into the tree.

"BEAR!" yelled the biker. Other bikers spilled out of the bar like warm Guinness.

"We'll catch your bear for you, mister!" cried a biker. Before Orlando could stop them, several began shimmying up the tree and scaring the bear into the higher branches.

Anxious bears sometimes lose control of their bladders. This one relieved itself all over the bikers, who fell out of the tree like sodden acorns.

"The bear pee made the bikers smell better," Orlando reported later. The bear with the weak bladder escaped.

Jarhead was still at large after five days and Orlando couldn't believe the little fellow was still breathing. Yet neighbors in the small forest community had seen him with his siblings and his mother.

As his siblings nursed, Jarhead could only watch. One woman saw the cubs tear berries from a bush. As the siblings ate the fallen fruit, the starving little bear pushed the morsels frantically along the ground with the jar on its head. A scientist for more than half his life, Orlando has learned to detach from his emotions. But the thought of Jarhead made him want to weep.

Orlando and his team set out doughnut-baited culvert traps all over the woods. Then they scoured the forest and the sand roads until midnight hoping they would encounter the bears. Maybe he could get a tranquilizer dart into Mama. The cubs wouldn't abandon her and he could catch Jarhead.

State wildlife officer Cathy Connolly and her husband, Mike, slept in their Blazer next to one of the traps. Mosquitoes whined around their ears. The bears never showed.

On Day Six, as Orlando drove into the forest, he saw Jarhead and his mother for the first time. His heart rose into his throat. He grabbed his dart rifle and hid behind a bush. Mama was 35 yards away. She started

Mike Orlando poses with a tranquilized bear. (Photo courtesy of Florida Fish and Wildlife Conservation Commission.)

ambling in the opposite direction. He fired and missed. At midnight he told his wife: "Well, that's it. I had my chance and I blew it." He tossed and turned until dawn.

On Day Eight, he had another opportunity. Mama and cubs were standing on the road ahead. Orlando began crawling along the shoulder with his dart rifle. Suddenly, a pickup truck pulled up next to him.

"What are you shooting at, mister?" asked the driver. The bears fled.

Day Ten. Every time his cell phone rang, Orlando braced himself for the news that someone had seen Mama with only two cubs. It rang at 5:05 on a Wednesday afternoon. "Mama is in my back yard," Rose West reported. "With all three cubs."

Orlando was three minutes away at the time. He drove like a lunatic down the sand road. He jumped from the truck, snatched his gun and hissed at neighbors to go inside. Cathy arrived next. She sneaked along the road and positioned herself to block an escape route. Next, biologist Brian Scheick pulled up in his truck and came running.

Mama smelled them. She and her cubs began moving with purpose toward a field. Hitting the dirt, Orlando crawled on his elbows after them like an Army infantryman. At the edge of the field, Mama stood sniffing the air, trying to figure out the threat. At her feet the oblivious cubs, including poor Jarhead, played with Spanish moss. Orlando lay frozen behind a grapevine thicket, his heart pounding.

Mama ambled in his direction. Stopped. Sniffed again. She stepped even closer. Sniffed again. She was only a few feet away now, on the other side of the thicket. Orlando flicked off the gun's safety and held his breath. Suddenly, she stepped through a gap in the thicket into the open. Orlando pulled the trigger. The dart flew into her buttocks. She jumped, yowled, and ran for the woods.

The dart contained a radio transmitter along with the drug. It was beeping now. Wherever Mama went to sleep, they would find her. But that had to wait. Orlando needed to catch Jarhead now that he had an immediate chance. The little bear and his siblings looked at him anxiously from a few feet away. They wanted to follow their mother, but they were afraid to run past him.

"HAAAAA!" Orlando yelled, waving his arms. The first two cubs flew past him. Jarhead, his vision impaired, bolted into a fence. Scheick grabbed the hind legs. Orlando grasped the cub by the jar. The little bear may have been weak and hungry, but it was 15 pounds of clawed fury. The two biologists couldn't hang on.

Brian dived—for an instant he appeared to be flying—and nabbed the cub by its hind legs again. As Orlando held the plastic jar in a headlock, Cathy threw a towel around the cub. Maybe the little bear would stop bawling and calm down.

They returned with their prize to the truck. Now it was Cathy's turn to hold the back legs while Orlando gripped the front legs. Brian tried to slide the plastic jar off the cub's head. It wouldn't budge. Brian made a careful slit in the plastic with his pocket knife, allowing Mike to get his hand into the jar. Mike held down the ears while Brian slid the jar off.

The little bear had endured enough. It sank sharp teeth into Mike Orlando's hand and wrapped four paws around his arm as if it were a tree branch. First Orlando yowled like a bear cub. Then he slung the little bear into the bushes. A wild banshee, Jarhead vanished into the forest.

As they caught their breath, the biologists stared in wonder at the plastic jar. They counted three puncture holes, probably made by Mama in her effort to free the cub. The holes apparently had allowed Jarhead to breathe. But what did the little bear drink? Condensation? What did it eat? It must have been very hungry. Yet given its feisty behavior, Jarhead seemed to be in no immediate danger.

Now Orlando turned on a special radio. It picked up the signal from the transmitter dart stuck in Mama's butt. Holding the radio, Orlando and his team tracked the signal into the woods and found Mama in a deep sleep.

She was pretty heavy for a female—about 150 pounds. The biologists recruited neighborhood men to help them drag Mama out of the forest. They left her asleep in the nearest culvert trap with the door open and tiptoed away.

It didn't take long, about a half hour. One by one her cubs joined their slumbering mother in the trap. As Mama slept, Jarhead suckled at her breast. He was going to make it. When Mama woke up, the biologists would set all the bears free.

Everybody on the bear team was exhausted. Everybody wanted to go home and sleep for a couple of days. But that had to wait. They climbed into Orlando's truck and drove down Forest Road 8. Orlando turned left onto a deep sand trail. He passed four mobile homes and then made a right, stopping at a double-wide parked in a clearing.

Georgia Wilcox heard the truck coming. She looked out the window, expecting the worst. "Oh, no!" she thought. "They're here to tell me Jarhead is dead." Georgia was scared to go outside and hear the bad news.

But she forced herself to open the door. Georgia saw the smiles and immediately burst into tears.

Summer 2010.

Sea Turtles

She crawled out of the ocean in the dark, stopping, starting, stopping and then crawling again up the sand, raising her head, sniffing the air, then plowing ahead toward the dunes. We watchers on the beach tried to remain quiet and still. If she noticed, heard, smelled something out of the ordinary, she might turn and lumber back into the Atlantic Ocean.

Sea turtles have been laying eggs on the world's beaches for at least 200 million years. They have been laying eggs on Florida beaches since the land emerged from the sea 25 million years ago. In the twenty-first century the turtles were still hanging on.

It must be so hard now. They drown by the thousands in shrimp trawls and at the end of commercial fishing long lines. Their nesting beaches are mostly developed. The seas in which they spend their lives are fouled with sewage, plastic, and, in some places, oil gushing from broken wells.

Yet here she came onto the beach. In the dark of a Florida night, she crawled out of the surf in Archie Carr National Wildlife Refuge in east-central Florida. In the sea, she was streamlined and powerful. Out of her element, on the beach, she was awkward and fought gravity. She caught her breath. Dragged herself ahead with those flippers.

The persistence and the courage of a sea turtle is enough to make a modern Floridian weep with joy.

She was a loggerhead sea turtle. She was about 4 feet long and 200 pounds. She likely had hatched from a meatball-sized egg here about two decades ago. Tiny, she had dug herself out of the sand, evaded predators on the way to the surf, and avoided being eaten once in the water. She made it to the Gulf Stream, to a weed line, where she was able to hide and eat tiny crabs and shrimp until large enough to survive. The Gulf Stream carried her north, then east, across the Atlantic toward Europe. She reached sexual maturity off Spain or Africa. Eventually she felt the urge to swim west. Somewhere along the way she mated. Somehow—possibly by following the stars or feeling the magnetic pull of the spinning Earth—she managed to find her natal beach after a 5,000-mile journey.

Ancient Americans believed our continent lay on the back of a giant turtle. We're guests on Turtle Island.

The Archie Carr National Wildlife Refuge and its 20 miles of beach is the most significant sea turtle nesting place in North America. In a good summer, scientists count about 15,000 loggerhead nests as well as some green and leatherback turtle nests. Named after the late University of Florida herpetologist Archie Carr, perhaps the best-known sea turtle biologist ever, the refuge is more suburban than wild.

When the federal government started planning the refuge in 1990, a good number of beachfront homes were already in place. Then developers began racing the federal government to the best of the remaining coastline. Developers and American taxpayers each won some beach, lost some beach. On one side of Highway A1A lay million-dollar mansions, golf courses, and shopping centers. On the beach side there was sand and sea turtles.

Mosquitoes and turtles come out after dark during the summer. On a breezeless night, an experienced turtle watcher wore long pants, a long-sleeved shirt, socks, shoes, and a hat. Bug repellent? It couldn't hurt.

The moon had yet to rise; it was very dark on the beach. At least the millionaires who had built their homes on the dunes had obeyed, for the most part, Brevard and Indian River County lighting ordinances. Homeowners are required to extinguish backyard lamps and close the drapes at night. Even the enormous Publix Shopping Center down the way shielded parking lot lights from the beach across the road.

Mother sea turtles prefer the dark; sea turtle hatchlings absolutely require it. Hatchlings instinctively crawl for light. The lightest part of a natural beach is usually the white, foamy surf and the horizon. On a civilized beach, hatchlings may head for the street lamps beyond the dunes and above the highway. Every year, sea turtle hatchlings by the hundreds are crushed under steel-belted radials.

It was a breezy night, which meant no mosquitoes. We descended the stairs to the beach. Our eyes slowly adjusted to the black. We walked, stopped, walked some more, our eyes straining.

We didn't see the turtle. We saw her tracks. Quiet now. She was somewhere in the dark next to the dune. We tried to be patient, giving her time to dig the nest. Facing the dune, she was using her back flippers to hollow out a cylinder-shaped hole about 2 feet deep. Disturb her while she is digging and she might immediately return to the sea. So we waited. Waited some more.

Eventually, I crawled on hands and knees along her track all the way to the dune. If she were still digging, I'd back off. If she were lying flat on the beach and barely moving, she probably was laying eggs. If she were laying eggs it would be safe to turn on a small flashlight—one with a thick red lens that casts no shadow. Once a turtle is committed to laying her eggs, she usually will tolerate the presence of witnesses.

She was laying eggs. I waved to my companions. We took turns lying on our stomachs behind her. Plop. In the faint glow of my light we saw her squeeze three eggs from the vent in her body known as the cloaca. Now she shifted her weight to rear flippers as if she was trying to stand. But the movement served only to stimulate another contraction. She expelled another clutch of ping-pong ball–sized eggs into the hole.

During the next half hour we watched her deposit about 100 eggs. A sea turtle hatchling's sex is determined by the temperature of the sand where eggs are laid. The eggs deepest in the cavity tend to produce male turtles. The shallow eggs produce females. Why? Nobody knows. We do know that even under the best possible circumstances, everything is against the hatchlings. If 1 out of 100 survives, the nest has been a success.

Now she began her next task, burying the eggs. With her flippers she tossed sand into the cavity for a long time. Eventually she pivoted slowly in place and tossed more sand this way and that in what seemed to be a random manner. She knew, of course, exactly what she was doing. After a few minutes we couldn't determine the precise location of her nest.

If we were vexed, perhaps the raccoons, possums, armadillos, and wild hogs that eat turtle eggs would also be confused. Finished, she turned and lumbered downhill, gasping for breath toward the surf. We walked behind her, feeling honored. Few Floridians ever get to see this.

As white foam covered her, as she vanished into the Atlantic, we looked down the coast and beheld the orange glow of civilization. Up the beach about an hour, and a million miles away, was the Space Center at Cape Canaveral.

Perhaps one day we will send a manned flight to Mars. Even if we fail, there are miracles to fathom here on Earth. Right now.

Summer 2010.

How to Photograph a Panther

Heather Green drove with a camera on her lap. If something wild scampered across the highway or flew out of the trees, she wouldn't be fumble-fingered with surprise. She remembered the time she encountered a crested caracara nibbling on a dead-on-the-road opossum. Click, click, click. She got the photo an instant before the rare falcon flew into the trees.

She lives near Lake Okeechobee and works at her husband's furniture business in Fort Myers. During her commute, she doesn't text her peeps or listen to Metallica. An optimist, she expects to see a deer in the next meadow or a barred owl in the oaks. "In Florida," she told me, "anything can happen." Taking a good picture of a deer or an owl is harder than it sounds, but at least deer and owls are common. The photographer who blows her first shot knows she'll eventually get another chance.

Serious wildlife photographers, though, aim higher. They all dream about the one flesh-and-blood creature that almost is as spectral as a unicorn: the spectacularly camera-shy Florida panther.

It's possible more people have won the lottery than seen a panther. What are the chances of having your camera with you and getting a focused, well-composed photograph when the panther shows its whiskers? Astronomically small.

But like I said, Heather Green is an optimist.

Once they roamed all over the state. When Ponce de Leon first saw Florida, there must have been thousands. By the time Heather was born near Fort Lauderdale in 1974, Florida panthers were all but gone, shot dead or crowded out by development. Many biologists, in fact, thought panthers were extinct. It took a mountain lion expert from out West and his trained dogs to determine that Florida still had a few big cats left. Over the years, expensive science and the taxpayer purchase of Florida's wildest lands have staved off what once seemed inevitable, the end of a species.

The state has about 120 panthers now, clinging to life in the southwest hinterlands of our state. Yet most folks live their entire lives within panther territory and never see a big cat or a track. Panthers, which sometimes measure 7 feet from nose to tail, are among the most skittish animals on the planet. They creep, they hunker, they hide in trees. Their prey—mostly deer, hogs, and opossums—meet a quick end when they suffer that lethal neck bite. Panthers don't roar histrionically like lions, but mew and purr and whimper like pampered house cats. They lurk in the most out-of-the-way Florida places and avoid the unpleasant odor of humanity.

So pity the poor wildlife photographer who carries equipment into wild Florida with the express ambition to get a picture of a panther. Easier to get a photograph of Lady Gaga.

In January, Heather was reading blogs about Florida wildlife. Another photographer, she discovered, had actually seen a panther cross a swamp road in South Florida. The photographer had failed to get a picture of the ghostly cat—as photographers inevitably do. Heather telephoned her husband. "If we go down there," she told Mike, "maybe I'll get my picture of a panther."

Mike didn't say, "Are you nuts?" He said, "Okay. We'll go to the Fakahatchee Strand."

Heather Green is one of those people who gushes about critters, especially her two Great Danes, Duchess and Earl, which enjoy the run of their house in Clewiston. Like Roy Rogers and Dale Evans, she and Mike also spend their weekends atop their beloved Appaloosa horses. When Heather took up serious photography five years ago, she practiced her techniques on Tatonka and Spotty.

She owns a series of Canon cameras. She owns lenses that could be telescopes. She tools around in a photographer-friendly four-wheel-drive Jeep with no roof. She studies nature guides, watches animal documentaries, and listens closely to people who know more than she does. She is learning her warblers, those high-strung miniature songbirds that test the mettle of photographers everywhere. She wakes early and goes to bed late to get good pictures.

Once she was afraid of snakes, but she has trained herself to photograph them without flinching. Perhaps one day she will vanquish her fear

No panthers in the trees, but a nice red-shouldered hawk.

of gigantic huntsman spiders that invade her home during rainy season. "They're so big you can hear their legs go clip-clopping down the hall," she told me, sounding guilty. She intends to stop running from spiders and start taking their photographs. Click, click, click.

The twenty-first century weighs heavily on the Florida panther. They require thousands of acres of wilderness. They don't have enough. So every few weeks we read about another road-kill panther. We hear about a bullet-ridden panther found dead in the woods after a spate of livestock predations. It's illegal to kill a panther, but it happens.

Perhaps the biggest enemy of the panther is another panther. Because space is at a premium, panthers—especially males—fight, often to the death. A mature panther will kill a younger male that competes for a mate. The banished young male typically leaves the wilderness to find new territory. Some wander hundreds of miles, into North Florida, somehow staying out of human sight while they search in vain for a girlfriend. But there are no known female panthers living outside southwest Florida's wilderness. So the young males come back south and take their chances.

The Fakahatchee Strand Preserve State Park may be the wildest stretch of wilderness left in the state. At 75,000 acres, it is tucked between

Left: A panther takes in Heather's measure.

Middle: Panthers at play.

Bottom: Goodbye: three panthers walk away from Heather's camera, tails in air. (Panther photos by Heather Green.)

Everglades National Park, Big Cypress National Preserve, and Picayune Strand State Forest. The nearest big city, Naples, lies 25 miles west. Copeland, a collection of shacks and trailers, is within walking distance of the Fakahatchee Park office. Here, the Milky Way still glows at night.

Fakahatchee is a Miccosukee Indian word with several meanings, including "muddy water" and "river of vines." Starting about a century ago, loggers began sawing down the biggest cypress trees. But since then the cypress trees and the pond apples and the swamp maples and the royal palms and the rare ferns and the amazing orchids and the entangling vines and the astonishing creatures with wings and fur and fangs have reclaimed their world.

Alligators bellow from the placid ponds and cottonmouth water moccasins slither from stump to stump. Every year or so, some two-legged explorer gets lost while hoping to see one of the rarest plants on Earth, the ghost orchid.

On the map, the only access is known as Janes Memorial Scenic Drive. Unpaved and about 20 feet across, it is lined for 11 miles by perhaps the most beautiful yet daunting swamp in North America. Florida may have 19 million residents, prestigious art museums, and institutions of higher learning, but in the Fakahatchee, time is going backward. If King Kong comes crashing through the trees, don't bother calling for help. Anyway, my cell phone never works.

I have seen panthers in captivity, of course. Like virtually every wildlife photographer in Florida, I have snapped my share of captive panthers. I am also among the few people who have seen a panther in the wild, though I seldom brag about it. Seeing the panther wasn't a matter of my expertise or even luck. It was almost guaranteed. In 1992, I was invited to write a story about a panther expedition in southwest Florida. The scientists intended to catch a few panthers that had been captured in the past. Those panthers wore radio collars that transmitted data about location and movement. Now it was time to replace the old collars with new ones.

Above us, a scientist in an airplane, listening to a radio receiver, located the collared panther and directed the rest of us, and some specially trained dogs, to the forest where the cat was hiding. As we approached, the dogs chased the panther up a tree. A scientist fired a tranquilizer dart into the bewildered cat. After the panther fell asleep, scientists replaced the collar. When the panther woke, we watched it run away.

I can't lie: it was thrilling. But still it wasn't the same as seeing a wild panther during a hike or drive. Most panther biologists, in fact, have never seen a panther in a random event. Unlike Heather Green, I am not optimistic enough to think I'll ever be around when the rarest large mammal in North America steps onto a remote road. But still.

Whenever I visit southwest Florida, I drive through the Fakahatchee Strand just in case a miracle wants to happen. In the Fakahatchee, there's always a chance.

So I telephoned Heather Green. I asked her if she'd take me along on her next trip. I wanted her to tell me what she saw on a winter day in 2011.

She looked like a swamp gal, in her boots and jeans and T-shirt and the raggedy ball cap under which she had stuffed an acre or two of strawberry blonde hair. In the back of the Jeep she carried ice, Pepsi, and her enormous husband, Mike, who could probably wrassle a bear if he wanted. In the Fakahatchee, a bear is a possibility.

Mike wasn't a bashful fellow, but it was hard for him to complete a sentence once Heather started talking. She talked about their dogs or horses or the time a barred owl flew over the road, about the otters that are the most playful creatures in the world, the pretty butterflies and the herons, about how she and Mike met two decades ago on the strip in downtown Fort Lauderdale, about their travels to Paris and Ireland, about how THEY'RE STILL IN LOVE, and yada yada yada.

She pointed the Jeep down Janes Memorial Scenic Drive, adjusted her Lady Gaga sunglasses, and punched the gas. We saw vultures floating above us through the open roof and heard the hawks sobbing invisibly from the treetops. Then we were driving through the swamp, where the limbs reached for us through the open windows like those angry apple trees in *The Wizard of Oz*.

Heather started talking. "That day was, I guess, the second time I'd ever been in the Fakahatchee. We got here in the late afternoon. We drove for, I don't know, about 10 minutes. Right, Mike?"

From the backseat he grunted.

"We, like, go around the bend. About 200 yards away I see what I think at first are two vultures in the middle of the road. I swing up my camera and look through the telescopic lens. TWO PANTHERS! My mind stops working, but I start shooting through the windshield. So click, click,

click. Then the panthers are gone. Just gone. I look at the screen on my camera. Blurry pictures. Argh."

Photographers sometimes suffer from buck fever.

"We should have sat there and waited, but, you know, I was still excited. So I stepped on the gas. Within, I don't know, a couple of minutes, a black bear poked its head out of the swamp. Then it booked it across the road. In like a blink of the eye. I never even lifted my camera. I was in shock.

"Goodbye, bear. So long, panthers.

"So, it's a little after 5 o'clock. The sun is going down. There's big-time shade. I mean, the whole road is in the shade. I adjust my camera for the low light and turn the Jeep around. We start moving, go around the bend. And there's another panther.

"Oh, my God.

"I didn't know if it was a different panther or one of the ones from before. I just knew I had to get a better photo this time. Click, click, click. Again, it walked off the road and was gone.

"Mike spoke up. The Voice of Reason. He said, 'Let's just stay here and see what happens.' So that's sort of what we did. Well, I pulled up a little more before I turned off the engine. It was really quiet. You could hear the swamp. I climbed out of the Jeep and sort of hid behind the door and pointed the camera down the road.

"Like about three seconds went by. Now, about 60 yards away, I'd say, a panther steps out of the swamp into the road. Click, click, click. I think it heard the camera but didn't know what I was or what the Jeep was and was just curious. It started walking right toward us!

"Then he stopped. I could see him opening his jaws but couldn't hear anything, but I think he must have been mewing. Now a much bigger panther steps into the road. And I realize I'm seeing a mother and a cub. She licks her cub's ear. And then behind the mother steps another small panther. Click, click, click. I'M GETTING PICTURES OF A MOTHER PANTHER AND HER TWO KIDS!

"I would have fainted.

"So now, and this is the most amazing part for me, the two cubs start swatting at each other like kittens will do. It goes on and on, the playing, like Mike and I and our Jeep aren't even there. Then they suddenly turn around and start walking away with their tails just sticking up. Then, whoops, they're gone. They've disappeared back into the swamp. Later I figured out that I had them on the road for three minutes."

Back at home 90 minutes later, she inserted the camera card into her Gateway, which clicked and clicked—and then finally purred something like a panther. Her images, hundreds of them, floated across the computer screen like tawny ghosts.

From those she decided on 11 keepers. She knew she had taken better photographs in her life, but she also knew that no one had taken photographs quite like these.

She and Mike headed to Beef O'Brady's and celebrated with chicken sandwiches and cold beer. Next time, she and her camera will be ready for that bear.

Winter 2011.

Save Florida, Eat an Iguana

George Cera was a burly bon vivant with a shaved head, a devilish goatee, and an appetite for provocative ideas, including one that had been cooking on his back burner for a long time. He was sure Florida would be a better place if citizens started eating iguanas.

"There's one," he hissed, stopping the station wagon in a waterfront forest in Sarasota County. Hunched intensely behind the steering wheel, he aimed his trusty Gamo air rifle out the open window and squeezed the trigger.

Pish!

Thirty feet away, the spiny-tailed black iguana, about 2 feet long, dropped in a heap—shot through its leathery head. Florida's great iguana hunter sprinted to his prize and swung it by the tail into an ice chest. There would be no need to stop at Subway for lunch.

"Save Florida, eat an iguana" happened to be his credo. It also was the name of his new cookbook, on sale in at least a few places.

Iguanas, like Nile monitor lizards and Burmese pythons, weren't supposed to live in Florida, of course. But in the twenty-first century, they were thriving—thanks to lax federal and state laws regarding the pet trade and irresponsible pet owners who routinely lost their critters or let them go as they grew large and feisty.

Now all manner of alien reptiles with no natural enemies were reproducing in the state's southern half as if on a mission to take over Florida. In a matter of decades they had changed the ecology of a place that had taken thousands of years to evolve.

Pythons, which grew longer than 20 feet, were eating deer in the fragile Everglades—and experts feared that humans eventually would end up on the menu. The state was allowing python hunting; for the record, gourmets who had eaten python described the meat as chewy yet sweet. In southwest Florida, nobody was eating the ferocious 6-foot Nile monitor lizards that crept through suburban back yards with impunity. On the other hand, there was no law against killing and barbecuing the homely invaders.

Immature iguanas look like they belong on a Florida postcard—they make you want to cue up Jimmy Buffett—but they pose a significant threat to the environment because they are in the process of eating everything in sight. Pythons and Nile monitor lizards are frightening but infrequently encountered. Iguanas are more like cockroaches, showing up everywhere in the south part of the state but the silverware drawer.

"They are widespread," Kenneth Krysko, who studies iguanas at the University of Florida, told me. "And there are tens of thousands of them." Young iguanas eat eggs of protected sea turtles, gopher tortoises, and burrowing owls. As 7-foot adults, they sup on endangered flora that includes the delicate butterfly sage. For dessert, they devour expensive suburban landscape plants.

Iguanas burrow under houses and undermine sidewalks. They invade attics and nestle in the insulation. They have established clawholds on the Tampa Bay waterfront.

Don't look now, I wanted to tell my neighbors, but something large and green might be poised to eat your hibiscus. Down in Sarasota, a bald-headed man was poised to eat the thing eating your prized shrubbery. "Listen," George Cera told me. "In Central America, in South America, in Mexico, iguanas are considered a delicacy. We ought to be eating them."

In Ohio, where he had grown up, he learned to use a gun to supply his family's vittles. He was never tempted to eat a reptile because they were pets bought by mail starting when he was 12. Anyway, his Eastern diamondback rattlesnake and Gaboon viper were roommates. "When I was in middle school the police would come to my classroom and ask for me. I'd say, 'What did I do?' They'd say, 'Nothing. We need you to catch a snake.'"

He worked in a pet store as a teen. That scar on his head? A capuchin monkey. The scar on his face? A 9-foot python. "Not good pets. Neither are iguanas," said Cera, who once owned one named Rusty. "They require a lot of care, and adult males are especially aggressive during mating season. They have big teeth and bite."

As an adult, Cera had worked as a carpenter and as one of those guys who catches possums and raccoons in suburban attics. During Florida's last building boom, he had moved south for the climate and a

The hungry George Cera fires a pellet rifle out his car window at a tasty lizard. (Photo by Maurice Rivenbark.)

construction job. Immediately he saw business opportunities that had nothing to do with hammer and saw. Florida! Bizarre Land! A Carl Hiaasen novel come to life!

Of course, I couldn't wait to hang out. He was 41 on the day of our great iguana hunt. He smoked Marlboros and his cell phone featured the mighty cry of an enraged chimpanzee.

The same phone had shrieked a few years before; on the line was somebody from the Big Gasparilla Island government in Charlotte County. Guy wanted to know if he'd help with their, ahem, iguana problem.

It seemed a couple of iguana pets had gotten loose in the 1980s. Now there were thousands on the 7-mile-long island known for marinas, tarpon fishing, rich folks and, increasingly, reptiles. They were eating tortoise eggs. They were eating the eggs of protected burrowing owls. Small ones occasionally slithered through pipes and appeared in toilets.

The iguana bounty was $20 each. Cera set catch-'em-alive traps. Iguanas may be primitive, cold-blooded lizards, but they were smart enough to avoid traps. Cera found it simpler, and less cruel, to shoot them with his pellet gun.

Not everybody was happy. Not everybody said, "Thank you for saving Florida from the lizard plague." Someone vandalized his vehicle. Anonymous callers woke him in the middle of the night with death threats. "I

George Cera with today's lunch. (Photo by Maurice Rivenbark.)

hope your children die," someone wrote the single father of two in an e-mail.

In a way, he had sympathy for the plight of the iguana. "There is no such thing as a bad animal," Cera told people. "Iguanas are just iguanas. They didn't ask to come to Florida. They were brought here. They were let loose by idiots. Now they are destroying Florida. We can't let that happen."

In two years, he bagged 12,000 iguanas on Big Gasparilla Island and didn't get them all. One day he may have to start all over again.

"I ended up giving the dead iguanas to crab fishermen to use as bait. But it bothered me. It would have been nice to have found another use for them."

Stewed iguana. Iguana pizza. Iguana tacos.

In the twenty-first century, Sarasota and Manatee Counties in southwest Florida may have had more iguanas than Democrats. They were taking over the waterfront, scampering along bulkheads, and basking in the sea grapes. Cera still caught the occasional opossum or rattlesnake in a caller's carport for a fee. But he was up to his elbows in iguana work on the reptile-infested waterfront.

He wore a yellow T-shirt with "Lizard Control" on the back. He had scars on his arms and scabs on his legs from handling live iguanas. The missing fingertip? Nile monitor lizard. He preferred to shoot at a distance.

In Central America, iguanas sometimes were known as the chickens of the trees. In 2006, Cera began collecting recipes for a cookbook. There was no shortage of recipes. "Iguanas are delicious," said biologist Meg Lowman, who earned her doctorate studying trees in the tropics where iguanas are plentiful. "Everybody ate them." When she became director of environmental initiatives at New College of Florida in Sarasota she began promoting "an iguana in every pot" for Floridians.

In Florida, some communities prohibit the discharge of firearms or animal cruelty, but there was no state law against killing an iguana in a clean and efficient manner. Where legal, George Cera went for a quick shot to the head or spine with his pellet rifle.

Summer. Morning. The air felt as moist as a bloodhound's breath. The fearless iguana hunter was on the prowl. "In no shape or form do I enjoy killing iguanas," he explained from behind the steering wheel. "In fact, I'm sick of the killing. One day I want to lay down this gun and just do public education. But for now I can't do that. There are too many. We might as well take advantage and eat them."

He steered off the road near a boat ramp. It was Carl Hiaasen country: The pepper trees were from Brazil, the pines from Australia, and the quaker parrots from Paraguay. Cera's sharp eyes detected something in the shade of a Brazilian pepper. Slowly he pointed the rifle out the car window.

Pish!

Bull's-eye. An iguana from Mexico, third of the day, was deposited into his ice chest. At home he spilled his iguanas into the kitchen sink. Like a farmer preparing a freshly killed chicken, he slit them open with a sharp knife.

Okay. Guts out. Now he dipped each carcass in boiling water just long enough to loosen the skin. Skin came off like a baggy pair of pants. Next he threw the naked iguanas into another big pot. Turned the heat up to boil. In the meantime, his best friend, Christy Conde, visiting from Ohio, began slicing carrots, celery, onions, and potatoes in an expert manner. She was famous for her chicken soup, George Cera claimed. She threw the veggies in the pot with the iguana and turned the heat down to simmer.

We waited. We talked about love, about reptiles, about life. About an hour later, the kitchen smelled like grandma's kitchen. George Cera started ladling.

Bon appetit!

I stared at the bowl and prayed for courage. Okay. Let's do this. I picked up the spoon and dragged it through the bowl. Next I put the spoon into my mouth. The broth, I had to admit, was delicious. The meat? Chewy yet mild. My grandmother would have enjoyed it.

Of course, I would have to spare her at least one little detail.

Summer 2009.

Floridians

Thunderman

Tad Staples savored summer, especially afternoons when the cumulus clouds piled up like dumplings before turning gray and ugly. He liked when the atmosphere above Florida developed late afternoon indigestion. First there were the little rumbles, then the dramatic rolls. When the main course arrived he could hardly contain himself. He attached two microphones to the screen front door and switched on his tape deck. Through headphones he listened to what he was recording. As the tempest peaked, as the crash-boom-bah apocalypse seemed imminent, I watched him standing in the dim light, swaying to music that had moved his soul.

Staples, who was 56, was Florida's Thunderman. He kept track of it for the rest of us. It was his hobby. He loved its majesty and power. He collected it on tape and stored it in his memory. He listened, critiqued, interpreted. He was like no one else I have ever known.

Sometimes he sold a recording to a sound-effects company, but for him a sale was merely icing on the cake. In his otherwise small world thunder was everything, and he was always surprised when he found out that other people lacked his enthusiasm. They may have claimed to be interested but they weren't. He'd telephone, leave a long voice mail, but they never called back. "They just flap their gums about being interested," he said after the latest bout of hurt feelings.

Kerpow! Summer in Florida! The sky is on fire!

Thunderman couldn't see it. He had been blind since infancy.

Crackety-blam! While the rest of us cowered in the closet, he aimed his dead eyes toward the heavens and for a moment felt like a lamb of God.

"Whoa! That was a good one!" For an instant, a profoundly lonely human cracked a small smile. He had diabetes and arthritis to go along with his blindness. He was pale and overweight and needed dental care.

He lived alone in near-poverty in a rented house with a leaky roof. His personality got in the way of friendships; he suffered from depression.

He had never been able to explain to family, friends, strangers, or doctors his obsession with thunder—perhaps because he didn't understand it himself. People disappointed but thunder never did. Thunder never said, "You're crazy! Quit bothering us! Grow up!" Thunder filled him up like the lamb chops in his refrigerator.

He had been born lonely, in Melrose, Illinois, on February 13, 1952. Tiny and weak, he ended up in an incubator, one of those rare infants who develops retinopathy of prematurity or ROP. The high doses of incubator oxygen damaged his undeveloped retinas. Some babies recover, but he didn't, and even when he stood on his porch and lightning electrified Tampa, he saw nothing of the flash. "My blindness was a blessing. It allowed me to develop my other talents. I listen very well."

He never forgot a sound. He could imitate the sputtering engine of the Piper Club flying over his house. Listening to televised bowling, he could perform an accurate imitation of ball striking pin. He performed train imitations, steam-locomotives and diesel. He was always trying to talk someone into driving him to the tracks so he could make a perfect recording up close.

Thunder was his raison d'être. "Each thunderclap is different, like a snowflake," he told me, and the imitations poured out of him, the cloud-to-ground, ground-to-cloud, cloud-to-cloud, the rolling thunder he heard on summer afternoons.

"I disappointed my parents. They wanted, I guess, the best for me, they wanted me to use my intelligence and find a way to support myself. They hated my interest in thunder. They said, 'Cut it out!' They thought that my love of thunder was a distraction from the important things they wanted me to be doing. I'd record it, and listen to it, and I'd say, 'Listen to this' and I remember my mother saying"—he mimics her voice—"'If you say one more thing about thunder you will be severely punished.' I'd have to wait until my mom and dad left the house to get back to my thunder. They'd swat my interest in thunder away like it was a fly."

Bzzzzz.

He imitated an obnoxious housefly.

By third grade he could read braille as fast as sighted children read their school books. Even now he devoured braille books and books on

Tad Staples listens to a recording of lightning. (Photo by John Pendygraft.)

tape like a starving man. He recently had read *The Perfect Storm* by Sebastian Junger. He liked the atmospheric novels of Cormac McCarthy because violent weather accompanied the violent characters.

Braille books and Library of Congress recordings were scattered about his claustrophobic three-room bungalow in a blue-collar neighborhood where men worked on their own cars under the oaks. He knew his nearest neighbors and their dogs by sound; he heard a distant bark and said, "There's Skippy."

He heard the mail truck coming a long block away. He heard the faintest train horn in the distance. He identified birds in the maple by their songs. He had listened incessantly to a book on tape about birds until he learned their vocalizations.

He listened to famous speeches on tape. To entertain me he performed Babe Ruth, throat ravaged by throat cancer, delivering his farewell speech at Yankee Stadium. He performed Winston Churchill emoting about blood, sweat, and tears. Suddenly Churchill became *Lord of the Rings* author J.R.R. Tolkien broadcasting a tennis match at Wimbledon.

His folks, the late Archene and Eugene Francis Staples, never understood their son's obsession. He was no longer in contact with his three siblings. "If I saw them they would only say, 'You still haven't given up thunder,' and that would be a great big downer." When I asked where they lived, for their phone numbers, any details about them at all, he said, "I prefer not to think of them."

His family moved to Indiana when he was a boy. He was 12 when he became obsessed with thunder after sitting at home listening to a passing storm. "It was the sound, the deep, satisfying sound." He also had an affinity for music. His working-class parents hoped he might have a career like Ray Charles. He lacked the dedication, though he had played organ at Calvary Community Church in Tampa for two decades. A small church salary and Social Security were his only sources of steady income.

Sometimes he skipped the Wednesday evening service when a thunderstorm was brewing. Otherwise, a church deacon picked him up and drove him to the service, stopped at Publix on the way home and bought him groceries, carried them into the dark house, maneuvered through the debris on the kitchen floor, and stacked the groceries in the refrigerator—the only place in the house with a working light.

When he was lucky, a clap of thunder woke him. If not, he depended on the radio for clues. He owned many radios, including instruments that broadcast weather alerts when storms were in the vicinity. If he heard something interesting, he sometimes telephoned the nearest weather bureau for more information.

People at the weather bureau knew him only by voice. Some had learned to hang up when they heard the voice, because they knew a long monologue about thunder and their failure to be interested in thunder was in the offing.

Frequently he telephoned newspaper columnists for long weather-related conservations. In one of our talks he told me he sometimes telephoned the Rwanda embassy in Washington to request recordings of African thunderstorms—but had yet to receive one. More often, he called the research desk of the Tampa-Hillsborough Library for information but ended up launching a tirade when he felt his questions were treated with disrespect. I talked to a librarian about him; she rolled her eyes.

Thunderman also was mystified about his poor relationship with weather professionals. In a perfect world he might have telephoned the Fox TV weatherman, Paul Dellegatto, and invited him over for chat. Thunderman would fix his friend lamb chops and pour glasses of diet tea. After eating they'd retire to the den to listen to one of his hundreds of recordings. He'd put on a favorite from July 4, 2004, and turn the volume way up.

First they'd hear the rumble, the wind in the distance, the sound of the interstate.

CRAAAAACK!

Thunderman wouldn't jump. He would sway.

I called Dellegatto. "I have actually never met Mr. Staples," Dellegatto told me. "But I'll bet I've talked to him 500 times. He seems to always call about two minutes before I'm going on the air."

We sat in Thunderman's yard and listened to jets landing at Tampa International. If he hears them circling he knows they must be flying around bad weather and goes on high alert. He was on high alert right now.

"We have three or four storm clusters in the vicinity," he said. "They're pulsing up and down. HEAR THAT RUMBLE? It's north of here, on the Hillsborough and Pasco borders, and that won't help me. WAIT! Hear it? The other one? It's 4 miles away, to the west of us, over Tampa Bay, heading for Caladesi Island. It's going to miss us."

CRACK!

"Excuse me. That one has possibilities. It's east of us, coming this way. I must prepare my equipment."

Once or twice a year he got a recording he might sell, for a couple hundred dollars, to a sound-effects company. Tampa's Michael Oster, director of F7 Sound and Vision, once edited a Thunderman recording and told me, "I can tell you it's challenging enough for a sighted person to make professional recordings. There are meters to read, tape lengths to consider, microphone placement to consider."

Thunderman, of course, had to set up his equipment by feel and memory. He did so now as I watched. "Okay, sounds like a good storm. It could even have hail. It could be big."

The storm petered out and we exited the claustrophobic house. I sat on the stoop. He sat on a moldy chair. "I have a theory about thunder," he said. "You can tell how powerful a storm is going to be by its lowest audible frequency. I would love to work with someone about this. We could warn people about the storm by the sound of the thunder. I can't get scientists interested. They are like everyone else I have met. They are like the people who say to me, 'You are a thunder-loving son of a bitch, aren't you?' My dad was like that."

A different kind of storm was suddenly brewing.

"My dad was like me. He sometimes spoke before he thought things out. The fucking this and the fucking that. He had a heart of gold; he could fix things. He had a wonderful singing voice. He'd get so mad at me. 'Get off your ass, you stupid dumb shit. You cold, selfish little shit. If you don't like my God-damned rules, pack your fucking bags and get the hell out of my house.'"

Thunderman did. With grant money from a charity he was able to move to Tampa from Indiana two decades ago. He did not return home even after his dad suffered his final heart attack. Sometimes, in a nightmare, his dad is alive, in his room in Tampa, demanding that he come back home and forsake thunder.

"Every day I live with the hatred," he said. For that reason he wondered if he—the disappointing son—was destined for the nether regions. "God gives you a report card. Did you go to church? Check. Did you read your Bible? Check. There are other things, too. I get angry, I curse, but I am working on those things. I am trying to work on emotional maturity."

Perhaps there would be thunder in heaven. Perhaps the angels need somebody to study the thunder in the clouds. In Thunderman's heaven, nobody would hang up on him because he was different.

Summer 2008.

Oil Boy

The night started badly for Frederic Kahler. His restless feet, tapping like Fred Astaire in that big showpiece number with Ginger Rogers in *Top Hat*, kept him awake. He took his nervous energy over to his studio on Avenue D, where he often painted abstracts, portraits, landscapes, whatevers. He told me he had been painting quite a few whatevers. They reflected what was going on in the northern Gulf of Mexico during the spring and summer of 2008—namely, the gushing of millions of gallons of oil that already had taken a toll on wildlife, beaches, and people who lived on the coast.

The oil hadn't washed ashore in Apalachicola, but that summer it was on everybody's mind. Apalachicola, population 2,000, was the most important commercial fishing port left in Florida. Its small-town charm was catnip to tourists.

Kahler called himself the Oil Boy. He had a Facebook page by that name. He often made small oil spill–themed paintings because they were easier to sell. But he had a friend, Tamara Suarez, who operated the little Café con Leche on Water Street. He worked for her afternoons. A passionate Venezuelan, she told him: "Frederico, you must do a painting that drips with oil that looks like blood."

That is what he was doing in the studio on the night he couldn't sleep. He started working on a huge, passionate, anti–oil spill painting full of misery and pathos. He'd hang it on the wall of the café, his Louvre. Maybe a tourist would throw down $500 and take it home. Whatever. It would be the Oil Boy's grandest statement yet.

He lived in what might be the last great Florida town. Apalachicola has everything from seafood restaurants where diners suck down raw oysters without wiping their chins to an amazing bookstore stocked with everything—Florida volumes and enough yarn to keep every knitter on the Panhandle happy. Another shop's inventory includes bandages that look like bacon strips.

On the waterfront, ramshackle commercial fishing shacks appear poised to tumble into the river on the next full-moon tide. On the dock, men with ZZ Top beards, nose rings, and tattoos haul sacks of oysters from boat to shucker. If you yell "Hey, Jethro," one or more may turn around. Folks answer to "Pinky" and "Tiny" as well.

If an artsy guy who served coffee by day and painted by night while singing opera to soothe his own tormented soul wanted to call himself "the Oil Boy," nobody cared in Apalachicola. The Oil Boy had found a place where he felt comfortable.

He was born in France in 1962. An Army brat, he lived all over the world. His mother, Sonya, was a sign painter. He got his artistic talent from her. He was the oldest of seven children. His dad took off, which meant Frederic had to take care of the kids while his mother scratched out a living. "Life was all about chaos," he told his friends. He joined the Air Force because he "loved the structure." The Air Force did not return the love because he was gay.

After quitting the military he cooked in Seattle and painted pretty desert pictures in Las Vegas. He and his partner, Dana, another artist, lost their Nevada home during the Great Recession and ended up in Apalachicola in 2008.

In the evenings the Oil Boy pulled on a yellow Speedo, sprinted through the reeds and took a dip in Apalachicola Bay. He weighed 125 pounds soaking wet. "Eat something!" his passionate friend, Tamara, was always telling him at her café. He swilled juice, had a carrot, maybe tore a hunk from one of her delicious cherry muffins, which he chewed listlessly. "Americans eat too much. We're too fat," he said, glancing at my waistline.

In a pickup truck kind of a town, he had never learned to drive a car and walked or rode a bike everywhere. Everybody downtown seemed to know him, yelling their hellos from doorways and truck windows. He called people whose names he had forgotten "Darling." He told me he smoked six cigarettes a day, like the late Audrey Hepburn, but without the pretentious cigarette holder. He told me without embarrassment about his years as a crystal meth addict and an alcoholic. "There is truth in wine," he said. "The problem is it can go too far. A man becomes a bad boy and a woman becomes a girl who goes wild."

Jeff Klinkenberg (*left*) with "Oil Boy" Frederic Kahler and his paintings behind them. (Photo by Susan King.)

Sometimes, when he felt downhearted, he cleaned the RV or washed clothes. "I love doing laundry," he said. Dirty clothes symbolized chaos to him. After the oil accident, BP and other emergency folks established a just-in-case beachhead in Apalachicola. "Is there a place around here where I can wash my clothes?" asked an odoriferous worker while drinking coffee one day at Tamara's place. "I'll do it," announced Oil Boy. Soon he was laundering the dirty socks, underwear, and T-shirts of emergency workers in Apalachicola. He hadn't sold any of them a painting.

His art studio was on the second floor of a nearby building. A self-taught musician, he sometimes picked up his violin and played Beethoven or Bach as he incubated an idea. Sometimes he sat at an electric piano and played something by his favorite group, the Carpenters, or perhaps a song by Diana Ross.

He seldom painted on an easel; he spread his canvas on the floor and knelt over it. The canvas he used for his grand artistic statement was about 5 feet long and 3 wide. He threw paint at it like Jackson Pollock on a bender.

He was afraid the paint was too thick. Anyway it refused to drip across canvas like blood or like oil. He carried the canvas downstairs to the water spigot. With a hose, he squirted enough water to thin the paint. That was more like it. But then he yanked on the hose with a little too much force. Crack. The pipe broke behind the spigot and water rushed out, flooding the floor. There was no way to turn off the spigot.

It was the middle of the night. The water ran out of the broken spigot like oil from the bottom of the gulf. Oil Boy is good with his hands, but he stood in the puddle of water like an impotent BP oilman.

He woke his landlord, who was able to shut off the building's water main. Suddenly, Oil Boy felt like something mystical had happened. The oil spill. A water spill. Art imitating life. He finished the painting like a madman.

"The epitome of chaos is the oil spill," he told me.

He tossed and turned in his bed until noon, got up, and drank juice. His partner drove him to the studio, where he grabbed his painting and walked to the café. At lunch, patrons drank their coffee and looked at his masterpiece. He hung it between a painting of an oil-threatened lighthouse illuminated by a BP sun and a painting of a flower being attacked by a river of oil.

His grand artistic statement had a Van Gogh *Starry Night* thing going on. Except most of the action was taking place under the sea during a horrendous oil spill. In the painting, Van Gogh's stars were replaced by the skeletons of doomed fish that poured from the broken pipe. They swam to the surface and became flying fish skeletons. Shining down upon them was another BP sun.

In the afternoon, a stout commercial fisherman walked over from the waterfront past the painting and ordered an espresso. While he fixed coffee, Oil Boy broke into song, softly at first but then with gusto. He sang something from the *Phantom of the Opera*, a number called "Prima Donna." At the counter, the audience of one witnessed the performance in utter silence.

Summer 2010.

11

Tim Chapman

Tim Chapman was almost finished building the most macho house in the Florida Keys. With his bare hands, of course. With his larger-than-life personality contained inside and outside the walls. His house was going to be fortress. His house was going to be ready for a fight. Just like he was. "I think every real man, at some time in his life, should build his own shelter," he declared in his pugnacious way.

He was a surprisingly agile 270-pounder who had muscles on top of muscles. His brawny house on the most remote island in the inhabited Keys sat atop bridge-quality pilings above a backyard canal and a flooded mangrove swamp. The walls, he told me, were 16 inches thick, filled with cement and steel. The metal roof was held in place by thousands of extra-long stainless screws, steel straps, wire and bolts.

He was building his house to withstand a catastrophe of biblical force: 300 mph winds, Category 5 hurricane tides, and the uncivilized aftermath that could follow. "If my house blows down in a hurricane, then nothing else will be left in the Keys either," he announced, sounding as if he were curious—if not eager—to test his house and mettle against a big one.

Chapman, 58 that year, was something of a fortress himself. He seemed like a character out of one of those wild Carl Hiaasen novels. Tough but tormented. A little crazy in a soldier of fortune kind of way.

He didn't seem to me to belong in modern Florida. He read Emerson, Thoreau, Walt Whitman, even the journals of Meriwether Lewis and William Clark. I asked about Hemingway, who had once lived in the Keys. "Ernest Hemingway would never live in today's Key West," he declared, thinking of the sodden and pusillanimous strollers on Duval Street. "He would live right here on Big Torch Key. It's the old Keys."

He probably was right. Hemingway would probably enjoy palling around someone like Chapman, who had grown up wild on the edge

A man and his castle. (Photo by Bill Cooke.)

of the Everglades and become an expert hunter and fisher, smoked big cigars, drank whiskey, and liked women as much as he liked to fight.

In certain Florida corners, Chapman was the stuff of legend. My favorite Chapman story was about the time he saw a motorist change lanes to run over a harmless milk snake. After scooping up the lifeless reptile, Chapman chased the other vehicle to a red light, dragged the driver out from behind the wheel, and attempted to shove the snake down the man's screaming throat.

"A true story?" I asked.

"I was brought up never to kill anything you don't eat," he told me.

Hemingway, the artist, seemed to have a psychological and physical need to measure himself against danger and other men. Chapman, a *Miami Herald* photographer for four decades, had covered eight wars, 50 hurricanes and human nature at its worst.

In 1978, three days after a crazed prophet named Jim Jones had persuaded more than 900 followers to drink cyanide-laced fruit drinks in Jonestown, Guyana, Chapman talked his way on to a flight to South America and was among the first journalists to witness the carnage on the ground.

He remembered gagging at the smell and the sight of so much death. Lacking a bandanna, he wadded a chamois cloth into his mouth. That helped. So did letting his camera become his eyes. It provided just enough detachment to keep him going. His photographs of the bloated bodies were published all over the world. "I had to get the photos," he told people. "Without them the world wouldn't have believed what had happened. I will take Jonestown to the grave."

He loved to fish in the Keys. He loved to cast a fly in the direction of a muscular tarpon, the most macho of all saltwater game fish. When a 100-pound tarpon felt a hook's sting, it leaped from the water in panic, shaking, rattling and tumbling. Then it dove deep and refused to give up for hours. A tarpon was not a fish for sissies.

As Chapman built his fortress in the Keys he tried to stay close in spirit to his late father, George Chapman, whom he tried to emulate in every way. The buffalo nickel his marksman dad had blasted out of the air years ago with a .22-caliber bullet was buried in the foundation of the fortress.

"My dad was the toughest man anyone ever met. He was a staff sergeant in Patton's Third Army, 87th Infantry, and was in combat for 110 straight days. But he cooked better biscuits than my mother."

Chapman's dad had tried to teach his only son to be tough. "He came from that generation of men who could do anything with their hands, do the plumbing, electrical work, rebuild engines, take care of their families even though he only had an eighth grade education. He could shoot doves out of the air with a single-shot shotgun. Down in the Everglades, he'd run the bays at night in his boat when there weren't any markers or lights to a place where he caught the fish they now call a goliath grouper. Huge fish. We ate grouper stewed, smoked, fried, baked for weeks at a time."

I've known other men like Chapman's dad. They scared me.

"One time, when I was a boy," Chapman said, "I was shooting doves over a field and this guy came out of a nearby house and said, 'Son, are you the one who has been peppering my house with bird shot?' and I said, 'No, sir. It wasn't me.' The guy didn't believe me."

George Chapman, eyes glittering, walked up. Asked what was wrong.

"Your little bastard . . ." were the only words the complainant managed to get out.

"My dad laid him out with a broken jaw."

You are Tim Chapman. You were born in rural Kentucky. Your relatives prayed to Jesus and made moonshine. In Miami, your blue-collar family is poor in material things. To some people you are inferior. You are a redneck. You answer with your fists.

Your work ethic, your brains and your resourcefulness are your other weapons.

In 1968, when other Miami teenagers are flipping burgers, you are catching snakes by hand in the Big Cypress and selling them to a scientist for 50 cents a foot. During the day you tar roofs and pour cement. A building contractor tells you: "You're too young for this work, legally speaking. But I'm going to let you. If it don't kill you it'll make you a man."

You are Tim Chapman, 18. You feel things deeply. You want to defend the natural Florida you love.

You block a developer's storm drain with a cement plug to keep his stinking pollutants out of Biscayne Bay. You buy a chain saw to chop down the most offensive of those fucking billboards.

You're asking for trouble. You're going to end up in jail if you stay in Miami.

So after high school, you head for Canada, live with an Ojibway woman, are lulled to sleep by the howling timber wolves, and wake early every morning to guide tourists to lakes where they angle for wily muskies.

You return to Florida, pick up a camera, get married, graduate from the University of Miami and in 1972 take a job at the "Herald." You are more dedicated to your newspaper job than your marriage. You have that bad temper. You have that roving eye. When your wife finally leaves, you tell her:

"I would have left me years ago."

Chapman put his son, Eric, through medical school, paying in cash. "I don't believe in credit cards," he told me. When he bought his Keys lot in 1982 he paid $17,000, cash. It was located in a sparsely developed area, about 20 miles from Key West, on Big Torch. It was 8 miles from busy U.S. 1, down a lonely, serpentine road on a barely dry spot in a mangrove swamp where mosquitoes hovered in clouds. It was on the water. There were tarpon, lots of them. There were neighbors, but not many.

He was 32, but already thinking of retirement and of a weekend place to escape the twentieth century. So now he owned a lot in the Keys. But now he had no money left to build the dream house. He began saving hunks of his *Herald* paycheck.

When Chapman was not covering wars or hurricanes, he spent his workdays driving through Miami, listening to a police scanner, smoking cigars and drinking eye-opening Cuban coffee by the quart. When he heard something interesting, he sped to the scene, snapped a photo, and e-mailed it to the newspaper office.

He liked to tell people:

"My dad said, whatever you do, do it the best you can. I want to honor that, tell the story . . . of one man in a photo so good it tells the story of mankind. I want to be the best newsman that ever lived, the fastest, with the best news judgment."

In the newsroom, stories abounded about the intense, gung-ho photographer who knew how to swear in several languages, start a fire without matches, and feed himself, if necessary, with road kill. Colleagues remembered the time he had removed the tail from a dead Tamiami Trail alligator and brought it back to Miami, and a barbecue, in a *Herald* vehicle.

In the middle of a civil disturbance, according to another story, Chapman snapped his last photo and drove to the only fruit stand still open in burning Miami. "Fuck it," Chapman told the reporter who cowered in the backseat. "This is my town, and if I want to buy melons, I'll buy melons." He purchased his melons, sauntered through a crowd of angry men, and returned to his vehicle. Then he tugged on his Army helmet—his preferred headgear in dangerous situations—and burned rubber.

In another often-told story he was on assignment in Haiti when a self-possessed young reporter handed him a long to-do list. He read it carefully, blew cigar smoke into her face and said, "I'm not your errand boy."

In Miami, according to another story, a rare freeze had discombobulated the tropical iguanas at a state park. Stunned by the cold, they were dropping like leaves from trees. Chapman called an editor about what was happening; the editor sounded skeptical. An hour later, the editor heard an ominous plop on his desk—followed by the terrifying sight of Chapman massaging the cold-stunned iguana back to life.

"If somebody ever writes a history of the *Herald*, Tim will have an important role," Carl Hiaasen, famous for his satirical novels about Florida, told me. "He's an authentic character who is completely fearless. Some people think he's crazy, and there may be some truth to that."

People who read Hiaasen's Florida novels often asked the author about his most glorious creation—the wild man known as Skink. Skink sups on road kill, lives by his wits, and emerges from his wilderness refuge to

Chapman at work, transmitting photos from his car to the *Miami Herald* by computer. (Photo by Bill Cooke.)

discipline the developers, politicians and con men who wreak havoc on natural Florida.

Chapman once had told me about one of his favorite pets, a golden retriever. Bullet had been a splendid animal except for one bad habit, digging. He liked to dig under the fence and loll in neighborhood swimming pools. It was only a matter of time before Bullet died crossing a street on the way home.

A friend had advised Chapman how to train Bullet. Use one of those electric collars, the friend said, and zap Bullet whenever he nears the fence. Chapman loved Bullet and was concerned that zapping would hurt too much. So he tested the collar on himself.

The electric jolt blasted him off his feet. A few years later, Hiaasen published *Stormy Weather*. In it, Skink kidnaps a cretinous tourist he catches videotaping the aftermath of a Cat 5 hurricane. Skink fits the lout with an electric dog collar and zaps him whenever he says anything stupid.

"I borrowed from Tim's personal experience," Hiaasen told me.

When it came to the opposite sex, Tim Chapman had never practiced monogamy. Back when he had been young and pretty, certain women apparently found it hard to resist his unique mix of smart and crazy. For a while, his expressed ambition was to share his charms with every TV anchorwoman in Miami.

The womanizer disappeared in 1997. He met a beautiful woman—his own age for a change—in the courthouse in Miami. She supervised bailiffs and looked criminal scum in the eye without blinking. Charlene Hall, born in Florida, was canny and tough and loved to fish. Charlene was also conveniently unattached.

They have been together since. She doesn't mind Tim's pet rat snakes or monkey skulls. Tim tolerates her eBay splurges and trips to Nordstrom. She has no problem with his guns and Bowie knives. He is fine with her makeup scattered on the sink. She never touches his hammers and saws and wrenches and pliers. She puts up with his obsessive neatness and need to plan for any emergency.

She likes his friends, especially Hiaasen, who always listens intently to Tim's craziest stories when they go to dinner as if he might be planning another Skink escapade.

Tim Chapman wanted to build the best house in the history of houses. He drew up plans based on what he had learned from covering hurricanes. When a house survived, he tried to understand why.

He began building six years ago—he'd saved thousands of dollars—working on weekends and vacation and living in a battered RV. He dug through the limestone and coral with a pick and shovel and laid a foundation 18 inches deep.

In the Keys, freshwater is expensive. He built a 20,000-gallon cistern, with 12-inch walls, to collect the rain. He put solar panels on the roof to generate enough electricity to heat the water. The pilings that hold the house 14 feet above the swamp are driven 7 feet into the rock. The slate floors in the two-bedroom, one-bath house are a foot thick.

He built the inside walls and rounded ceiling from pine. He installed Italian marble in the bathroom. He furnished the house with furniture his late dad had built. His father had always loved cedar. To honor him, Tim drove to Kentucky, harvested trees, and stored them two years in a warehouse. After they dried he trailered them to the Keys and milled the logs into boards and built the master bedroom where he and Charlene sleep.

Last spring, as Tim was putting the finishing touches on the house, Charlene felt a lump in her breast.

"Maybe it's nothing," Tim told her.

The tests at the clinic showed otherwise.

"Don't you dare ever bring another woman into this house!" she ordered him out of the blue. She had the mastectomy.

On her first night home, he gave her a sponge bath and decided to take a leave from work to take care of her. "That's my new role," he told me. "I've never been a caretaker before."

He planned to be the best caretaker in the history of caretaking. Caretaking was hard, though, and even harder for him was acknowledging that some things were outside his control. He had always strived to be in control of his own destiny and feel he could protect loved ones from every danger.

Charlene's cancer. It was beyond his control. He'd have to be patient. And maybe even pray.

Back in his bachelor days he did what he pleased, said what he pleased, hurt feelings and smoked cigars wherever he wanted. Charlene hated the smell of his cigars. So now he smoked on the back deck as he watched the canal for the tarpon. Smoking outside was a gift for the woman he loves.

Fall 2009.

12

Flip-Flop Man

The Flip-Flop Man has long been a legend in west-central Florida. Yet very few people know his name or much about him other than his affection for flimsy rubber sandals. Flip-Flop Man lacks an automobile or driver's license, but he is surprisingly mobile. He lives in Madeira Beach, near the center of Pinellas County, but folks frequently see him miles away in Gulfport, Seminole, Clearwater, Dunedin, Tarpon Springs, Tampa, Brooksville, and far beyond.

On sunny days his ensemble includes an enormous sombrero and a long-sleeved shirt buttoned at the neck so that the tails fly behind him like a cape. On overcast days, he goes bareheaded and bare-chested, sticks to plaid boxers and, if he is feeling especially debonair, carries a cane or walking stick.

People encounter Flip-Flop Man at high noon and at midnight. If they happen to be out at 4 a.m. the moonlight sometimes illuminates not a pink elephant floating across the highway but the Flip-Flop Man out for a wee-hour ramble.

The Flip-Flop Man is a garrulous fellow with salt-and-pepper hair and a scruffy beard. Many women I know describe him as "handsome," even though he apparently often smells like a sweaty locker room and is toothless from eating sugar. Ironman triathlon champion Jackie Yost, 78, once told me: "He has beautiful legs."

The Flip-Flop Man has a muscular 5-foot-10-inch frame and seems to lack any body fat whatsoever. In a normal week, he runs or walks 125 miles—6,500 miles in a year. In 1995, his best year, he flip-flopped about 33 miles a day, approximately 230 miles a week, 12,000 miles in all—equal to a trip from St. Petersburg to Athens, Greece, and back. At the time he was 62 years old.

"He must have the constitution of Superman," marathoner Bill Castleman once told me. A typical Flip-Flop endurance event lasts eight hours, though sometimes, when he can't sleep—the Flip-Flop Man deals with more demons than most of us—he flip-flops 20 hours.

One time he asked his friend Lisa Lorrain a question that continues to haunt her: "Are you happy?" he said. "I have never been happy."

The Flip-Flop Man raced into Joe Burgasser's world two decades ago. Burgasser, a renowned athlete himself, was founder of the Forerunners, a long-distance running club. Two afternoons a week he conducts grueling practices at St. Petersburg Catholic High School's running track, where his athletes sprint at top speed for a quarter mile, jog for a quarter mile, then repeat the process until they poop out.

One day in 1990 a new runner caught Burgasser's eye. Hard to miss, the new guy apparently had shaved the front half of his skull and was wearing flip-flops. At 4:30 p.m. the first group of Burgasser's hard-core runners arrived. The new guy joined them, running effortlessly, never falling behind some of the fastest, most competitive athletes in Florida.

After Burgasser's gasping athletes finished their workout, another group began running their intervals. The new guy joined them, and joined every new group for the next two hours, running at a 5-minute mile pace during the sprints.

The new guy identified himself as Larry Perrier. Folks delighted in his strange company. Some also wondered if their ears were going to fall off: Flip-Flop's tongue, as it jumped from topic to topic, was as fast as his feet.

After a few months, club members brought the new guy their old $100 Nikes and Reeboks. He took the shoes home and tried to modify them into something resembling flip-flops. After a while he told his new friends, "Thank you, but I don't need charity."

Burgasser, running on the Pinellas Trail a few months later, encountered an unhappy Larry.

"What's wrong?" Burgasser asked.

"I am having trouble with my flip-flops," Larry said.

Burgasser thought, "Of course you are. We gave you running shoes but you prefer flip-flops with no padding. Your feet must be killing you."

"It's winter," Larry explained. "Kmart doesn't sell flip-flops in the winter. I'm running out of flip-flops."

Over the years I have seen the Flip-Flop Man dozens of times while riding my bike. One day I stopped and introduced myself as a writer.

"I don't know if I want to talk to the media," he said politely. "You

Larry Perrier, the notorious Flip-Flop Man, in action.

know, I think I ought to demur because part of me is really private. But on the other hand, everybody knows me anyway, and for years I have sort of been working to build up my legend."

So here is how Larry Perrier became the celebrated, talkative, irrepressible Flip-Flop Man.

He was born in the South Bronx on May 15, 1945. When he was a boy, his mother developed multiple sclerosis and took to the bed that would be prison for the rest of her life. As she deteriorated, his father quit work to care for her but found it impossible to care for a boy who suffered from what today we might call attention deficit disorder.

He grew up in seven foster homes, quit school in ninth grade, enlisted in the Army, left the Army, and found it almost impossible to hold onto a job. He has lived with a kindly woman—"my old lady," he called Blanche Tucker fondly—for three decades. She supported the two of them as a nurse.

"I have always been different," he said as I pushed my bike next to him. At first he didn't tell me why he was different; he was off on another topic—doctors. "I don't go to them. Oh, I'll go to the doctor if I have to, like when I had a hernia, and they took care of it, though I didn't follow their advice—they said to rest for a while—but I was back running in a

The Flip-Flop Man with Jeff Klinkenberg. (Photo by Bill Castleman.)

few days and then developed another hernia. Now you're going to ask me if I wear a truss. I don't believe in trusses.

"What was I saying?"

About being different.

"One time I hitchhiked across the country barefoot. Then I discovered flip-flops. Flip-flops are almost like being barefoot. I used to buy them at the dollar store. Now I get them for five bucks at Kmart. Sometimes when I know I'm going to do a long day I'll hide flip-flops on the trail in advance just in case one of them breaks."

What's a long day?

"Fifty miles is a long day, though I'm older, I'm not as strong, I don't do as many long days. One time I walked to Brooksville. I think that must be 70 miles to Brooksville from where I live. I ended up somehow running in a forest in Brooksville and these guys came up and said, 'What are you doing running out here during hunting season?' I think they were trying to scare me, but they were hunting deer and maybe I could have gotten shot by accident."

That would have ruined a nice run.

"Over by the mall in St. Petersburg, these young kids on bikes rode up to rob me. At lunchtime. Noon. One guy says, 'Give it up!' and even though I didn't have much money I tried to talk my way out of it, and one took out a knife, and I wasn't going to run, no, I wasn't going to show them I was scared, so I sat on a bench and held my ground, but then I got nervous and I started running, jumped a ditch and lost a flip-flop and had to walk home to Madeira Beach with one flip-flop. But I was lucky. I stopped to talk to this old guy who gave me a rag to wrap around the other foot so the pavement wouldn't burn it."

I had lots of questions about his diet.

"Well, I eat a lot of sugar for energy. I keep a bag by my bed. That's what rotted my teeth. Now I have to eat soft things, food out of cans. People tell me, 'That isn't enough,' but it seems to work.

"In the winter I like to put on a little weight for warmth and energy. Right now I weigh 148 pounds, but my winter weight is higher. I eat cheese and chocolate. I have to be careful, though, because of my, you know, addictive personality. If I buy a gallon of ice cream I'll eat the whole gallon in a day."

Some people try to soothe emotional pain with food, shopping, television, computer games, sex, gambling, tobacco, cocaine, religion. For years, the Flip-Flop Man's drug of choice was alcohol. After his last booze-related dustup with the law, in 1989, "I quit drinking."

To cope with his demons he started walking, jogging, running and sprinting. A shrink might have told him "Larry, you're substituting one addiction for another. Work on your problems."

But he didn't go to a shrink. Didn't believe in shrinks. He believed in the power of flip-flops.

I had a small camera in my pack and asked to take his photograph. As I fumbled with the settings he began fidgeting and said, "Hurry up. It's hard for me to stand still."

A guy in a nearby yard cranked up a hedge trimmer as I put away my camera. "I'm high-strung," Flip-Flop told me. "I don't like loud noises. Time to go."

When he took off running, I jumped on my bike and followed. I glanced at my speedometer. Twelve miles an hour. A 5-minute mile. In flip-flops. I stayed behind for a half-mile.

"Call me sometime," he yelled over his shoulder. "We'll run together. I sometimes run with people even more overweight than you."

Fall 2007.

13

Huckleberry's Raft

I encountered Lee Allen Young one day at Blue Springs Creek, in the Ocala National Forest, where he lived on a vessel he called *Huckleberry Raft* with a faithful mutt he had named Becky Thatcher. A barefooted man of 59, he told me he was looking for Tom Sawyer—that is, he was looking for the kind of free and irresponsible life all but gone in modern Florida.

He had no bank account, no credit cards, no telephone. "Civilization," Mark Twain once declared, "is the limitless multiplication of unnecessary necessities." Young had no spouse, no commitments, no immediate plans except to fry a few fish for supper. "I've done so much for so long with so little I can do almost anything with nothing," he said.

One thing you could say about Lee Allen Young. He knew how to get by whether on a raft, a horse, or in jail.

If we run out of oil, if the Internet stops working, if the supermarket suffers a shortage of vittles, if the vacuum cleaner breaks, if the Florida Legislature refuses to fund anything but golf course construction for Republican millionaires, Lee Allen Young probably will survive. He owns no computer or golf clubs or gas guzzling car. He has a broom, a dog, a fishing pole, and what's more than likely the best raft east of the Mississippi. If he has to, he can row, pole, or paddle it.

About 16 feet long, the raft was born a decade ago as a canoe to which he had added Styrofoam outriggers. Then he built a 10-foot-wide deck on top of the canoe and the Styrofoam. On top of the deck, out of cedar, plywood, bamboo, rope, and a vinyl tarp, he erected a hut.

The hut contains a propane stove, one chair, a single table, and three storage tubs for his meager belongings. He has a flashlight, canned goods, and a small collection of turkey feathers. At night he yanks a string and a bed drops from the ceiling. He owns the clothes on his back and a few garments he has fashioned out of cowhide and deerskin. He

Lee Allen Young boards his vessel, the *Huckleberry Raft*. (Photo by Maurice Riven-bark.)

has many tools that require no electricity. Young is an elbow grease kind of guy.

He builds furniture when he has a mind to, and walking sticks and little wooden icons he sells to tourists sometimes for $10 or so. A rambling man, he lacks close friends but knows a lot of people who stop to say hello and listen to his stories. If they get too chummy, if they ask too many questions, if they rub him the wrong way, he pushes the raft off the bank and says goodbye.

"Always do right," Mark Twain once told an audience. "This will gratify some people and astonish the rest." Young is a nineteenth-century man who has mainly tried to do right while somehow managing to do an occasional wrong.

"What do you dislike most about the twenty-first century?" I asked.

"People are rude. They steal. They rip you off."

Civilized people who need help dial 911 or hire lawyers. Lee Young isn't the kind of man who calls the cops or consults an attorney to fix his problems. His first impulse is to take care of bad business on his own, which is not the twenty-first-century way.

He finds it easier to avoid modernity. Most nights he ties to shore near a boat ramp close to Otter Street, near Raccoon Street and Possum Street. He lives in the sticks, but some nights the inhabited side of the creek gets too civilized for him; he can hear televisions, stereos, and twenty-first-century Florida creeping closer.

So he pushes *Huckleberry Raft* off the bank, heads down the creek a mile, ties to a cypress stump, and listens to the calming after-dark symphony performed by alligators, owls, and pig frogs. "All my life I've tried to find a place where I can go 24 hours and never hear a motor," he told me. "It's near impossible. There's no place to hide."

He was born in Virginia; his mama, alone with four other young mouths to feed, sent him to live in Bradenton with an uncle who grew unhappy with the assignment. The boy made himself scarce and got away as soon as possible.

He threw newspapers on front porches, dug ditches, and toiled as a bottler in an orange juice plant. An experiment in structured living—he joined the Army—lasted almost a decade. On his 23rd day in Vietnam in 1970, a mortar shell exploded over his head. A buddy lost his foot and he lost a chunk of his right calf.

An American flag flies from the stern of the *Huckleberry Raft*, his Purple Heart is stowed in a safe place, and his terrific scar always is visible below the cuff of his short pants.

He takes off the shorts when he bathes in the creek, soaping up naked and watching for hungry snapping turtles. He has been bitten by sand flies, chiggers, wasps, honeybees, yellow jackets, mosquitoes, and ticks but never a turtle. Sometimes alligators bother the catfish hung on a stringer behind the raft, but cottonmouths have yet to join him in the galley.

"I've been lucky," he said. "I've never been hurt. I'm fast and I'm careful." He has no money to pay doctors, no savings except the bills in his pocket or in the galley coffee can. On paper, he lives in abject poverty, earning about $2,500 a year for his furniture and trinkets. "But that's enough for me to live pretty well."

He considers himself a rich man.

Young doesn't lie to anyone about his love life. He's a drifter. At present "I'm not hemmed in by nobody," he told me.

In 1987, he announced to wife No. 1 his intention to leave Arcadia, in Central Florida, and head out to Wyoming—on horseback. The divorce followed. Over the next decade, life in a mule-drawn covered wagon failed to be the dream marriage for his next two spouses.

Speaking of mules, he loves them, though, like women, they sometimes forget to return his affection. One ornery fellow butted him in the mouth, making the huge gap in his smile. Otherwise, he is a good-looking man with a neat beard and wiry build.

In 2000, as he worked his way back to Florida from Wyoming, he dug graves, built fences, shoed horses, and labored as a land surveyor to feed himself. For a spell he lived in Atlanta, where he remembers developing a Web site for a fortune-teller.

Unfortunately the seer neglected to warn him about the trouble awaiting him in Florida.

Like Huck Finn, Young smokes a pipe. Lighting up, he inhaled the vanilla-flavored smoke into his lungs, cranked up the 4-horse engine, and coaxed *Huckleberry Raft* up the creek. Listening to the coughing Johnson, he was reminded of his greatest lost love, which happened to be not a woman but a canoe.

In 2007, when he was living on his raft on the Oklawaha River in the national forest, he built a canoe from scratch. He used an ax to hollow out a log, built outriggers, and felt like a Seminole warrior while poling it through the shallows. Folks who visited the fishing camp to look at his canoe often ended up buying his cane furniture and hand-carved doohickeys. The paper in Ocala published a story about him, which he pasted in his scrapbook.

One day a couple of guys came to see him. They told him he was a sucker to sell his furniture for such a low price and promised they could do better. He has little interest in business, but this time he said, "Go ahead and try." They loaded his furniture on their vehicle and drove off. When they returned, the furniture was gone and so was all the money. Traveling expenses, they told him. Young thought he had been swindled.

The police report filed on October 3, 2008, by the Marion County Sheriff's Office reveals the unsavory details about how Young showed up at the alleged swindler's house with a black-powder pistol and even a blacker disposition. "Things got out of hand," says the police report. During the ensuing wrestling match for the pistol, blows from Young's fists made contact with the other men, leaving them bruised and bleeding.

Lee Allen Young lights his pipe. (Photo by Maurice Rivenbark.)

He was arrested, charged with battery, and served 155 days behind bars. When he got back to his beloved raft on the Oklawaha River, all his tools were gone. And so was his beloved canoe.

Now it was a different time and a different place. As he navigated the *Huckleberry Raft* from his seat on the stern, his dog Becky Thatcher, named after a character in *Tom Sawyer*, sprawled across his feet. Smoke from his pipe swirled above the homemade leather cap he had decorated with wooden beads that spelled out "Captain Natural."

"I found me a nice dead cypress tree off the creek in the woods," Captain Natural shouted above the motor. "I've started another canoe."

The log lay back from the creek, hidden among the maples and the cabbage palms, the ferns and the poison ivy. As the squirrels chattered and the red-shouldered hawks cried, he changed into the loincloth that always makes him feel as wild and as free as Huck Finn on the Mississippi.

Next he began hacking at the downed tree with an ax. His new canoe was going to be 16 feet long; it was going to be better than the canoe that was stolen. This time he would be more careful with the canoe. He would lock it to a tree if he had to. By God, this canoe would be his masterpiece.

The dog Becky Thatcher watched for a while and then trotted off to squat in the ferns next to the *Huckleberry Raft*, which bobbed silently in the current as if modern Florida had never existed.

Spring 2011.

The Man Who Invented Florida

Know what Florida needs right now? It needs Jack Swenningsen. Jack Swenningsen! Yes, Jack Swenningsen, old coot idea man, famed photographer and, if you must know, accordion master. Jack Swenningsen, who wants to return Florida to glory, wants to bring those vanishing tourists back, wants to keep old Floridians from leaving—in fact, wants to make old Floridians fall in love with Florida again.

Jack Swenningsen! Get out of his way, man. Give him a camera, a palm tree, and two cavorting girls in bikinis. Ol' Jack—that's what he calls himself—will grab his camera and capture the dream. "While I'm thinking about it, I'd want a beach ball in the picture, too!"

Jack Swenningsen! Age 91! Brimming with ideas and energy still! Jack Swenningsen, the man who invented Florida.

Ponce de Leon. William Bartram. Andrew Jackson. Chief Osceola. Henry Flagler. Forget the names in the history books. The one you need to know is Jack Swenningsen. In 1948, the young advertising hotshot moved from Brooklyn to St. Petersburg to escape the cold. He knocked on the door of *Florida Speaks* magazine, introduced himself as "The Picture Man," and was instantly hired. *Florida Speaks* was a monthly chamber-of-commerce-type magazine marketed to frozen northerners. The war was over. Folks felt optimistic about the future. Sure, a returning GI could seek his fortune in snowbound Ohio, Michigan, or Wisconsin. Or he and the wife could buy themselves a sleepy bungalow in Florida.

Jack Swenningsen drove 100,000 miles around the peninsula for decades, taking dreamy come-to-Florida photographs. Most were published in *Florida Speaks*, but many showed up in advertising brochures and Sunday newspaper supplements all over the United States. The Florida he documented didn't quite exist, of course. How could it? So he invented an ideal to go with the pictures.

Jack Swen-
ningsen and
an always
photogenic
Florida palm.
(Photo by Scott
Keeler.)

Let's say a couple, whom we'll call Bea and Ernie, pick up the *Chicago American* on the way home from Sunday Mass in 1950. On a gray January morning the windy streets are piled with snow. Ernie asks, "Bea, aren't you tired of the snow?" Bea, who slipped on ice the day before and bruised her behind, is exhausted. Her adorable infant son always has a runny nose.

"Look at this picture in the *American*, Bea. Wouldn't it be nice to live in a place like this?" Bea isn't sure. It would mean moving away from friends and family.

"Look at this photo," says Ernie, doing the hard sell. "If we lived in Florida, we'd reach out the back door and pick oranges for breakfast. We'd catch fish in the canal behind the house. Coconuts, Bea! We'll have our own coconut tree!"

Jack Swenningsen!

He got a Kodak folding vest camera when he was 14 and developed film in the basement next to a pile of coal. He graduated with an advertising degree from Pratt Institute, served in Italy during the war, and hustled to make a living afterward. Then he moved his family to Florida.

"You can't imagine what Florida was like to a Brooklyn Yankee like me! The way I saw Florida, it was a fairyland! All pristine! Virgin! I'd

Bathing beauty and fish, a can't-miss combination. (Photo courtesy of Jack Swenningsen.)

Young people, sand, a beach. (Photo courtesy of Jack Swenningsen.)

never seen such trees! Beautiful springs! Big animals! Beaches. WHAT BEACHES WE HAVE! How could anyone want to live anywhere else?"

Yet there was always room for improvement. Traveling through Florida, Jack carried important props in his station wagon—beach balls, bikinis, straw hats, oranges, and fishing poles. He carried chaise lounges, firewood, croquet sets. Just in case he had to spice up a photo.

Jack Swenningsen's pictorial Florida lacked mosquitoes, humidity, hurricanes, and other unpleasantness. It was balmy and breezy, ol' Jack's Florida, a nice place to drink fresh-squeezed OJ while looking at palm trees and puffy clouds.

In St. Petersburg, he was well known to the Kay Lyons Charm School and its bevy of beautiful girls—"goils" in Jack's Brooklynese—whom he posed in photographs. He didn't pay the goils, but often he provided tasteful red bikinis for them to wear in the beach pictures.

Jack Swenningsen!

Jack and his wife—he and Amelia married in 1942—live in a perfect bungalow in western St. Petersburg near the railroad tracks. Jack's excellent photos line the living room walls; in a storage room next to the garage are a dozen boxes of old photographs perfectly preserved, ready to publish right now if God or the governor needs them.

Ol' Jack will tell you what's wrong with Florida today. Wholesome virtues have too often been replaced by the tabloid world of *Miami Vice*, crime, drugs, and high taxes. No wonder the latest statistics are glum about Florida's tourism and population growth.

The challenge makes ol' Jack want to grab a Speed Graphic 4 by 5 and take a field trip. No dirty photos of pouting, half-nude women on the beach for Jack Swenningsen. No hairy men with earrings and tattoos sitting on scary motorcycles at the traffic light next to your elderly mother in her sensible Dodge. No gangbangers! No insurance agents! No tax collectors! Just nice folks living the Florida lifestyle in the shade of a coconut tree.

He will pose a freckled-face kid on the dock with a fishing pole. (Of course he'll tie a rock to the line and toss it over.) Pole bends! Fish on! Next, he'll pose a grandfatherly figure—somebody right out of a Norman Rockwell calendar—wearing Bermuda shorts, smoking a pipe, and carrying a fishing rod. Grandpa, by the way, will be grinning and displaying a big fat fish (that Jack bought at the seafood market on the way over).

Finally, in the foreground, he will pose his trademark wholesome sunbathers in red bikinis. They will be offering good-natured advice to a handsome guy wearing a goofy chef's hat who is preparing to grill the fish.

Jack Swenningsen!

For an instant the corners of ol' Jack's upbeat mouth droop south. "A lot of people moved here. Maybe too many. Maybe I was too good. Sometimes I feel guilty. . . . Better not put that in the paper."

Jack Swenningsen!

Spring 2008.

15

Golf Ball Diver

On what could well have been the worst day of his life, Glenn Berger felt something hard and heavy crawl upon his back. It turned out to be an amorous alligator apparently hankering for a mate. At that moment, Berger entertained doubts about the wisdom of his chosen profession, diving for lost balls in Florida golf course ponds.

The Golf Ball Man didn't brood long. "Alligators are a hazard in my line of work," he thought, "but what are the chances of really getting mauled?" Probably small, he told himself. "What are the chances of getting killed?" Even slimmer.

Still, there was the matter of the dinosaur on his back. At Ibis Country Club in West Palm Beach, as Berger scrambled out of the water that morning, the lovelorn 7-foot alligator slid off without giving him a hickey.

He escaped with a terrific story—and about 4,000 golf balls. Some were worth only a few cents, but 15 percent—about 600—were Titleist Pro V1s and worth about $2 each, even used. So what if a sex-starved alligator had tried to take a few liberties?

At Pelican Preserve Golf Course in Fort Myers, I watched the Golf Ball Man pull on his mask, adjust his air tank, and vanish into a pond. I felt no envy. Two kinds of golf ball divers work in Florida: those who have experienced underwater unpleasantries and those who soon will. Berger, 35, had a decade of golf ball work and scary stories under his dive belt. His strategy for coping with fear? Denial.

"Really, the best thing you can do," he told me after surfacing later with 125 balls, including a half-dozen Pro V1s, "is not to think too much. If you think too much you'll scare yourself."

Florida boasts more golf courses than any other state, about 1,250. Berger, who was born in alligator-free Indiana and lives in alligator-infested southwest Florida, had dive contracts on about 30 of them. His territory extended from Key West to St. Petersburg. He competed for business with about 100 other full-time divers who usually paid a fee—often a nickel per ball or a flat rate—for the privilege of working a particular course.

Berger retrieved balls on inexpensive golf courses and at ritzy country clubs. Public courses attract budget-minded golfers who may play infrequently and hit many balls into the water. "Ball farms," Berger called them. But the balls he harvested usually were cheapies. At private clubs, golfers were more apt to hit expensive balls. But the more polished golfers were less likely to hit balls into a water hazard.

At Pelican Preserve, Berger sank into another pond as a white egret scolded him from the bank. In the water, schools of tilapia got out of his way. Berger had been told that all the alligators had been removed from the course, but in Florida, wise people assume that any creek, pond, lake, or river contains them.

At 6 feet 8 and 250 pounds, Berger would be enough for dinner and then some. On the job he wears a black and blue wet suit, weights, and an air tank painted a camouflage pattern in hopes he'll be invisible to lurking gators. They tend to find him anyway.

"Typically they'll float over me while I'm on the bottom," he told me. "They're curious, especially the smaller ones, and they'll dive down and bump me on the tank just to see what I am."

Never a happy moment.

"One time I felt my arm in an alligator's mouth. I couldn't see anything, but I almost flew out of the water. There was no blood, so I think the gator just mouthed me without biting down."

The Golf Ball Man was lucky that day. In 2008, an acquaintance was diving for balls at Tampa Palms when a big gator grabbed him, dived for the bottom, and started spinning. He escaped but suffered a dislocated left shoulder, puncture wounds, and an ambition to retire.

Again, as I watched, the Golf Ball Man waded in. Soon his bubbles streamed up from the bottom, 20 feet down, where he was crawling on all fours in almost black water, feeling ahead with his hands. He was hoping for the wonderful, dimpled feel of a Titleist and not something, you know, scaly and toothy.

He knows he is more likely to be hurt by one-celled organisms and poisons than by ornery reptiles. Polluted runoff tainted with pesticides, herbicides, and various heavy metals wash into golf course ponds every

Glenn Berger and his harvest. (Photo by Maurice Rivenbark.)

time it rains. Berger keeps his immune system humming by taking vitamins and praying. He keeps ear infections at bay with cotton swabs dipped in isopropyl alcohol and white vinegar and never misses a chance for a long, hot shower.

Married, Berger likes to cook and once supported his wife and daughter as a chef. Eventually he concluded that golf balls were more profitable than meatballs.

At his warehouse I watched him dump the day's harvest into a machine, which conveyed balls along a kind of an assembly line where they were bathed with bleach, water, a degreaser, and a series of chemicals. After the balls dried, Berger sorted them according to value. "I'm good at math," Berger said. "Time is money. I don't eat breakfast. I don't eat lunch. They take time away from hunting golf balls. My personal best is 17,000 balls in a single day. You can eat a big dinner after work."

That assumes he is not eaten for dinner by a dinosaur, of course. "Don't tell me about the alligators," the Golf Ball Man often orders golf course employees eager to pass on worrisome stories. "I'd rather not know."

In the winter, alligators crawl from ponds to sunbathe on fairways and greens. If he sees one on land, so much the better; he feels safer while under the water. Alligators are most aggressive during spring mating season when their hormones rage and they are ready to fight for a girlfriend. In the summer they regulate their cold blood by remaining in the water, out of the hot sun and out of sight.

Berger's credo is "Look Before You Leap." Whenever he spots an alligator floating nearby, he raises his arms above his head and shouts. Usually the alligator flees. If the alligator merely sinks out of sight, he'll try another pond.

Hunting for golf balls he has found chairs, tables, umbrellas, bird skulls, dead fish, lawn mowers, golf carts, and clubs probably flung into the water by hapless hackers with bad tempers. Golf course ponds are typically turbid; as he crawls along on the bottom he feels for treasure with his bare hands. He still has all his fingers, though he once tore a tendon on a rusty golf club submerged in the mud.

He never knows what he will find. In the water hazard at the 17th hole at St. Petersburg Country Club he once encountered something that felt like a tire. The tire, it turned out, was attached to the rest of a car. Deep in the pond, Berger stood on the bottom and began feeling his way around the car. Eventually he approached the driver's side, where the window was ominously open.

"I thought about putting my hands inside that window," he told me. "Then I remembered an old friend who has been doing this work for years. One time he put his hands inside the window and touched the body of a suicide. You don't want to put your hands inside the window of a submerged car and touch a body. You'll want to retire and I don't want to retire."

Summer 2010.

16

The Dabbler

The guy on the phone, Joe Penrose, said he was a dabbler. "I dabble in this, I dabble in that, ya know what I mean? I find something that somebody threw away—you wouldn't believe what people throw away!—and I restore it. Come over and meet me. I got an interesting story to tell. Also, I got big mangoes."

How big?

"One of my mangoes falls on your foot, you got a broken foot. Come over and I'll give you a bag."

So I went over. The Dabbler lived on a dead-end street in a neat little bungalow situated in the middle of a gravel lawn about a block from the Gulf of Mexico. Perched on the gravel lawn was a stone menagerie that included frogs, skunks, and turtles. The Dabbler had liberated them from trash cans and painted them.

He stood tall in the driveway, a burly guy with white hair, waiting to tell someone a little bit or a lot about himself. The Dabbler was 74, hailed from south Philadelphia, and sounded like the movie pug Rocky: dis for this, dat for that, wit for with, beeyuuteefull for beautiful. His wife's name was Laurel and she didn't mind his dabbling though sometimes his talking got on her nerves.

What about the mangoes?

"We'll get down to the meat and potatoes of the mangoes in a minute," he said. "But let me tell you some background first. I was in the Army Air Force, military police. Then I was a longshoreman, just like my father, but that's another story. I worked at a factory where we made long playing records, the kind they don't make no more. I worked for Sears and sold appliances, though we called them big ticket items."

What about dabbling?

Joe Penrose and his mangoes. (Photo by Scott Keeler.)

"You know how it is when you retire. I picked up a paintbrush. Look at this. I got it last Friday at a yard sale, this birdbath. THREE BUCKS! Look how I painted it."

Every block in Florida had somebody like the Dabbler. Usually it was a talkative old guy with a good heart. He might knock on your door and ask, "You need some mangoes?" or knock on your door and ask, "Want me to trim your hibiscus? It's leanin' over the fence. Do you like my fence? See how I painted it? I like to paint everything the color of tangerines. Want me to paint your fence?"

He doesn't have your home phone number, and maybe that's the way you want it. Anyway he can just knock on your door any old time.

"So what can I tell you?" he asked. "Look at this picture of me. I'm playing the banjo, but I also play the guitar and drums. Back in Philly, I was in a string band. I am a pretty fair banjo player. In the Durning String Band, we played that song from the Jewish movie, *Exodus*. The wife and I are Catholic. Check this out. I painted this sign about salvation. Can you read what it says?"

The Surest Way To Heaven Is Holy Communion.

"The wife and I go to Mass at St. John Vianney. I take up the collection basket at the 10 o'clock Mass during, you know, the offertory. Well, okay, really I'm just a substitute."

The Dabbler led the way into the backyard, which was a wonder—a theme park of kitschy Florida. There were plastic flamingos and concrete herons but no unicorns, only because he hadn't found any at a yard sale. The trunk of a palm tree was painted like clouds and sea. He showed me the shrine he had built to honor the Virgin Mary and the bench where he sat in the morning to pray the rosary.

He wanted me to see his lemon, orange, and tangerine trees, the avocadoes that hung like Christmas ornaments. The mangoes weighed a ton or two each, red-yellow orbs like the sun on the summer horizon.

"Have you seen mangoes like this?" he asked. "I didn't think so. I ain't NEVER tasted a mango like this in my life. Well, my wife eats more mangoes than me. Her name is Laurel, did I mention? She'd come out to meet ya only she has a touch of stomach virus."

What do you do with all these mangoes?

"We both volunteer at the St. Petersburg Free Clinic. They call us the Mango Man and the Mango Lady because we bring our mangoes. We also bring mangoes to the Salvation Army. Hey, you know what I say? I say stop thinkin' about yourself all the time. Do for other people. You get so much joy doing for others. Look at this pinwheel! Somebody threw it away. Can you believe that? I painted it. LOOK AT IT NOW!"

He followed me to the driveway. "Hold the sack from the bottom," he said. "Those mangoes are heavy, ain't they? You ever see such mangoes? Did I talk your ear off? Sorry."

As I stored the mangoes in the back of my truck he kept a close watch and kept up the monologue. "My mother died young," he said. "I was 7. My dad was a longshoreman 42 years. Lots of the longshoremen get caught up in the booze. I don't blame my dad that much. Six kids. His wife dies. He got drunk one night and froze to death."

Oh, that's terrible.

"I don't hold it against him. I hope he's in heaven."

I turned the ignition key and backed out of the driveway. The Dabbler was walking alongside my truck, his lips moving. I opened the window so I could hear.

The Dabbler said, "Look, I'm going to put an ad in the church bulletin about how I restore things, but if you want to say in your story that I restore things, that would be fine. I wouldn't mind at all. I could use a few bucks."

Summer 2007.

Whitey Markle

A quiet man tried to live quietly in the quiet woods, except when he had to turn on the power saw. Then for a while things got loud. After he finished cutting lumber for bathroom walls or a new kitchen table or a bedroom chifforobe, the woods grew quiet again. A quiet man might hear the jackhammer attack of a pileated woodpecker on a pine or an armadillo crunching through the palmettos.

"Woods is a quiet place," Richard "Whitey" Markle told me in his trademark country drawl. "You're supposed to hear nature."

Some quiet men learned by experience to appreciate quiet when they heard it. A hell-raiser as a young man, Whitey once had liked loud music, pot, liquor, and friendly women. He was 66 at the time of my visit and still enjoyed the occasional vice—tobacco juice sloshed ominously in the fruit jar he toted through his house. But his life was quieter than before. Now he preferred a plate of smoked mullet and vine-ripe tomatoes to an illicit doobie. Speaking of pot, even groovier for him was a smoking cauldron of homemade shrimp creole, heavy on the okra, followed by a quiet tune strummed on his guitar. Sometimes he played "Song of the Lake."

Oh you come through the marsh,
O'er the reeds and the pads,
For the gator and the frogs you explore,
But unlike the marsh hawk, so silent and peaceful
You invade with a deafening roar.

The quiet man lived on a lake that in the twenty-first century had come to lack quiet. At night, on weekends especially, a different song of the lake was being performed by a fleet of airboats with powerful engines and throbbing airplane propellers. First he would hear a distant rumble. Then came the crescendo that grew to a mighty whine. Airboaters were gigging frogs. Airboaters were hunting alligators. They were having fun raising their own kind of hell.

In the woods along the lake, a quiet man was tempted to shout his anger to the heavens. But he didn't. His revenge took a quieter, more effective form.

William Bartram, America's first real travel writer, explored the woods close to Whitey's property on Orange Lake in the 18th century. In the twentieth century the late Marjorie Kinnan Rawlings wrote her beloved novel, *The Yearling*, while living nearby at Cross Creek. For some people, Orange Lake and the forest are Florida's spiritual heart.

Whitey could have been a character in a Miz Rawlings story. He was born in the Duval County woods along Broward River, wore overalls, went barefoot, shot rabbits with his .22, ate mullet and grits, and taught himself guitar. His daddy, Conrad, who made a living as a mail clerk, could do anything with his hands. His mama, Earleen, taught her white-blonde boy how to sew, garden, and cook. She also advised him to "go ahead and watch your daddy make that table." Thus he learned carpentry. Mama said, "Stand next to your daddy next time he's got the car hood up and see what to fix." That's how he learned auto mechanics.

After junior college he headed for Tallahassee, where he majored in Industrial Arts at Florida State and, not surprising for a repressed country boy who suddenly found himself living in the Age of Aquarius, illegal substances. For a while, he kept the drug devil at bay. He got married, had a child, joined the military reserves, and learned to be a machinist. One night he got busted for cocaine. After the judge gave him four years, his wife filed divorce papers. At a minimum-security Marion County prison, he gazed at the woods through the window screen and thought about taking off like a rabbit. Instead he got a job building things for the prison. Impressed, his jailers dispatched him to teach reform-school girls how to use hammers and saws and screwdrivers and paintbrushes.

After his release he hung on to the reform-school job; at night, for extra cash, he ran a trotline for catfish at the lake or netted mullet on the coast. In 1978 he had enough for a down payment on 5 acres. His nearest neighbor was a half-mile away.

He heard the occasional airboat at night.

He lived quietly on Orange Lake in a cozy homemade shack that lacked indoor plumbing and electricity. He dreamed of a better house, but that would cost real money. He took on still another job, this one at the University of Florida's college of architecture, teaching students basic carpentry and welding. He started a bluegrass band—acoustic instruments only—called Whitey Markle and the Swamp Rooters.

The ex-con also worked on himself. He made friends with his estranged daughter. He courted a lady or two. He grew peppers, okra, and sweet potatoes. He raised hogs and chickens. Every morning, on an ancient stove he had found abandoned on the road, he cooked a fresh egg with bacon and cheese and served over white bread.

He tended his orange trees and made his own marmalade. He sometimes ate the deer he had found freshly killed on the road. He bathed in a child's wading pool, drank from his own well, and avoided the fangs of the cottonmouths that slithered into his yard when the lake came up during rainy season.

He began the construction of a two-bedroom, octagon-shaped house. He laid the concrete, sawed lumber, put on the roof, and built the walls and furniture. His air was conditioned by the breeze blowing off the lake and through the woods and onto his upstairs porch, where he slept behind a screen during summer. Chuck-will's-widows lulled him to sleep with their mysterious cries.

"Whooo-cooks-for-you?" the barred owls called in the middle of the night. "Whooo-cooks-for-you-allll?" Whitey hung up a sign at the entrance to his property.

"Owl Holler," the sign said.

As the years went by, it became harder to hear the owls.

The first airboat was developed in 1905 by a team led by the famous telephone inventor Alexander Graham Bell in Nova Scotia. Bell's associate, Dr. Glenn Curtiss, brought an airboat to Florida in 1920. Flat-bottomed, with the prop positioned above the water instead of under the water, an airboat proved to be the perfect vessel for skimming across the shallows. Airboats were used extensively in the marshes of the Everglades, Lake Okeechobee, and Indian River by hunters, froggers, fishing guides, and scientists who needed to explore otherwise inaccessible wilderness.

Miccosukee Indians in South Florida still use airboats extensively. In 2005, quick-thinking airboaters saved hundreds of Hurricane Katrina victims in Louisiana.

Over the decades in Florida, the number of airboats has gone up. At the same time, the number of out-of-the-way places for airboat users

In his house on Orange Lake, Whitey Markle plays "Song of the Lake" on his guitar. (Photo by Maurice Rivenbark.)

has gone down. Airboats are loud and waterfront homeowners often come to resent the noise. A handful of Florida counties had banned or curtailed nighttime airboat use.

RUH, RUH. VRRRRROOOOOOM!

Airboat drivers and passengers always wear ear protectors. Otherwise they'd go deaf.

RUH, RUH. VRRRRROOOOOOM!

To a man skimming above the lily pads in his prize airboat, even the muffled roar of a big engine can be pure symphony.

In a house in the woods, a few hundred feet from Orange Lake, a quiet man said, "Enough is enough."

In the twenty-first century, quiet was an endangered species, disappearing not in a whisper but a roar. The car stereo in the next lane burped "BOOMPITTA-BOOMPITTA" without mercy. In Starbucks, a woman shrieked into her cell phone as if she were alone on a desert island. There were motorcycles without mufflers and leaf blowers and blowhards on radio shouting their opinions without shame.

"We live in a noisy world," Whitey Markle told me. "And people just ain't as polite as they used to be."

In 1990 he started working on a master's degree at the University of Florida, where his topic was "Airboat Noise around Orange Lake as a

Community Planning Issue." For years he made a study of airboat engines, decibel levels, and local laws. Okay, airboats weren't as loud as 140-decibel jet engines. But from a mile away, on a quiet night, a person could hear them loud and clear. Low frequencies penetrated the woods and Whitey's house.

"Sometimes, when there were a bunch of them in the lake a few hundred feet away from my house, it was hard to talk on the telephone or hear the television. But that wasn't so bad. It was after I went to sleep."

Froggers and alligator hunters work at night. Duck hunters liked to get on the lake before dawn.

RUH, RUH. VRRRRRROOOOOOM!

"Okay, that wakes me. The airboat shuts down for a while, but I'm lying there waiting for it to go again. But I drift off. I fall asleep again. RUH, RUH. VRRRRRROOOOOOM! Lord, I sit up in bed. Engine shuts down again. I'm so angry I can't go to sleep again."

He got his master's in 1996. But he couldn't hear the owls.

Sometimes he says "ain't" or says "don't" when he should have said "doesn't." But with his freshly minted master's degree, he felt confident enough to testify at Alachua County Commission meetings over in Gainesville. Of course, the airboaters testified, too. Fishing camp owners complained that an airboat ban would put them out of business.

Whitey Markle—and now he had allies who included other waterfront homeowners, kayakers, and environmentalists—kept at it. Nothing happened until 2009, when a sympathetic county commissioner suggested that the quiet man try to get something put on the 2010 ballot and let voters decide. Whitey and friends had to gather more than 11,000 signatures in a short time to make it happen. They got 12,000 signatures. The proposed ban—no airboat use in Alachua County lakes at night—went on the ballot.

Brass-knuckle politics followed. Alachua County Citizens for Change, the pro-airboat organization, raised $40,924 to fund a campaign. One ad featured a fist with the letters "H-A-T-E" etched on each knuckle, suggesting that an airboat ban was tantamount to racial discrimination. Quiet Lakes of Alachua raised $7,653.80 to spread its word.

The pro-airboat side took the position that banning airboats at night would lead to higher taxes for future law enforcement. Without airboats, sportsmen would have to find a quieter, less efficient means to approach frogs, fish, and alligators. Airboat sales would go down. Fuel sales would go down. A few folks wondered publicly how anybody could pay attention to Whitey Markle, a convicted drug felon who was probably growing pot quietly in the woods next to his hippie house.

"We also think that the people behind the ban want to build a development along the lake. They know the airboats will hurt home sales," said Jeff Septer, who owns Twin Lakes Fish Camp, known as "The Peace and Quiet Camp." His wife, Michelle, said, "Please, no more government intrusion into our lives."

On November 2, 2010, Alachua citizens headed to the polls. In a year when angry conservatives across Florida said "no" to almost everything, 56 percent of Alachua voters said "yes" to the airboat ban. Starting in January, airboats under power were banned on county lakes between 7 p.m. and 7 a.m.

Whitey Markle hoped for a good night's sleep.

He had a new lady friend, Cecilia, who lives in Fernandina Beach but drives over on weekends. He intended to give up chewing tobacco for her. He was also cleaning up a debris pile next to a shack that would have fallen had it not been for the rusty screen and cobwebs. In the downstairs bathroom, he had decorated tiles with his own artwork of garfish, a lake species most people never eat because of bones and strong-tasting meat. When properly cleaned they taste to Whitey like $35-a-pound lobster.

Perhaps he would throw a quiet romantic dinner. He would cut oak with an ax and start a fire in the wood-burning stove. He could play a guitar tune, not the bitter "Song of the Lake" but something for Cecilia, "Thinkin' about You, Babe."

As the moonlight peeked through the pines, he'd retire the guitar so he and Cecilia could listen to the fire crackle and maybe the crickets. Deep in the night, he hoped to hear the "Whooo-cooks-for-you? Whooo-cooks-for-you-allll" call.

The sign was back on the road.

"Owl Holler."

Fall 2010.

♭ 18

Woo

Here is what Woo wants. He wants to go fishing, catch something beautiful and primitive, snap a good photograph, drive to his gallery, stand before the easel, study the photo, paint something nice. Woo wants to paint the tarpon, capture the utter wildness, the silver-dollar scales, the great maw of a jaw and the enormous eye that sees everything vital in its universe.

Woo, 42, was west Florida's irrepressible fish man. Painting fish filled him with joy. Painting fish focused his mind on the exciting present rather than the depressing past and a worrisome future.

Woo had brain cancer. When he gazed in the mirror he noticed the place where a surgeon had sawed open his skull a while back. She got most of the cancer, but not every bit. Woo hadn't painted a self-portrait. Instead he painted tarpon, grouper, and ravenous yellowfin tuna blasting open jawed through a school of minnows.

Woo wondered about those minnows because "everything in the sea is trying to eat them." Woo wondered if they spent their few weeks of existence obsessing about mortality. He wanted to think they lived to eat, grow, reproduce, swim joyfully. He wanted to think they lived in the moment until the very end.

Humans, of course, are more complicated. At his gallery at 689 Central Avenue in St. Petersburg, Woo wanted to paint Atlantic sailfish and coral grouper today, tomorrow, and as long as the menacing growth in his brain would allow. With good luck, he thought, he might have a half-century of painting snook and spotted sea trout ahead of him. With bad luck, less.

Sometimes he thought about his dad, who died of cancer at 50, and said, "Life is short. You got to take advantage of it when it's here."

His given name is Bill Correira. In west Florida almost nobody, except maybe his oncologist or his mother, called him Bill or used his last name. He is always "Woo" as in "What's up, Woo?" The answer, of course, was painting a fish, perhaps a bigeye toro or a mahi mahi. Or talking to pals or drinking a beer, thinking about the next tattoo, courting a new girlfriend, wondering about his own mortality.

To "woo" is to seduce, to lure, to reel in people who might like to buy a painting of a fish, perhaps a nice big red. "But that's not how I became Woo," he told only close friends.

He became Woo one evening years ago while enjoying an adult beverage at an outdoor tavern. He heard the squealing of brakes followed by a car's insistent honking. Turning, he saw an uninhibited female friend waving from the passenger's seat. She yelled, "Wooooooo!" as she bared her breasts.

Picasso. Dalí. Woo.

His art probably will never be part of the Louvre in Paris or the Museum of Modern Art in New York City. His work may never hang in the Museum of Fine Arts in St. Petersburg. He told me he was cool with that. Woo was a self-taught regionalist who painted what he knew. In a place where people liked to catch fish, look at fish, and eat fish, he had a following. He made a living. He had paintings in the city's history museum, in seafood restaurants, in hotel lobbies, in magazines, in private homes. A few days before we talked, somebody had purchased a painting of a koi, an Asian carp, at a Tampa auction for $4,000.

He calls his St. Petersburg business Gallery Woo. It served as a gathering place for all manner of downtown's denizens, from tattooed skaters to purple-haired femme fatales to grayish gentlemen who wore coats and ties in September's awful swelter. Gallery visitors sometimes included grizzled anglers who had dropped in to share photographs of their latest trophies, perhaps a blue-lightning wahoo or a blackfin tuna. A homeless guy poked his head through the doorway and said, "I like your fish, Woo." An elementary schoolteacher asked if Woo might talk to her class. The owner of a dive shop wanted to know if Woo would contribute a painting as a tournament prize. "If you ever want lessons," Bill Hardman, who owns Aquatic Obsessions Dive Shop, told Woo, "let me know."

"Awesome."

If his brain stayed healthy, he'd love to take a photograph one day of a goliath grouper at close range. They weigh 700 pounds, man.

The world of Woo was peopled by straights and gays, blacks and Hispanics, the occasional redneck, the occasional Ringling College of Art

Bill Woo and his paintings. (Photo by Maurice Rivenbark.)

and Design sophomore, Rastafarians with dreadlocks, and headbangers beered up from the Emerald Bar down the street. His most regular visitor was a fellow artist who goes by Rooster. "Let's go to Barnes & Noble's tonight," said his friend, who sometimes answers to Marc Levasseur and is known for his colorful barnyard creations. "We'll study some art books."

"Awesome!"

Sometimes fish-art collector Goliath Davis III, the city's former deputy mayor, ambled in to ask, "What's up, Woo?" So did Charley Morgan, the crusty 82-year-old founder of Morgan Yachts. "I'm a fan of Woo's paintings," Morgan told me. "But it's more than that. It's his personality, his hustle, and his refusal to be defeated by the things that have happened to him. I really admire him."

Part Buddha and part Munchkin, Woo stood 5 feet 4 and weighed a few six packs more than 200 pounds. He favored paint-spattered shorts and smocks. His hair was a wonder, short on the sides but cresting to a small wave in the middle. A night owl, he had dark rings under his eyes from bad sleep. He had a hipster's goatee and wore hipster eyeglasses. Large gold hoops dangled from his ears while the tattoos of jellyfish, octopi, and koi on his thick arms swam into view as he painted.

A Friday.

Now he was standing before a blank canvas, which is scary but in a different way from how brain cancer was scary. "Fish are living art," Woo said. Every fish is different. Every one serves a natural purpose. Fish are utterly alive. Woo wanted to do them justice. He studied his model, a small photograph of something colorful given him by an angler as inspiration. He dipped the brush. Started. Stopped. Stepped back, cocked his head, stared down the intimidating blank canvas, unafraid.

He finally initiated a painting of a speckled peacock bass, an Amazon River species introduced to South Florida in 1984. A peacock bass features every hue in the Crayola box, but they're mostly gold and green with a dab of blue. They have black spots and black bars and black speckles and striking black eyes that show no mercy to minnows or grass shrimp.

"I've got an appointment for an MRI soon," Woo suddenly blurted out. "I try to remain positive, but it's hard not to be nervous. You know what I mean?"

He was genetically programmed to paint fish, barracuda or orange grouper, perhaps, or red snapper and Spanish hogfish. A second-generation American, he counted among his relatives commercial fishermen from Portugal and the Azores. He had been born in the commercial fishing town of New Bedford, Massachusetts, once America's whaling capital. His dad, William Correira Jr., was a graphics designer for Goodyear Rubber Products but was better known for his paintings of whales and his engravings of 19th-century ships on sperm whale teeth. Bill's mother, Gale, was named in honor of a storm that drowned 500 New Englanders and destroyed a fishing fleet in 1938.

The Correiras moved to Florida when Bill was 7. As a boy, he caught sheepshead on a hook baited with a fiddler crab and blue crabs using chicken necks. While snorkeling, he saw homely toadfish feeding along the oyster beds and pretty, striped sergeant majors cruising through the turtle grass shallows. Exploring Tampa Bay on a little unseaworthy boat made from Styrofoam, he caught Southern puffers and gafftopsail catfish.

"He was always a wild little kid," his mother told me. "When he was really small I had to put him on a leash to keep him from going off." At St. Petersburg's Northeast High he preferred his skateboard to what his teachers had scrawled on the chalkboard. His other hobbies were girls and beer.

He told me the story about attending the prom in a Mercedes loaned to him by his girlfriend's dad. During the evening, Bill loaded the car with friends and sped over a hill, landing hard enough to decapitate the oil pan. Without lubrication the engine seized, ruined. "Call your dad," he told his date. "I'm gone." He vanished into the dark, walking 5 miles home in his rented tux. End of date. End of relationship.

Bill clashed nightly with his own dad, a retired Army veteran who had become a Baptist and wanted to see not only maturity but some As on his son's report card. "If you're going fishin'," his dad sometimes barked at him in his clam-chowder accent, "why isn't there a fishin' rod in the cah?"

They became close only a dozen years ago. That happened when dad came home after the doctor's appointment at which he had been diagnosed with deadly pancreatic cancer. "I only got about six months," the father told the son. "So let's get to know each other."

At the time, Bill had only just started dabbling in art. A community college dropout, he earned a paycheck by tending bar, scraping boat bottoms, and graphic design. "You got some talent," his dad told him. "To learn how to paint you gotta paint."

Bill painted naked girls.

"Now try and sell 'em," his dad said.

He drove to a gallery where Leslie Curran, now a city council member, stood behind the counter. "Not bad," she told him. "But lots of artists paint nudes. What else do you have?"

He did paintings of gag grouper and pompano and mangrove snapper. "People around here really like fish," Curran said. "Give me some fish."

They sold like cod cakes.

One night, his dad waved his boy over. "Out of respect for your mother," he said, "take me outside for a walk because I'm going to smoke."

As Bill pushed the wheelchair he realized his dad's desire for a smoke was not the reason for their walk. "Stop," his father said and pointed at the western sky. "See that crescent moon? And the little star right next to it?"

Bill saw the heavenly objects. "When I'm gone," his father said, "and you see that moon and that star, I want you to know I'm up there watchin' ya."

The son fought back the tears.

"So, Billy Bad Boy," his father said, "you cryin' back there?" His dad died at home on November 29, 2000. Woo and his mom scattered the ashes over the fishing grounds in New England.

Back in Florida, Woo began painting his fish furiously. Curran's new gallery on Central Avenue, Interior Motives, took on the appearance of an aquarium.

Most artists don't starve, but neither do they need a stockbroker. They drive old cars and do without health insurance. Woo somehow managed. He bought a condo and opened a little studio but kept his bartending job.

Thanksgiving 2007. That night he was tending bar at a joint that's gone now, a neighborhood kind of place where everybody knew everybody. As he poured wine and tapped the beer he felt dizzy. Maybe he'd eaten too much turkey.

The chair flipped when he passed out. The ambulance arrived, loaded him up, sped to the Bayfront Medical Center. As word got around, friends showed up in force—some from city hall, some from the city's back alleys. They loved Woo. The hospital staff had to pass a Woo rule: only so many visitors at a time.

Woo remained in a coma 48 days. He woke tied to a hospital bed so he couldn't rip the tubes from his arms, nose, throat, penis. A nurse gently removed the tape from his eyes. He somehow focused on the television near the ceiling. *The Wizard of Oz* was on. Dorothy's house had just fallen on the wicked witch. The movie tripped from black and white to color. He watched Dorothy on the yellow brick road. In Munchkinland, Woo was alive.

"You have a tumor on your brain," a doctor told him. "You had a seizure."

The tumor had to wait. First, he learned how to talk, walk, eat, and go to the bathroom again. Ten days later, he and his mother celebrated his homecoming with steaks. Fear was their dessert.

First, Woo had no insurance. Medicaid was going to take care of some expenses, but not all. Second, something that could kill him was growing in his brain.

Goliath Davis III, the deputy mayor, helped him get a doctor's appointment. The biopsy revealed malignant cells. His oncologist prescribed chemotherapy in pill form. The pill made him sick to his stomach. Woo had bills to pay, so he painted every day, maybe a rock hind grouper or a bonefish, sometimes at home, sometimes in his studio, but often on the street in front of restaurants where he could attract a crowd and woo potential customers.

His favorite sidewalk fronted 400 Beach Seafood & Tap House in downtown St. Petersburg. He might paint a king mackerel, an Atlantic bonito, or a snowy grouper. Then he'd bolt for the restaurant's restroom and throw up. After brushing his teeth, he'd return to the sidewalk and maybe his painting of a queen triggerfish.

Over the next two years, the tumor grew smaller. Then it stopped shrinking. As it grew back, Woo felt as fragile as a mullet in the path of a hungry amberjack.

At Moffitt Cancer Center, Dr. Surbhi Jain looked at his latest MRI scan, recommended surgery and explained the risks. He might lose his sense of smell. He might not be able to taste food.

He might not be able to paint. The frontal lobe controls the movement of fine muscles. So in order to live he might lose the one thing he loved the most.

Dr. Jain removed a tumor about the size of a slice of cheesecake. Woo retained his ability to smell—out of one nostril, anyway. He lost much of his sense of taste. When he got home from the hospital he set a canvas on an easel. Stared at the blank canvas. Backed away. He took a deep breath and started a barracuda.

He could still paint. That mattered to him more than the taste of smoked Spanish mackerel. He painted great hammerhead sharks, snapper, even a few green sea turtles. He socialized, got tattooed, fell in love and out of love and in love again. He ate rib-eyes at Outback and never turned down a beer. His friend, council member Leslie Curran, warned him, "Slow down. Rest. Take a day off every once in a while."

"I'm bored when I take a day off," he protested. "I love to paint. Painting isn't work to me."

Not long ago, he met a friend, Trisha Servedio, at a bar. She wanted to tell him the good news: she and her significant other were expecting their first baby. "Now you can't drink," Woo told her as he gulped the first of six Jägermeisters, a potent liqueur noted for its pungent flavor. He

Bill Woo paints a grouper in his St. Petersburg studio. (Photo by Maurice Rivenbark.)

chased down his favorite beverage with six highly caffeinated Red Bulls, which sped the booze through his system.

"Now you can't drink," Woo told his friend.

"You already said that," Trisha pointed out.

"Now you can't drink," Woo said minutes later.

"What's wrong with you, Bill?" she asked.

"I think I blacked out."

On a recent Wednesday, Woo and his mother woke early. He ate Raisin Bran; she was too nervous for anything but coffee, which, of course, made her more nervous. Bill dressed in shorts and a baggy fisherman's shirt and tried to stay calm.

"Let me iron your shirt," his mother said. "It's so wrinkled."

"I'm having an MRI, Mom," Woo said. "Nobody cares about my shirt."

The appointment at Moffitt Cancer Center in Tampa was scheduled for 8:30 a.m. In the waiting room, Woo filled out forms with tired eyes. He hadn't slept for days. He hoped his dad was up there in the stars, looking down.

A nurse checked his blood pressure. Off the charts.

"I guess I'm nervous."

Another nurse took him back, and a technician helped him into the magnetic resonance imaging unit. "Butter me up" is Woo's standard joke when he squeezes his goliath grouper form into a space meant for a skinny needlefish. He took a deep breath when the technician rolled him into the machine that was going to take pictures of his brain and determine his future.

In another room, Woo's brain appeared on a TV monitor. Front and back, upside down and right side up—for 45 minutes the MRI hummed and thumped and took photographs at every angle. On the other side of the smoked glass Woo lay still as death.

As the technician rolled him out of the machine, Woo wanted to ask, "Did you see anything?" but didn't. She wouldn't have told him anyway. The doctor would.

That happened half an hour later in a small consulting room, where Woo sat anxiously waiting with his mother. Suddenly Dr. Edward Pan strolled in carrying photographs. "Good news," he said. "The tumor hasn't grown at all. In fact, I'm going to wean you off the antiseizure medicine."

So why had Woo suffered the blackout? Probably all those Jägermeisters and the Red Bulls and his high-octane life. Woo vowed to slow down. Then he typed a message on Facebook about his news. Okay at least for now. No woe for Woo.

Hours later he showed up on a downtown sidewalk with his easel and another blank canvas. He set everything up in front of a bar known as Sake Bomb.

A crescent moon hung over the western horizon. He dipped his brush in the paint and stepped back. Then he started painting.

A tuna, yellow and blue with those black, expressionless eyes, slowly came to life.

Summer 2011.

19

The Worm Grunters

I always wondered about that "early bird catches the worm" saying until I met Gary Revell and it turned out to be his credo. He liked to be in the Apalachicola National Forest in northwest Florida at daybreak, armed with a wooden stake he called a stob, a heavy steel file he called a rooping iron, and a mess of one-gallon cans in which he placed the bounty he scared out of the ground. Earthworms. By the thousands.

In our state there was no more unusual way of making a living than—take your pick—worm rooping, worm charming, worm grunting, or worm fiddling. It was a way of ordinary life where science met folklore, where the twenty-first century intersected with the old Florida of horseback and Model A Fords.

Kneeling in the dirt at dawn, Revell buried the stob 15 inches deep in the topsoil. Grasping the heavy iron roop with both hands, he leaned his weight against the stob and commenced a passionate rubbing. The roop-on-stob collaboration produced the Sopchoppy Symphony, which has been performed in a remote section of Florida for more than a century.

The Sopchoppy Symphony, as Revell played it, starts with a groan and proceeds to a kind of mighty grunt, the kind a distressed 100-pound bull-frog might produce, an awesome, hair-raising, teeth-rattling sustained kind of grunt. First the earth begins to tingle. Then it quakes for dozens of feet in all directions. Then things really get weird.

Within seconds the ground explodes with earthworms. They writhe in what seems to be ecstasy, but is more likely terror—as if the demons from hell are pursuing them from the netherworld.

As Gary Revell played the stob like a Stradivarius, his wife, Audrey, trotted among the worms, plucking here, plucking there, filling bucket after bucket with fish bait.

The Itzhak Perlman of worm fiddling was a gray-bearded man with strong arms and shoulders. He had been rooping worms for more than half a century. His great-granddaddy taught his granddaddy the process, his granddaddy taught his daddy, and his daddy had taught him. At one time there were hundreds of mostly men in the 565,000-acre forest harvesting worms. Now only a handful tried to make a living at it.

"It's real hard work, you got to get up before the sun and there's not a lot of money in it," said Revell, who makes $30,000 in a good year, selling worms to bait shops all over the South. "But I love it. I love being in the woods and I love being my own boss."

Revell, 58 when I met him, also enjoyed the prestige that accompanied his role as King of the Earthworms. The earthworm in question, by the way, is known by scientists as *Diplocardia mississippiensis* and common in the long-leaf pine forests near the Apalachicola River. The worms are pale in color, rather corpulent, and sometimes measure a dozen inches or more. For generations, country southerners have used them to lure catfish, bass, and bream into frying pans.

Revell lived 6 miles from the biggest nearby city, Sopchoppy, population 400. His nearest neighbor, a hog farmer, lived a mile away. Revell's acre included pear, peach, and persimmon trees and two large gardens in which he grew tomatoes, corn, squash, okra, collards, and snap peas. He raised chickens for the eggs and horses for the manure that fertilized his gardens, already enriched by hundreds of pounds of worm-fortified soil.

Revell and Audrey, who had married after high school, shot deer and turkey every fall, caught Gulf of Mexico mullet in cast nets, and gathered oysters commercially during the cold months when the demand for worms waned.

Five generations of his family had made a living from worms; his son, Donald—known as "Snap" from boyhood—who built cabinets during the afternoon, helped his daddy catch worms at dawn. Snap was as small as a snap pea when he was young, but now he had his father's large upper body, the result of years of rooping. "My daddy would carry me out to the woods on his shoulders when I was little," Snap, 33, told me. "I'd catch me frogs, but soon I was rooping next to him."

When Snap's daddy had started his roping career, his ambition was only to harvest enough worms to catch a stringer of bullheads. Soon Gary Revell traveled in the company of older members of his family, grim-faced men to whom worms were a commodity.

They thanked the Lord for Henry Ford.

Gary Revell kneels in Apalachicola Forest and rubs steel bar against wood stake to grunt up worms. (Photo by Maurice Rivenbark.)

"About a hundred years ago," Revell told me "one of my kinfolk noticed that worms would come out of the ground under an idling Model A." Then somebody thought to drive the Ford to a different location in the worm-infested woods. "That was a lot of work. Eventually, folks tried rubbing wood sticks on wood stobs in the ground. From there, they tried rubbing ax heads on the stakes and that was more effective."

Bed and truck springs, rubbed against the wood stobs, proved to be even better than the axe. "I make my own rooping irons now. I got me some that weigh 10 pounds, I got me some that weigh 20 pounds. Some I use when the topsoil is shallow. Some I use where the topsoil is deep. I could go on and on if you had all day. They's a lot to it."

It is often said that if the ground is beaten or otherwise made to tremble, worms will believe that they are being pursued by a mole and leave their burrows.
CHARLES DARWIN, 1881

In 2008, a scientist at Vanderbilt, a whiz kid who once won a MacArthur Foundation genius grant, was enjoying a little light reading,

Gary Revell emerges from his bait shop. (Photo by Maurice Rivenbark.)

namely, Darwin's *The Formation of Vegetable Mould through the Action of Worms with Observations on Their Habits.*

Ken Catania, the Vanderbilt biologist, is a mole expert. Over the years he had read several obscure reports about the vanishing art of worm fiddling in the Apalachicola National Forest. He wondered if he might test Darwin's theory and answer the eternal question: "Why the heck do worms bolt out of the ground when the Sopchoppy Symphony is performed?"

Soon he was part of King of the Earthworm's posse. "First time I saw Gary roop up worms I could hardly believe what I was seeing," the scientist once told me. Catania also began watching for evidence of moles, namely, the notorious scourge of worms everywhere, *Scalopus aquaticus.* They were plentiful in the places where Revell labored.

Moles apparently make a ruckus while burrowing through the soil. A scientist with a good ear and sensitive feet can hear and feel them a dozen feet away. Catania began recording the sound of burrowing moles and the Sopchoppy Symphony. Worm grunting, he discovered, produced vibrations in the 80 kilohertz range; mole activity peaked at 200 kHz. However, there was a point where worm fiddler and mole music overlapped.

One night, in Revell's living room, observed by the spooky deer heads and the stuffed largemouth bass hanging from the walls, the scientist conducted another experiment. He dropped a mole into a box where worms had been living comfortably under the soil. As soon as the mole began digging, the worms popped up.

Was that terror on their slimy little faces?

Gary Revell goes to bed when his chickens roost. He wakes before the roosters crow, about 4 a.m., and ambles out into his yard with his coffee. He almost always catches earthworms, but some days are better than others. He prefers a warm morning with dew on the ground and no wind. Worms dry out quickly; if they emerge on a windy day they lose their lubrication and can't slip back into the soil efficiently.

A little humidity and rain are good. Slightly damp soil enhances the vibrations. When the ground is soaked, vibrations are diluted. Worms don't like cold. They hate a north wind.

"They's animals," Revell said of his prey. "You have to pay attention or you're not going to get none." When he sees a flock of robins on the ground, or armadillos rooting, he has a good feeling about the morning. Sometimes, after he starts rooping, his wife has to race the robins to the worms.

Seldom does he have to race other worm roopers to the gold. The few who remain—whippersnappers!—often try to follow Revell. They may extinguish their truck headlights, but he knows they are behind him. Sometimes he leads them on a wild worm chase; sometimes he feels charitable. "They can follow me, but they can't get worms like me. It's been my life here in Wakulla County," he told me.

We parked in the woods. Now we trooped a mile through the pines and the palmettos and through the water. Finally we stopped in an area the forest service had burned recently to renourish the soil.

It was time for the Sopchoppy Symphony. As he worked, the muscles on his arms quivering, Revell grunted with the effort, like a weightlifter bench-pressing a heavy barbell. Meanwhile his rooping iron caressed the sweet-gum stob and brought to life the song of a giant bullfrog.

I wouldn't have believed it unless I saw it. Within seconds, worms popped out of the ground writhing in what looked like agony. Not just near us, but 100 feet away. In the next two hours we collected 3,000, about 60 pounds of fat, slimy catfish-enticing worms.

Later, at home, Revell poured them into a big sink and began ladling them into plastic cups for bait-store delivery. "These are real pretty worms," he told me, pride in his voice. "We got us some real pretty fish bait today."

Fall 2009.

Some Places I Like to Go

Mack's Fish Camp

Marshall Jones and his brother, Keith, who operate historic Mack's Fish Camp in the Everglades, were barefoot boys in the tradition of Tom Sawyer and Huck Finn. The 30-year-old twins wore shoes only if necessary, perhaps because buying proper footwear was a challenge. Marshall squeezed his ample paws into size 13s. Keith's feet measured a sawgrass-stomping 15EEE.

Their toes were prehensile, bent and misshapen, topped by yellow nails more reptilian than human. Banged up and scarred, their feet looked like something large and toothy had gnawed on them. Something had.

"One night I'm standing on my dock in the dark," Keith told me one morning. "And I hear this big old splash under me. Something grabs my foot. This gator has jumped up and tried to pull me in."

"It must have been a long and painful drive to the ER," I said.

"Not really," Keith said. Neither twin, it turned out, had faith in doctors or hospitals. In their toolboxes, they carried sutures—mostly to sew up hunting dogs sliced open by the tusks of irritated wild hogs. But the Jones boys also stitched up their friends and each other. Without Novocain.

"You take the pain like a man," Marshall told me defiantly.

The Jones brothers, after all, were Gladesmen—self-reliant, don't-tread-on-me fellows who depended on the Everglades for everything from physical to emotional nourishment. Men and a handful of women like them—folks who knew how to eke out a living from a most inhospitable land—once had been common in South Florida. But in the twenty-first century, Gladesmen were rarer than panthers.

The Jones brothers had been raised among the snakes and alligators, the roughnecks and the kindhearted countrywomen at the fish camp founded by their great-grandfather, Mack Jones Sr., in 1937. They attended school miles away in Hollywood but shed their shoes and the stink of the city the moment they arrived back in the Everglades. They learned how to gig frogs for the legs, catch bass, shoot deer, and grow things. They learned every bird and plant. Something broke? They could fix it. Something need building? Their huge hands swallowed up any hammer. "We grew up young," is how Marshall once put it.

In the Everglades, they could handle any crisis, from a hog-gored dog to a faulty magneto on a battered airboat. But as Florida became civilized, so did their challenges. The brothers told me, for example, that they wanted to keep their dilapidated fish camp in business. They wanted their children to grow up as they did, and they wanted to keep the Gladesman tradition going. Walking into Starbucks scared them more than an enraged cottonmouth.

I am a city rat who likes a good cup of coffee, an art museum, and a nearby hospital, just in case I need stitches. But a big part of me is a country mouse who loves exploring a swamp, listening to the pig frogs, and encountering a big alligator. My country roots lead directly to Mack's Fish Camp.

I started visiting during the period Eisenhower lived in the White House and the Dodgers played home games in Brooklyn. My dad liked to fish and dragged his kid along into the Everglades. We'd take the road out of Miami, then head down Krome Avenue to where the Broward and Dade County borders bumped heads. If you saw another DeSoto, Studebaker, or Nash Rambler out in the sticks, more than likely it was bound for the same place. You turned onto an atrocious limestone road, crossed a bridge, and 3 miles later you were at Mack's.

I think my Chicago-born dad liked the adventure of visiting Mack's as much as he liked the fishing. It was the last frontier, lacking electricity, running water, or even telephone service. We'd watch the Gladesmen jump into their airboats and roar off into the sawgrass to hunt deer. Even more exciting, at least to city people, was the return of the hunters, who hung their just-slain bucks upside down from a tree limb to bleed out.

My dad hoped to catch bass, the high-status Everglades denizen, but we settled for bream, a blue-collar cane pole fish that fit perfectly in a frying pan. We caught them on worms acquired from Grandma Nell Jones, the Queen of the Everglades. She was 5 feet 2, but closer to 6 if you counted her mountain of auburn hair.

Marshall Jones takes a dip—alligator be damned. (Photo by Maurice Rivenbark.)

After I learned to drive, my Everglades world expanded to other places, but I still visited Mack's to cast a fly-rod popping bug at bass and to chat with the Queen of the Everglades, who held court from a wooden chair backed against a wall decorated by stuffed creatures with fur and fins.

"Sit down, honey," she'd tell me. And I would. Born in Georgia, Grandma Nell never lost her cane-syrup accent. She talked about the Bible and about how Jesus was a fisherman, though he probably didn't catch any black bass in the Sea of Galilee because, honey, the bass is a Glades fish. She'd say if you want to catch a really big bass, get yourself a giant minnow for bait, one of them wild Everglades shiners, and cast him out next to the lily pads at first light.

Sometimes her husband, Mack Jr., ambled in, chomping on a cigar and looking dapper in a fine straw hat. Mack Sr., his daddy, a farmer from South Carolina, had started the fish camp during the Depression. The cigar-smoking son, Mack Jr., was a talented home builder who worked in Miami most of the time while Nell ran the fish camp. But he could tell you how to skin a catfish and how to keep a woman happy.

Every four years he bought Grandma Nell a new Cadillac, including, at least once, a pink one. She loved her Everglades, but she loved the bright lights, too. Every once in a while, she'd drag Mack Jr. to town and they would dance the jitterbug.

The twins were born in 1979. After their mama got sick and died three years later, their dad abandoned them. In the Everglades, Grandpa Mack and Grandma Nell raised those boys best they could.

Now they were civilized wild men. Marshall to me seemed more civilized than wild, and Keith seemed more wild than civilized. Fraternal twins, Keith was the larger of the brothers, robust like a college defensive tackle. Marshall was slightly smaller and quicker, intense in the way of a Parris Island drill instructor. Marshall was a "yes sir, no sir" kind of serious guy. I was tempted to drop and give him 20.

Both brothers had piercing eyes. Both had the same short hair. They didn't have to diet, go to the gym, or worry about ever getting fat. "It's the Everglades life," Keith said, glancing at my citified waistline.

They obviously enjoyed talking about growing up in the Everglades. "It was wild, it was free," Marshall said. They swung from ropes over the Miami River and dropped, on purpose, onto the heads of unsuspecting alligators "just to see what would happen," Keith said.

"Grandma hated when we did that," Marshall said. As small boys, they jumped into the river, swam deep, and hunted by feel for antique bottles on the bottom. Occasionally in the murky water they touched a gator by mistake. "You didn't want to tell Grandma that," Keith said. "We were hellions," Marshall said. "We were her heathens."

Every Sunday, the Queen of the Everglades drove them in her pink Cadillac to the nearest Baptist church, which happened to be miles away in Miami Lakes. Their faces scrubbed, hair combed, and shirts tucked in, the twins squirmed in the pew until the last hymn.

Back in the Everglades, they fished, built forts, and rode ATVs down the levees after wild hogs. Sometimes, when a hog leaped into the water to escape, they'd follow on foot. They'd tackle the struggling hog and dispatch it with a knife. Barbecue was on the menu that night.

One time Keith grabbed by the tail what was supposedly a dead cottonmouth and began waving it above his head like a lasso. "Somehow

I ended up hitting myself in the ear with the fang-end of that snake," Keith said, laughing.

"You started screaming, 'I'm gonna die,'" Marshall pointed out with glee.

"Well, I was only 15. I thought I got the poison in me."

"We didn't tell Grandma that either."

Mack Jones died in 1985. Grandma Nell carried on running the fish camp and raising wild boys, doing her best to instill Baptist values in her own steel magnolia way. "Never mind the dog," said the well-known sign propped against the cash register next to her. "Beware of the Owner."

The handgun pointed at the customer in the sign was just for show. Grandma Nell never needed the assistance of Smith & Wesson. Her wrath was the stuff of Everglades legend. Here's a story one old Glades-man remembered about an obnoxious drunk. "Honey, you got to quiet down," Grandma Nell told him. When he cussed her, Grandma Nell exploded from her chair and set upon him with her enraged broom. She broke the broomstick over his sorry noggin.

Here's another Gladesmen tale: a drunk got mad at his woman and gave her a vicious shove in Grandma Nell's presence. Grandma Nell grabbed for the broom, but her beauty-shop manicured hands somehow found a shovel instead. Swinging, she chased the drunk out the door. Somebody called the sheriff. "Here's the part I always loved about that story," Keith told me. "The deputies showed up, but they just stood there watching Grandma take care of the problem."

Marshall continued the story. "Grandma told the drunk, 'You come back here again and I'll shoot you.'"

"The deputies told her, 'Now, Miss Nell, you know you can't shoot him. Just call us,'" Keith said.

The twins chose Everglades girls whom Grandma Nell liked. At the time of my visit, each twin had four children. They hoped their kids would grow up to be Gladesmen, even the girls.

Grandma Nell died in 1999. The headline in the Fort Lauderdale paper caught the essence of her personality: "She Enjoyed Conversation."

The boys were only 20.

In the ensuing years they tried their best. They rented boats and sold bait. They took tourists for airboat rides. Being a Gladesman is what came naturally to them, not business. The federal government eventually proposed that Mack's Fish Camp be listed as a national historic site,

Keith Jones with "Elvis," his pet alligator.

which delighted the twins, who hoped the designation might bring in new customers.

Last time I visited, workmen were eliminating trash and clutter and selling off long-abandoned trucks and airboats. The twins were gathering keepsakes for a museum they hoped might lure in a few tourists along with their regular anglers. They planned to build cabins and hold barbecues. All you can eat for 10 bucks and Lynyrd Skynyrd on the stereo.

Once again, they told me, they wanted to be headquarters for what is left of South Florida's hunting community. But they worried. Hunters and their airboats, swamp buggies, and Jeeps had access to only a small part of the Everglades in the twenty-first century. "The world has changed a whole lot on us," Keith said.

In late afternoon he gave me a tour of his home, showed me prized photographs from the old days, and fed me barbecue. In the back yard— a swamp—he showed me another side of Everglades hospitality. He stomped his 15EEEs on the boards of a dock until the welcoming party, an enormous alligator, rushed out from underneath.

A moment later the giant lizard employed its powerful tail and front legs to climb up on the dock next to us. "Git now," Keith said, pushing the gator back into the water—with his bare hands. It hissed a dinosaur hiss and stared balefully. "I call this one Elvis," Keith told me. "I've known him since he was little. I can read him like a book. I ain't afraid."

In a moment of Gladesmen bravado, or Huck Finn foolishness, Keith entered Elvis's lair, the swamp. The gator, all 10 feet of him, rushed over and opened his jaws in a way that suggested a consuming hunger for a large meal. Keith, a Gladesman after all, didn't for even a moment consider backing down. Leaning over with those bearish hands, he simply closed the menacing jaws.

Fall 2009.

Hurricane Graveyard

Robert Hazard, a middle-aged African American, was one of those men who hated to miss the daily weather report during summer when the tropical storms were brewing in the Atlantic by the hour. He had experienced a few hurricanes in his four decades in Florida, he told me, though never a bad one. But he knew many who had.

Some he had interviewed about the storm of 1928—the hurricane of so many nightmares. Others, long gone, communed with Hazard only as spirits. "Oh, they talk to me," he said with a shy smile. Hazard spent every day on a one-acre lot at the corner of Tamarind and 25th Streets in the black section of West Palm. Sauntering through the field in a hurricane-like counterclockwise direction, he meditated about what had happened.

"It was quite a hurricane," the spirits of the dead whispered to him more than once. "And what happened to us after it was over was just as terrible. You should tell everyone about it."

Before a great storm named Katrina came to symbolize nature's fury and human folly, there had been the Hurricane of 1928. "As we saw on television, Katrina was bad," Hazard told me. "The one in 1928 was probably worse. But how many people have ever heard about it? I'm guessing not many."

He had made it his life's purpose to tell the story. "Communication was primitive compared to today," was how he liked to begin his tale. There were no weather satellites in space, no televisions, not many radios to broadcast alerts. Meteorologists had to run up red and black flags on a city hall pole to warn residents about a coming hurricane.

September 16, 1928, fell on a Sunday. Folks noticed the gray skies on the way home from church. That evening, the storm blasted ashore in southern Palm Beach County, sweeping aside trees and buildings. It was bad, but what happened next was horrific. The storm raced inland toward the state's largest lake and the poor people who lived in shacks on the shores.

"It woke up old Okeechobee and the monster began to roll in his bed," wrote the famous African American author Zora Neale Hurston in the hurricane chapter of her novel *Their Eyes Were Watching God*.

Protecting a handful of low-lying, humble farming towns from the 700-square-mile lake was a 4-foot earthen levee. Some people who lived on the lake had gotten word about the coming apocalypse, Robert Hazard told me. But some hadn't.

It didn't really matter. Roads were narrow, unpaved, prone to flooding. Few people had dependable vehicles in which to evacuate. By the time the 140 mph winds fell silent, thousands lay dead, drowned when the 30-mile-wide lake overflowed.

For the most part they were poor and black migrant farm workers. They had died running for higher ground. They had died when houses crumpled, capsized or floated away. They had died in their attics and clinging to debris. They had died holding babies and grandparents in their arms.

The official 1928 hurricane death count was 1,836. The revised 2003 National Hurricane Center death count was 2,500 with an asterisk. Historians say the death toll likely was higher, though nobody will ever know the precise number. A new levee, 30 feet high, now circles the lake. It has never been tested by a hurricane as powerful as the Category 4 storm of 1928.

Robert Hazard competed in football, basketball and track in high school in the 1960s. Now, he admitted sheepishly, he had slow legs and a middle-aged waistline. He lived in a neat neighborhood where enormous alligators sunbathed on the banks of his canal. He didn't think he could outrun an alligator anymore.

An old woman once told him about the alligator that saved her life during the 1928 hurricane. As the winds shrieked over the lake, the woman said, her family headed for a sturdier government building. Soon the water streamed through the crack under the door. Then the door broke and torrents spilled in. She was 6. She climbed atop a chair. Around her, folks moaned and called on God.

Death surrounded them. The water reached her chin. Around dawn, when the waters were subsiding, she heard someone yell, "God is good" and point her way. Her arm was in an alligator's mouth. The alligator hadn't hurt her, the woman said. It was holding her up.

Listening, Hazard didn't know what to make of such a far-fetched story except that it gave him the chills and the impetus to learn more. Which is exactly what he did.

The 1928 hurricane, he found out, was the second deadliest natural disaster in U.S. history, behind only the 1906 Galveston hurricane in loss of life, which killed more than 6,000. The 1928 hurricane killed more people than Pennsylvania's Johnstown flood of 1889 and the San Francisco earthquake of 1906. Combined.

As with Katrina, whose winds and water breached levees around New Orleans in 2005, victims were mostly people of color. "The (Florida) hurricane may have accounted for the most deaths of black people in a single day in U.S. history," wrote Eliot Kleinberg in *Black Cloud*, his history of the 1928 storm.

"The montropolous beast had left his bed," wrote Zora Neale Hurston in her famous novel. "The two hundred miles an hour wind had loosed his chains. He seized hold of his dikes and ran forward until he met the quarters; uprooted them like grass and rushed on after his supposed-to-be-conquerors, rolling the dikes, rolling the houses, rolling the people in the houses along with other timbers. The sea was walking the earth with a heavy heel."

When possible, the white dead were collected, identified, and buried in pine boxes in the closest cemeteries. The bodies of the black people were stacked in roadside pyres and burned. Others were dumped in mass graves, some marked, some not marked.

Most victims were migrant farm workers from the Caribbean. Back in the islands, their families never found out what happened to them. Some 674 black corpses were trucked from the lake to a dump in West Palm Beach. The bloated bodies were bulldozed into a 20-foot-deep hole and covered over.

As the years went by, the dump became a sewage plant, an electrical substation, and finally a slaughterhouse. Then one day it was merely a forgotten litter-strewn field. There was not as much as a wooden cross to mark the resting place of the black dead.

When Robert Hazard ambled through the field, he could hear the spirits calling him.

Robert Hazard at the West Palm Beach African American graveyard for the 1928 Hurricane dead.

"If there had been 674 white folks in this mass grave," he thought, "there would have been a marker a long time ago."

Hazard was born in Massachusetts in 1948. His dad pressed clothes for a living; his mother was a homemaker and a maid. Black people were treated like second-class Americans. He remembered the day he showed up at the baseball field in Worcester to join Little League. He was 8, an innocent child, excited about demonstrating what he could do with ball and bat. The coach sent him home. No black kids allowed.

Another time, older white boys held him down while other kids heated something in a fire. He showed me the spot below his eye where he was branded with a red-hot Abraham Lincoln penny. He had other scars as well, but they were inside on his soul.

He became a heroin addict, got clean, and became a drug counselor. He was inspired by Martin Luther King Jr. and by Malcolm X, protested police brutality, joined the Black Panther Party, and organized free breakfasts for the poor. After he moved to West Palm to live closer to his retired parents, he opened a charter school for black children and worked in the justice system.

Near Lake Okeechobee in 1928, workers recover another body. (Photo courtesy of the Historical Society of Palm Beach County.)

He also began looking for the mass grave on Tamarind Street. Nobody, not even the elderly hurricane survivors, could remember the exact location. He'd drive them to the field and walk them around. Someone would point to a spot and say, "There." Someone else would say, "No, a little south." Hazard always hammered a stake into the spot and hung a wreath.

In 1991, Hazard and other interested people held their first candlelight vigil in the field. Local newspapers covered the story. The field's owner, an exterminator, hadn't known about his property's history. He and Hazard became allies in an effort to persuade the city to buy the land.

The city balked. So on September 16, 1998, Hazard and a group he had founded—the Storm of '28 Memorial Park Coalition—staged a 70th anniversary service. Hazard soon began haunting city hall with a new idea: he proposed the city buy the land, install a memorial, and build an education center.

In 2000, West Palm Beach at last hired a company to hunt for the mass grave. Using sonar equipment, the specialists isolated what seemed to be a mass of bones about 20 feet down. The location turned out to be only a few steps from the place where Hazard had hung his first wreath. Black historians throughout the state began writing letters to the mayor. On December 11, 2000, the city purchased the land.

As the 80th anniversary of the hurricane approached in 2008, Robert Hazard invited me to West Palm to see the new memorial park. As we ambled in a hurricane-like counterclockwise direction, a landscaper from the city's beautification department weeded the flower bed on the grave site. Hazard smiled.

The memorial plaque looked shiny and nice. The paths were clean; the benches were in place. Hazard enjoyed sitting on a favorite bench after dark and watching the moon come up. He also liked sitting on the bench in the morning and in the afternoon.

He was the self-appointed docent. If someone wanted to know what the hurricane was like, he could tell them that roofs flew like birds and the cottonmouth snakes swam into the attics where the terrified waited with dread. He could tell how the black folks, conscripted to gather the dead, accidentally discovered the bodies of brothers, sisters, parents, children. Bloated bodies.

Death in the air. Vultures soaring above the wet earth for weeks. September 1928.

Now 80 years had passed. As we sat on the bench, traffic rushed along Tamarind and 25th and a breeze rustled the palms. Robert Hazard told me: "Everything looks real nice here now. I think the spirits of the dead ones are going to like it."

Summer 2008.

Chiappini's

Loitering is an art at Chiappini's, a grocery/gas station/tavern in the little town of Melrose in North Florida. Loitering happens to be my hobby, so I pulled off State Road 26 and stepped through the door. I wasn't disappointed. The place was filled with loiterers who were too busy loitering to even notice me.

As I loitered, I ate chips, admired the big hornet's nest that hangs empty near the impressive fan-belt inventory, asked about the stuffed bass over the door, checked out the live minnows in the bait tank, heard the cool Doris Day story, silently vowed never to play poker with the man named Maurice, and discovered a new use for a favorite fast food.

Chiappini's (pronounced cha-peen-ees) had the best beef jerky selection I had ever seen—seven varieties of this loitering food for the gods, including "teriyaki" and "smoked." A woman who loitered on a nearby barstool told me her kids had cut their teeth on Chiappini's finest jerky. "It felt good on their gums," she said.

"My Momma gave me a pork chop when I was teething," an older loiterer proclaimed.

"My mother gave me Zweiback," I volunteered. Nobody ridiculed me. At Chiappini's they know enough not to criticize a loiterer's momma.

Not that Chiappini's is a completely mellow place. Loiterers do get carried away, like the time a woman dressed as a nun turned out to be a stripper who had arrived to embarrass a customer on his birthday. And there is that "No Profanity" sign below the TV—just in case—and that warning you will never see in your neighborhood Publix.

"No Spitting."

Papa Joe Chiappini, an Italian immigrant, founded his store when Gulf Oil gave him a loan in 1935. He paid it back, over the years, by taxing gasoline a penny. Papa Joe was big and strong and had a hearty laugh. He sold meat, coffee, flour, and hardware. He installed a juke box and

Gasoline, beer, and beef jerky. And they'll wipe your windshield for free.

sold beer to soldiers. He tolerated loiterers, though if they misbehaved he threw them out the front door.

Joe's sons, Francis and Maurice, inherited Chiappini's. They ran it just like Papa Joe, maybe even better. Steady customers who lacked money got credit. If you paid for a pound of sugar, you received a pound. Children who swiped candy weren't spanked or arrested but given window-washing or sweeping chores. Customers included pecan farmers from down the road, rich college boys from Gainesville and, at least once, a flashy blonde who paid for her gas with a credit card and raised the collective blood pressure of the town. "It was THE Doris Day," Maurice Chiappini told me.

Maurice may be retired, but he still loiters at his old store, talking to customers about hunting and fishing and the best thing that happened to him during World War II. His troop transport ship broke down, which meant 30 days of marathon Atlantic Ocean poker and $4,000 in a country boy's pocket.

Mark and Robin Chiappini, Maurice's nephews and Francis's sons, took over the store about 10 years ago. They told me they intended to carry on the Chiappini way of doing things. As I loitered against the counter, a Porsche pulled up in front of the store. His pony tail bobbing, Mark Chiappini, 48 at the time, rushed out to pump the gas. Then he wiped the windshield and checked the oil.

"A lot of these modern stations have the words 'Full Serve' over their pumps," Mark said when he returned to the cash register. "But all it means is they'll pump the gas for you. Ask them to check your oil or put air in your tires and they look at you like you're crazy."

Across the street was one of those modern convenience store/gas stations that looked to me like every other convenience store/gas station in America, with squeaky clean aisles, junk food, a USA Today machine in front, and a cashier who didn't know you, didn't want to know you, but said, "Have a nice day" anyway.

The new station also sold gasoline for 20 cents a gallon less than Chiappini's. "Yes," said Robin Chiappini, bouncing his 9-month-old boy on his knee. "But I guarantee you that people who buy their gas there won't know if they need oil. Nobody will tell them if they got a bad headlight. We tell them."

"The world has changed," I said.

"If you dropped me out of an airplane anywhere in America, I wouldn't know where I was," Robin said. "Everything looks the same now. But not here. If you see Chiappini's, you know you're in Melrose."

At Chiappini's, loiterers passed their time perusing one of North Florida's finest selections of bait, including live minnows, shiners, and earthworms. Anglers could celebrate a nice stringer of bream with Dom Perignon champagne, kept behind the counter, at $117 a bottle.

"We stock some unusual items," Robin Chiappini explained. Budget-minded loiterers, reluctant to spring for big-time champagne, made do with cans of Old Milwaukee or humble Yoo-hoo. Window shopping, of course, was free. Chiappini's has Buck knives, garden hoses, chili sauce, cigars, corncob pipes, trailer hitches, and little bottles of wild animal musk that hunters sprinkle around their blinds to attract deer.

Hunters, like loiterers, never felt out of place. Stuffed deer heads watch from the wall, next to the heads of a black bear and a huge wild hog. Other members of the veritable zoo include a stuffed coyote, two bobcats, and a fox squirrel. There are stories to go with each head and stuffed fish. The two mounted bass above the door, for example, were

Chiappini's colorful interior.

landed by a customer whose deathbed wish was that his trophies have a home at Chiappini's for eternity.

In the late afternoon, especially on Thursdays and Fridays, the parking lot out back fills with dusty cars and pickup trucks as customers, eager to loiter, get off work. Clutching frosty beers they loiter on stools at the bar or on benches in front of the store. They're a loyal bunch. One elderly customer, Old Man Smitty, used to joke that he had every intention of dying at Chiappini's. He did.

In 1993, Francis Chiappini, father of Robin and Mark, passed away, too. He was beloved in the community, and his sons put on the biggest funeral in the history of Putnam County. The overflow crowd at Trinity Episcopal had to watch the funeral from a parish hall over closed-circuit television. Francis was laid to rest at Eliam Cemetery, which is across the highway from Chiappini's.

Sometimes Mark and Robin are grateful that the sad controversy involving Chiappini's and BP Oil happened after their dad's death. He was an old-fashioned man and would not have understood modern business practices. In the mid-1980s, BP bought out the company that Chiappini's had been associated with for many decades, Gulf Oil. The Chiappini brothers painted their store BP's franchise colors and persuaded customers to apply for BP credit cards.

Everything was fine for a few years. But the relationship came to an end in 1994. BP told the Chiappini brothers that their station just wasn't modern enough to meet company standards.

The Chiappini brothers could have spruced things up by moving the bait tanks from out front and making a few changes inside. Instead they chose to do nothing. "It hurt to lose the franchise," Robin Chiappini told me. "But we weren't going to change."

He has to buy more expensive gas from independent dealers now and charge more for it, but on a busy afternoon Chiappini's hardly seems to be hurting for customers.

Like I told you, Chiappini loiterers are a loyal bunch. Some cut up their BP credit cards and wrote nasty letters to the company. To this day you'll find them loitering at Chiappini's, drinking beer, eating beef jerky, and being careful about where they spit.

Winter 1996.

Cane Grinding

The cane grinding began when a determined mule named Molly, all 15 hands of her, commenced ambling in a circle to pull a belt that powered a machine that spat out brown juice. "Here is what you need to understand," Steve Melton told me as Molly trudged along. "This is how we used to do it in Florida." Melton, 62 that day, held a cane grinding every December at his Pasco County ranch as a reminder of a time when Floridians couldn't buy sugar in a bag at Publix.

From the Panhandle to the Keys, folks of every race and creed once grew sugar cane, harvested the stalks in the fall, squeezed the stalks into juice, and then boiled the juice into sweet syrup they sprinkled into coffee or over pancakes or even meat. In the age before mass communication, a cane grinding was a social gathering where Floridians might exchange news and gossip, tell jokes and share their dreams.

In the twenty-first century, a cane grinding was ancient history, a demonstration at the state fair, perhaps, or a picture in the history books. Melton and a few other stubborn folks scattered across the state hadn't stopped. They invited friends, neighbors, and interested historians to watch. It was a way to stay in touch with their Florida past. It was a way to recall memories of loved ones long dead, grandmothers who made from-scratch biscuits swimming in cane syrup. "It's our heritage," Steve Melton was saying from beneath his cowboy hat.

At the cane grinding, boys swung on a rope under a moss-draped oak while a toddler lurched through the grass licking an ear of corn dripping butter. From a nearby porch a guitarist, a mandolin player, and a fellow plucking a washtub bass performed a timeless bluegrass tune. Little girls skipped rope. Old men in overalls studied an old tractor with critical eyes.

Steve Melton collected old tractors. He also collected antique machines that in another era dug holes and planted seed and harvested

Steve Melton and his mule, Molly.

corn. The ghosts of the men who sweated and bled over those machines were invisible except in Melton's memory.

He had grown up on the farm and graduated from the University of Florida with a degree in food production. He had a scientist's sensibilities yet at the same time dwelled in the past. He had a working grist mill and liked to grind his own wheat. As he walked from the grist mill to where the cane juice was starting to boil, he carried the next generation of his family, his baby grandson, Josiah Flowers.

Cane grinding requires expertise, hard work, and long hours for a small payoff. A 10th of an acre of cane produces about 60 gallons of juice. Sixty gallons of juice might boil down to six gallons of thick amber syrup. Melvin Brenson and Daryl Hildreth watched the iron kettle closely, taking turns to skim off the bubbles of scum. Next to them, Paul Meeker added pine and oak to the fire already sputtering under the kettle.

"They know what they're doing," said the man standing next to me. Millard Sanders, 77, had grown up in Alabama watching his daddy cook cane juice. Sanders had met his wife of 58 years, Lois, at a cane grinding. They still liked dripping cane syrup on their biscuits.

After three hours, the cane juice stopped boiling and started bubbling like molten lava, which meant it was getting thick. Steve Melton dipped a thermometer that indicated 212 degrees. Almost ready. Another instrument, a hydrometer, helped him judge the density of the syrup. "The old timers didn't need an instrument," Melton said through the sweet-smelling steam. "They'd stick in a spoon and watch how the syrup was dripping."

Musicians retired their instruments. Old men abandoned the study of tractors and walked toward the kettle. It was almost time. As a crowd gathered, Melton began taking the temperature every two minutes. Then every minute. Temperature was now 221 degrees. Almost perfect. Wait too long and syrup would become too thick or even burn.

He tossed aside his thermometer. "Pull the fire! Pull the fire!" he yelled. His fireman, Paul Meeker, yanked a pallet, which supported the burning wood, from under the kettle. Ashes spilled onto the concrete floor.

Steve Melton pours cane syrup.

Nothing better than a homemade biscuit swimming in butter and cane syrup.

"When the syrup is ready you have to get rid of the heat immediately," Melton explained.

He and a helper began ladling syrup out of the kettle and into a 6-gallon vat.

Watching, Bob Waldron looked forward to obtaining a bottle of syrup. He was 70, he told me, an Alabama native, who lived in Dade City now. He had grown up poor, attended cane grindings as a boy, watched his mama bake biscuits, ate the biscuits with cane syrup.

His wife died in September after a long illness. "She baked the meanest biscuit you ever ate," he said. This would be his first Christmas in 48 years without Sandra by his side.

He planned to eat a biscuit, with cane syrup, in her memory.

Fall 2011.

Honey Man

I know summer has arrived in North Florida when I see the Honey Man at his accustomed spot at the corner of U.S. 98 and State Road 267 south of Tallahassee. With his tupelo honey and mayhaw jelly stacked on the hood of his bug-spattered pickup, he sits in the nearby shade and makes eye contact with the unsuspecting motorists who pass by every few minutes. Hypnotized, they pull off the road where he can sell them a little bit of heaven starting at $5 a jar.

"Now tupelo—that's the Cadillac of honey," he tells me, explaining that beekeepers in the spring set their hives along wilderness rivers when the giant white tupelo trees erupt with blossoms. "Now tupelo honey—there's nothing like it, really. First off, there's never a lot of it because of the difficulty of getting them hives deep into those swamps. I mean, it's not easy! And THEN—AND THEN—you got to get the hives out and work that honey. So I don't expect to get much this year.

"Look at that amber color, son. Isn't it pretty? Let me tell you, it tastes even more special. It's real distinctive, real delicate. No, son, we don't add nothing to it. It's perfect like it is. Even diabetics like me are allowed by their doctors to eat tupelo honey. IT WILL NOT GRANULATE."

By now the grateful motorist clutches several small jars and is eyeing a gallon jug.

"What else we have right now is the mayhaw jelly. Now your mayhaw berries get ripe in May, come from a swamp tree that's sort of like a hawthorn, which is why they're called 'mayhaw'—get it? Our mayhaw jelly is real special. You ought to try some.

"What happens here in the South is folks go wading in the swamps and net the mayhaw berries that are falling in the water. Back home, they boil the berries and squeeze them and add some pectin and lime juice and I'll tell you—mayhaws make the best jelly in the world."

Having stashed the honey jars in the backseat, the motorist dutifully returns for containers of jelly.

"You'll want to put it on your toast," the Honey Man advises, bagging everything up. "But it's good any time."

Motorist nods, climbs behind the wheel, starts the engine.

Honey Man approaches, raps on the window.

"Here, take this," he says, holding out a white pamphlet.

I assume he's given me a collection of recipes.

"No, son. It's something that will get you home safely."

It's what the Honey Man calls the "Traveler's Guide."

"Turn ye, turn ye from your evil ways," says the line from Ezekiel 33:11.

His name is Preston Bozeman. Florida born, he is 74 and grizzled and sweaty and the first to tell you in a graceful southern accent about his human shortcomings. "I used to be a traveling salesman," he says. "I was on the road all the time, selling welding supplies. Well, let me tell you, son. All the jokes you've heard about traveling salesmen is true. I was a heathen from the word go. I smoked and I drank and I pursued the pleasures of the flesh.

"Now one day in 1980 I'm sitting at home in Tallahassee on a Sunday morning. I didn't go to church back then, but I did watch TV, and when I was flipping channels I got to where this preacher was talking. At first, I couldn't make sense of what he was saying. Then it hit me. HE WAS TELLING ME I HAD TO REPENT MY WICKED WAYS! So right there I turned to God. I told him if he saved me I'd try to serve him. And that's what I have tried to do."

A recreational vehicle, hauling a boat, pulls off the road. "I see you been fishin'," Preston Bozeman says.

Richard and Jill Spurlock, nearing the end of vacation, admit they have been catching spotted seatrout near Dog Island. "But vacation won't be complete without some of your honey," Jill says.

"It's real special this year," the Honey Man says. They drive off with a gallon of honey and a Traveler's Guide.

"I wish I had me some fish right now," Preston Bozeman says a few minutes later. It's 11 a.m. on a Friday. "One time this guy stopped for honey and he was wet to the waist 'cause he'd been throwing a cast net for mullet over by St. Mark's. The prettiest mullet you ever saw he had. So I traded him honey for mullet. Put them in the ice chest where I keep my lunch."

Preston Bozeman, the Honey Man, in North Florida.

When the day was over, he took the mullet over to Patsy Owen's house and she fixed them supper. She is Brother Clyde Owen's widow. Brother Clyde was Preston Bozeman's pastor and his best friend. A beekeeper, he was also the original honey man. Preston Bozeman still gets his honey and mayhaw jelly from Patsy Owen.

"I need to tell you something about Brother Owen. He was the kindest man I ever knew. He supported missionaries in India with his profits. He also preached at Victory Baptist Church in Tallahassee, which is where I met him. He wasn't a good orator, but I get teared up when I remember the prayer meetings we used to have. When he started praying I got the chill bumps because I knew the Lord was in the room. Well, his prayers helped get me through some real hard times.

"Well, he got sick about 10 years ago. It was his heart, you know. That's when I started helping him with his church and his honey. God called him home in 2009. He was 82 years old. I get choked up thinking about him."

Noon. Ninety degrees in the shade. Florida Hades. Preston Bozeman is wearing his summer outfit—tie shoes, socks pulled high, long pants, long-sleeved shirt, straw hat, towel around his neck. "The deer flies are bad right now," he says, perspiring, "and the no-see-ums will drive you wild first thing in the morning. The seed ticks that will give you Lyme disease are in the tall grass. But they're God's creatures."

He reads his Bible, the King James version, from Genesis to Revelation, while waiting for customers, twice a year. He's working his way once again through the Acts of the Apostles, one of his favorite chapters, because it tells the story of Paul's conversion on the road to Damascus.

"He was a sinner like we all are. God took away his sight for three days. Then he became a different person. Let me tell you, it's hard to be a good Christian, because you got to have faith and accept things you don't understand."

Preston Bozeman was tested on July 29, 1988. Finishing work, he headed home, driving along the shaded streets of Tallahassee, thinking of supper and what he had to do tomorrow, until he reached his own street and beheld the sight of his own yard, filled with cars and trucks and weeping friends and relatives.

"Something had happened to my own son. John Preston was a soil tester. He and another man, they were just doing their jobs, testing the soil along a road for the county. What happened is their equipment somehow touched a power line. They were killed on the spot. Just like that. Electrocuted."

The Honey Man wipes away his tears. "The world isn't supposed to work like that. Parents aren't supposed to outlive their children. He was almost 28, in the prime of his life, and then it was over. It was devastating for me, for my wife, unbelievable. You can never recover. I had to tell myself that God brought him into this life and it was up to God to decide when it was time for him to go.

"It was harder for my wife to accept. You know, we ended up getting a divorce in 1994. I guess I didn't have the compassion or whatever she needed at that time. Anyway, I feel very bad about what happened between us.

"You know, we're still on a friendly basis, though. Not long ago, she stopped on the road where I was selling and we talked and I gave her a jar. She wanted to pay, but I just said, 'No, just take some,' and finally she did.

"I keep thinking that maybe, one day, who knows, one day maybe we'll get back together. God works in mysterious ways."

Swoosh go the brakes of a Peterbilt truck. Smokey Rowland, who hauls airline parts and gravel across the country, has stopped for his tupelo fix. "I drink tupelo honey right out of the bottle," he announces.

"Well, sir, that's a good thing," Preston Bozeman says. "It's real special this year."

He bags it up, adds the Traveler's Guide, says, "Have a nice day."

Summer 2011.

♭ 25

Joanie's Blue Crab Café

One time a big alligator chased me through Joanie's Blue Crab Café in the Big Cypress preserve, bellowing until the rafters shook. Shouting for help, I escaped by jumping on top of a table. From the safety of the kitchen, Joanie hollered, "You're on your own, Mister." There was little I could do but eat a bowl of lima bean stew while standing next to the bottle of Louisiana Hot Sauce.

That's actually a big fat lie, of course, except for the part about lima bean stew, which I eat whenever I stop at Joanie's. As for the alligator: I would like to think a live crocodilian will one day make an appearance inside the only restaurant in the 725,000-acre national preserve.

Things happen at Joanie's that probably never happen at another restaurant in Florida. Like the time I was wolfing down a bowl of lima bean stew at dusk and a bear showed up behind Joanie's to devour her garbage. "I didn't know Florida had any bears," said the patron who almost knocked me over as he fled the porch nearest the bruin.

"Of course Florida has black bears," sniffed the middle-aged pedant, yours truly. By the time the natural history lesson was over and I got back to the table, my lima bean stew was cold. You want to know something? It was still the best lima bean stew I'd eaten in a goodly spell.

With so much of modern Florida pallid and boring—lacking any appreciable sense of place—it is always a pleasure to visit the hinterlands and find that Joanie's is exactly as I left it: dimly lit, cigarette butts standing at attention in the back porch ashtrays, the possibility of encountering something reptilian on or off the plate.

Joanie, who was born in 1939, serves up vittles from the swamp (frog legs, catfish, and gator) and from the saltwater Everglades (blue crab and grouper). Her lima bean stew, an acquired taste, is a South Florida specialty as is rattlesnake. The skin from the rattlesnake, by the way, hangs on the wall.

In the Big Cypress, Joanie Griffin holds court from behind the counter at her little restaurant.

"It got killed on the Tamiami Trail," Joanie explained to me once. "The chef ran out and got it, skinned it and cooked it up. One of the waitresses said, 'Have some, Joanie, it tastes like tuna fish.' I said, 'I've ate tuna fish, so that means I don't have to eat rattlesnake.'"

Snake, last time I checked, remained an irregular item on the menu.

A half century ago, there were plenty of places like Joanie's scattered about our state, little mom-and-pop joints with personality. Most went out of business, crushed by restaurants with golden arches and "no surprises here" modernity. Joanie Griffin had a saying: "If you want fast food, go to Miami or go to Naples." Both, by the way, are 50 miles and a half-century away.

One time I ordered a meal at Joanie's and got it in less than 10 minutes. But usually it takes longer because Joanie comes over for a talk or the cook leans out and asks, "Where you from?" or somebody yells, "Bear!" and everybody, including the help, runs to the door to look.

Also—you should know this before embarking on an expedition—restaurant hours are written on paper and not on stone. On paper, Joanie's is open Tuesday through Sunday, lunch only. That said, I've eaten supper there. I have also arrived on a Friday at lunch and found the place closed with no note on the door.

Not long ago, a server called to say she wasn't coming to work because of a forest fire along the road. And there's always that stray gator that blocks the traffic on the Tamiami Trail. So I encourage you to call (239) 695-2682 just to make sure. Also, pack a picnic. If Joanie's is closed, walk around to the back and look for bears.

Joanie is a shoeless pixie with brownish-blonde hair and dimples in her cheeks. "Help yourself to what you want to drink" are usually her first words upon hearing the screen door creak. If you demand your air ice-cold, try one of those fern bars closer to the coast. Joanie likes natural ferns and natural air.

She was born in Miami back when everybody called it "Miam-maw," and like a lot of Miam-awns she tired of the hustle-bustle. She and her husband, who had been fishing in the Everglades since forever, decided to move out to the middle of nowhere for good. They bought the oldest known building in the Big Cypress, an edifice constructed in 1928, the year the road was completed across the swamp. Carl made it into a gas station in 1987; Joanie sold the sandwiches. After Carl died, Joanie closed the gas station, though patrons like to joke you can still get gas at Joanie's.

Her loyal regulars, as long as I have been going there, have included cane-pole fishermen stinking of bream, Miccosukees who like her fry bread, and legions of foreign tourists who have worked up an appetite by counting gators along the road. "I parlez-vous with people pretty easy," Joanie told me.

She wanted me to notice recent improvements and pointed out a few things. She had patched the cracks in the floorboards and added a few stuffed bass, turkey feathers, wild hog skulls, and deer antlers to her walls.

She had graced the men's restroom with photographs taken by her friend, the irrepressible swamp man Lucky Cole, known for his circa-1950 pictures of naked women typically posed with alligators.

Reptiles have always played a role in Big Cypress and Joanie culture.

Being the nosy reporter, I once peeked inside her freezer and discovered, coiled in a plastic bag, a cottonmouth water moccasin.

Joanie swore to me that she never has served snake to an unsuspecting customer. That said, I won't be ordering her famous "Swampy Dog" frankfurter until further notice.

Spring 2007.

26

Gatorama

Allen Register, retired Navy, values structure. He maintains precise records, dislikes clutter, can always find his tools. It bothers him whenever
he notices algae clinging to the prehistoric teeth of his favorite crocodile,
Goliath. "It's not his fault," Register told me. "If Goliath was in the wild,
he'd be eating things that would keep his teeth nice."

In the Florida wilderness, American crocodiles typically crunched
tooth-scraping shell and bone during meals. At Gatorama, Register's old-
timey tourist attraction near Lake Okeechobee, Goliath devoured tender
vittles and ended up with green teeth. Every once in a while, in the name
of improving Goliath's smile, Register had to play dentist.

Goliath is approximately 15 feet long and weighs more than half a
ton. His frightening teeth, 2 inches long, chomp down with about 2,000
pounds of force. When Goliath is famished or perturbed, he bites down
faster than Register's eyes can follow. He hears only a tremendous
"pop"—as if the world's biggest bottle of champagne has yielded its cork.
Register, who was 51 when I visited, hated the sound of popping crocodile jaws. It reminded him of the worst day of his life.

But he tries to repress that memory when Goliath's unhygienic chop-
pers require cleaning. He simply climbs into the dinosaur's sprawling pen
and takes a long look. Lying in a shallow pool, Goliath first opens his yellow eyes, followed by those gargantuan jaws. Register grips the cleaning
hose with his nine good fingers and advances on the great beast.

The golden age of Florida roadside attractions lasted from 1945 to the
arrival of Disney World in 1971. After the war, new residents and tourists
who traveled the state's sometimes lonely highways found no shortage
of cheap, corny, and sometimes even frightening thrills.

At Lawtey, in North Florida, I remember the Gulf gas station that
housed Reptile Land. Ocala boasted Six-Gun Territory and Wild West
shoot-'em-ups. Near Lake Okeechobee, the eccentric Tom Gaskins

harvested hundreds of cypress knees and called his wacky collection a museum. For hundreds of miles he beckoned tourists with roadside signs such as "Lady, if he won't stop hit him over the head with a shoe."

After admiring a cypress stump that resembled say, Charles de Gaulle, a visitor could eat lunch down the road at Old South Bar-B-Q Ranch, where waitresses in cowgirl outfits fired cap pistols between tables.

Florida, of course, got modern. Interstates diverted tourists away from the old haunts while Mickey Mouse and destination "theme parks" turned out to be lethal to the unsophisticated mom-and-pop "Want to see a rattlesnake?" joints. In the twenty-first century only a handful of authentic roadside attractions survived. Register's Gatorama is among the last.

It was established on U.S. 27 during the Eisenhower era by the misanthropic Cecil Clemons, a chain-smoking, vodka-swilling poacher who gave up skinning alligators for skinning tourists. The colorful coot who might say something inappropriate in front of your kids while handling a reptile was part of the thrill.

As Florida changed, he sold the place to longtime Floridians David and Marietta Thielen, who kept it going another decade before selling the business to their daughter, Patty, and her husband, Allen Register, in 1996.

The Registers continue to scratch out a living in a swamp in the middle of the Florida nowhere—halfway between Clewiston and Lake Placid on your Central Florida map. Plug in the address—officially it's 6180 U.S. 27—and your GPS robot voice may admit "I'm lost."

Before he lost much of a finger, before he could write "I know how to clean crocodile teeth" on his resume, Register found adventure in a nuclear submarine as a sonar specialist. As a fifth-generation Floridian, he eventually answered the reptilian call of the swamp. He and Patty hadn't gotten rich—most of the tourists still head for Disney World—but they hadn't gone hungry. And neither had their big lizards.

Gatorama is a small attraction at which Register does much of the day-to-day labor. At a big pond he struts onto a rickety dock with a bucket of chicken parts. Watched by a half dozen tourists ensconced safely behind a secure fence, Register waves a chicken wing with his good hand. A 13-foot croc—Big Daddy—rockets out of the water like a Polaris missile and snatches the snack.

POP!

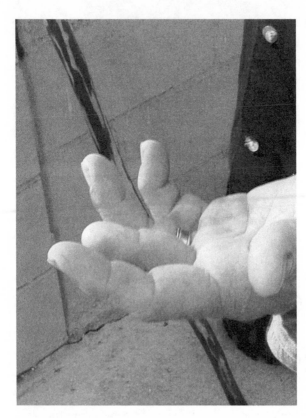

Allen Register still can count his gators and crocs on nine good fingers.

"Thank you for leaving me with nine and a half fingers," Register calls out to Big Daddy, who has slipped below the surface.

Gatorama is home to thousands of reptiles with hearty appetites. They include a human-eating saltwater crocodile from the South Pacific and crocodiles from Cuba known for their ability to jump, which explains the high fence around the pond. Alligators, of course, dwell in great numbers.

Register raises them for their meat and hides. In late August and early September, in a hothouse behind the office, leathery eggs by the thousands begin to crack. Lucky tourists sometimes are allowed to hold an egg, listen to the chirps, and midwife the newborn into the world. Hatchlings bite—they'll hang onto your hand for dear life—but their teeth aren't powerful enough to draw blood.

Not so for the grownups.

It was a 9-foot croc that scarred him. Looking for a place to nest, she'd dug under a fence. Register needed to return her to her home. Register was in a hurry. After straddling the croc he made a grab at her jaws without having sufficient control. Panicked, the croc began snapping.

POP!

Register looked down. He was surprised to see that a chunk of his left middle finger had vanished. The nearest hospital was 45 minutes away. As his blood collected in a bucket at his feet in the truck, his wife Patty hit the gas. Two surgeries followed. "You know what I need now?" Register once asked me. "I need to have a fingernail tattooed on my nub."

I watched as Goliath, jaws opened wide, crept to the edge of the pond, a living dinosaur with a walnut-sized brain, hair-trigger instinct, and an appetite for flesh. At a major zoo, perhaps Goliath would be sedated in advance of his teeth cleaning appointment. Then a nice graduate college student on an internship, under the supervision of the kindly staff veterinarian, would gently clean the monster's teeth with a special brush.

Allen Register sneaks up on crocodile "Goliath" to administer a tooth-cleaning. (Photo by Maurice Rivenbark.)

Gatorama is an old Florida roadside attraction. Goliath was awake. If Register had owned a special brush, Goliath would have bitten it in half and tried to bite the dental hygienist in half for good measure.

Standing in the dinosaur's lair, Register turned on an ordinary garden hose and adjusted the nozzle to the "jet" setting. Edging closer, he took special aim from three feet away. Then a little closer. His practice is to crouch a little to the right of the croc's lethal end in case he needs to leap out of the way.

Goliath seemed to know the drill. Open wide.

Using the hose as a giant Waterpik, Register fired away, taking his time to wash each tusk carefully. When he finished a half hour later, Goliath's teeth gleamed white in the sun, and Register still had his fingers—nine and a half of them anyway.

Fall 2010.

27

KISSIMMEE

Orange World

Where was Eli? The man never stayed put. "Eli's over at Waffle House finishing his coffee," an exasperated clerk finally told me. Now here he came, looking impatient as he marched through the door. "I don't have much time to talk, but I'll give you a few minutes. What do you want to talk about? The Orange?"

The biggest orange in the Sunshine State belonged to Eli. Built from fiberglass, 60 feet tall, 92 feet wide, and 35,000 pounds, it served as the roof of Orange World, Eli's magnificently tacky gift shop. It's so big that pilots landing at Orlando International use it as a landmark. Even better, tourists in SUVs and in Trailways buses have a hard time missing it when they are cruising U.S. 192 and wondering where to blow their money on T-shirts and all things flamingo.

"We do okay here," Eli told me, glancing at his watch again. It was clear he hated answering questions when there was other work to be done. I had heard from a friend that he hated having his picture taken. Eli was a busy man, I was supposed to know. He had bought a new yacht. It was going to be ready for him soon. If he got a call about going to collect his yacht, interview over.

"What do you want to know? Well, I'm 73 years old. I'm from Indiana. I was in the gas station business. I come down here on vacation about 1970 and heard about Disney. Land was cheap. I had one of the closest businesses to Disney, a Texaco. Good God, at night, somebody would stop for gas and get out of the car and squish mole crickets under his feet. Talk about the sticks. I almost lost my shirt selling gas. Then I started selling T-shirts and oranges, and the rest is history."

Eli, the tourist trap king that everybody knows now, was born at that moment. Like Madonna, another self-invented creature, Eli no longer needed a last name, but, for the record, it was Sfassie, pronounced

157

"Suh-fassey." His stepparents were Romanian-Hungarian, though he told people he was as American as a hundred dollar bill.

In the corner of the planet that included Disney World, SeaWorld, Epcot, and Universal Studios, Orange World was just a drop in the Sea of Tourism. But that was fine with Eli. Drops added up. He had money in the bank. The new boat, a 50-foot Viking, would come with bells and whistles.

"My stepdad was a janitor, and I never got past eighth grade," Eli said. "But the kid done okay."

His friend Rick Pinner, who had grown up hunting turkey in the woods of Orlando and ended up selling time-shares, once told me: "Eli knows how to add and subtract. That's the important thing."

It was impossible to be outlandish in Eli's neighborhood, which included the roads U.S. 192, International Drive, American Way, and Orange Blossom Trail. Hotels can look like Sultan's palaces. Skull Kingdom was the name of one attraction. Another was Medieval Times. Oddball go-cart tracks and things with pirate ships lined the endless strip malls. So it made perfectly good sense that Eli wanted the world's largest orange on his property.

"My wife and I sold the place near Disney. Then I had one of the first tourist shops up on this section of 192. I also had one of the very first tourist shops on I-Drive. I had one store across the street from Water Mania. A gold mine. In the morning, kids would come over to buy bathing suits. At the end of the day we would lock our doors and only let kids in two at a time on account of we didn't want to get stolen blind.

"You know what my desk was? My desk was a 4-by-8 sheet of plywood set across two sawhorses. On Monday morning I'd come in and count my take for the week: $100,000, cash. I had 11 shops and the Magic Mountain Golf Course at one time. I sold 'em. Made some dough."

I asked about the giant orange.

"That came about in '88. You know, there used to be orange groves here before all the buildup. I miss the oranges and the smell of the blossoms. I was sitting in the Waffle House next door—I own it now—and I wondered about putting an orange dome on the roof.

"The word got around. This guy come in and said, 'Eli, me and my dad could build your orange.' I said, 'Yeah? You in the fiberglass business?' He said, 'No, we make outhouses, but we could do it.' I ended up giving him a check for five grand to get started."

I wanted to know what happened next.

"Well, he calls me after a while and says, 'Eli, we have a problem. Your orange is going to be too big to trailer over to your place. We're going build it and cut it in pieces.' Twenty-six pieces. They rented a crane for $875 a day. Every time the wind blew I thought my dome was going to end up in Polk County.

"Well, I said, 'This ain't going to work.' Then these other guys came in for some coffee. Ironworkers from the Midwest. I said, 'What do you guys think of this?' The leader said, 'They're doing it wrong.' The next morning the ironworkers got started. My down payment to them was two cases of beer."

The ironworkers were the heroes?

"Yes, in a few days they done it. I was in the Waffle House, watching. The leader comes in to give me a bill. I was anxious 'cause we had never talked price. He said, 'There's six of us. I figure we need $1,000 each.' I could have kissed him. If he had said $60,000, I would have paid it gladly. I went to the bank and came back and dealt out $6,000 worth of $100 bills like it was a poker hand."

Under the orange was the tack of a classic Florida gift shop. In Florida, "tacky" is considered a gift shop virtue. Of course Eli sold Mickey shirts, but everybody sold Mickey shirts. He sold ball caps that sported the likeness of an alligator and the words "Bite Me." He sold alligator claws and stuffed alligator heads and alligator meat sticks that tasted like smoked leather. Eli sold must-have cans of Florida sunshine for $2.99. He sold signs that said "You've Got a Friend in Jesus" and bumper stickers that celebrated flatulence.

"It's crap I wouldn't have in my own home. But the tourists can't get enough of it."

Eli liked to defy tourists to find another place on the strip that sold fresh-squeezed orange juice. For that matter, fresh oranges. He sold them one-by-one and by the box. In 2004, a series of hurricanes threatened to blow his giant orange away. But Orange World stayed put. All it needed was a coat of paint, which had cost him $11,000.

"I paint it every three years. What else am I gonna do? It's my bread and butter. Tripled my business. Brought the tourists in. Did I tell you Orange World was in a movie? *Marvin's Room*. Meryl Streep and Diane Keaton were in the movie. Nice, ordinary women who didn't put on the dog. The point I'm making is everybody knows Orange World.

"Disney World is good, too. I won't lie to you. If Disney was a dog I'd say, 'Disney is a dog.' I tell it like it is. Disney has been very good to me. I grabbed Disney by the shirttail and they dragged me all the way to the bank.

"Will that do? I talked enough today. Drive safe."

Winter 2007.

Indian Pass Raw Bar

The problem with spring in Florida, I was telling a friend, is that summer is sure to follow. It will be hot, buggy, and wet. If we're especially unlucky, we'll be threatened by a hurricane. In the spring, to cheer myself up, to banish thoughts of hurricane shutters, batteries, and bottled water, I liked to eat oysters.

I eat them fried, steamed, and baked, anytime, anyplace. But most of all I like to eat them raw, with a little lime juice and a smidgen of cocktail sauce on the side. After I've knocked off a dozen or two, I feel like I am ready to take on a Florida summer, a sand spur, and even a cyclone. It's a Florida boy thing.

Oyster restaurants are hardly an endangered species even in the twenty-first century, but I keep returning to an old favorite, Indian Pass Raw Bar, in the Panhandle's little Gulf County. It is a serious oyster-eating place where I can perch at the counter, make eye contact with the shucker named "Gator," and tell him to "Hit me." He can then shuck me a dozen oysters that have been tonged from the bottom of Apalachicola Bay not last week but that morning.

Visiting the raw bar, a slow-food kind of eatery, over the years has become a springtime ritual for me. On Fridays and Saturdays, when the joint is jumping noon and night, I can count on a long wait for service. I bring a companion or a book or chat with a stranger to help pass the time. Sometimes I think about arriving early enough for Gator to teach me his oyster-shucking secrets.

Indian Pass Raw Bar first got in the oyster-restaurant business in 1986. Before 1986 it was a retail market known as Indian Pass Seafood Company, which regularly shipped oysters as far as New York's Fulton Fish. During the Depression, the place was a store/gas station/restaurant that housed Gypsie McNeill's tearoom. In 1903, the building was a sundry store for a turpentine company.

Indian Pass Raw Bar.

Gypsie's grandson, Jim McNeill III, has been operating Indian Pass
Raw Bar for a quarter century. He was 54 on the day I interviewed him
and built like a football offensive tackle. Whenever I see him he looks as
if he has just received very bad news in the mail. Anyway, I often catch
him sitting at the counter and glaring at paperwork. "Jimmy Mack," I
want to tell him, "can I buy you a dozen?"

Jimmy Mack, which is what everybody calls him, has never felt the
need to advertise his business by television, magazine, or billboard. "You
almost got to know we're here," he said with a great big Panhandle drawl.
"We're a word-of-mouth kind of place." Indian Pass Raw Bar is halfway
between the little towns of Apalachicola and Port St. Joe but well off the
main drag, U.S. 98.

Jimmy Mack's raw bar is on an especially lonely stretch of two-laner,
at the intersection of county roads B-30 and C-30, hidden among a pine
forest, swamp, and salt marsh. People who punch the address into their
GPS—for the record it's 8391 Indian Pass Road—often drive past anyway, probably because the tumbledown restaurant's sign has all but
faded away.

Still, Jimmy Mack has always been surprised by the folks who dis-
cover Indian Pass Raw Bar by accident. He likes to tell the story about
the time a tall man dressed in black stopped in to use the toilet.

"Know who that is?" Jimmy whispered to the dazed oyster-eating regulars.

"Nope."

"It's Johnny Cash."

"No, it ain't."

The stranger emerged from the lavatory, ordered lunch, and nodded hello in Jimmy Mack's direction.

"You Johnny Cash?" Jimmy Mack asked.

"HELLO," said the stranger, "I'M JOHNNY CASH."

He said it in the exact way he always introduced himself on his television show and onstage at the Grand Ole Opry. Since that day, when Jimmy Mack says he has seen a celebrity, nobody dares argue. If he says that Lauren Hutton, the model with the fetching gap in her smile, is in the house eating oysters, bet on it.

On warm mornings Jimmy Mack sees rattlesnakes slithering across the road. Sometimes he sees a black bear lounging near his Dumpster and licking a crusted-over paper plate. A few times a year, he spots a wild hog sniffing eagerly among the piles of last night's oysters. Grabbing his rifle, he shoots it, ignites the barbecue grill out front, and serves on-the-house pork to go along with the seafood. He could serve possum if he wanted—they're almost always underfoot up here—but why bother? A nice slice of hog and a half-dozen raw ones is usually more than enough to satisfy Florida appetites.

Jimmy Mack, of course, liked to keep things simple and, if you'll excuse the expression, manly. He serves protein only—never anything green. Shrimp, crabs, oysters, and gumbo are pretty much what you are expected to order, except for the beer, wine, and soft drinks stored in a cooler. "Help yourself, honey," a blonde waitress calls out when I walk in.

Jimmy Mack also sells T-shirts, bread, and hot sauce. He shows off deer heads and stuffed fish on the walls. Jimmy Mack's late dad was a University of Florida graduate, which explains the everything-Gator motif. Even the tile floor is orange and blue.

Sometimes someone feels the need to strum a guitar and sing a Jimmy Buffett song from a corner on the front porch. Often folks in the audience stand next to the road and sip beer or something stronger smuggled from home and argue about politics, fishing, hunting, dogs, and religion.

Occasionally Jimmy Mack maneuvers through the crowd to his Chevy pickup and retrieves something of importance. Old mail, invoices,

Jeff Klinkenberg (*left*) and Jimmy McNeill talk about supper. (Photo by Maurice Rivenbark.)

crumpled newspapers, fast-food cups, and what looks like fishing tackle cover every inch of floor, dashboard, and seat. The truck's bed, meanwhile, contains a mountain of tools, soda crackers, plastic forks, and a rainforest's worth of paper towels. Some Saturdays Jimmy Mack serves 300 dozen oysters. If he were to exhaust his supply of forks and towels, the polite Yankee tourists might panic; the Florida folks, of course, would go on sucking oysters from shells and wiping dripping chins on shirt sleeves. It's a Florida boy thing.

Jimmy Mack's oysters never remind anyone of a bluebird singing sweetly from a fence post. Nor are they beautiful like a cloudless sulphur butterfly sipping nectar from a pink hibiscus. His oysters are brown and slimy and covered with barnacles. They're uglier than a kidney stone.

An oyster doesn't look alive from the outside; inside it hardly seems ready for Broadway either. But that pink, prehistoric slimy mollusk is an animal. And it is a living thing—like your homely second cousin.

On the Florida Panhandle coast, kids start eating raw oysters about the time they give up Zwieback toast. But for most modern folks, the idea of swallowing a live animal is unsettling, if not barbaric.

"He was a bold man that first did eat an oyster," wrote Jonathan Swift in 1738.

In other words, eating a live oyster requires courage, if not a cold bottle of beer and the desire to be nothing like Woody Allen, who famously said, "I will not eat oysters. I want my food dead—not sick or wounded—dead."

What I like to do is squeeze lime juice over my living oyster. With one of Jimmy Mack's plastic forks, I extract the meat from the open shell and dip it in the horseradish-ketchup sauce. One, two, three, swallow. Block that thought!

Oysters from Apalachicola Bay are plump and salty and taste of the sea. When fresh, they rarely taste fishy. That said, folks who suffer from immune disorders should never eat raw oysters. If you're squeamish, or even slightly worried about the remote possibility of contracting *Vibrio vulnificus* from consuming a live oyster and spending the next day in the company of a toilet, play it safe and order a burger, well done. But you'll be missing something.

Hemingway, that manly-man author, ate raw oysters after writing a short story, according to one legend, and I'd like to think he also found time for some shadow boxing or shooting an elephant. Casanova, that human billy goat, was said to consume 60 oysters before a romantic tryst.

I can't tell you if oysters are an aphrodisiac. Nor can Jimmy Mack, who, by the way, seems to have about a hundred kids, including at least two or three who labor in his restaurant.

But I can tell you one thing: swallowing a few dozen raw ones will give you the strength to face another grueling Florida summer. Now excuse me while I walk barefoot into this patch of sand spurs.

Spring 2011.

Ravine Gardens

Joan Turnage's favorite time of the year had arrived in her North Florida yard, where everything was in bloom, especially the azaleas, which glowed red and pink with magnificent life. "In Palatka," she told me, "we think you should go to jail if you don't love azaleas." In Florida, azaleas went with spring like fried catfish and hush puppies. Miss Joan worried over her 30 azalea plants and kept a close watch on the blushing azaleas belonging to the widow next door. When she drove through town, Miss Joan enjoyed judging the quality of the spring's azalea crop or gossiping about what slacker homeowners should do to improve the lot of their tortured azaleas.

"Honestly," she said from behind the wheel of her Chevy SUV. "Nobody needs to let their azaleas grow wild like in that yard. Just chop them back once in a while in the summer to control them. They'll come back strong in the spring."

Did I tell you her favorite season is spring? She was a lover of spring from way back. She had been born in Palatka, population 11,000, which billed itself as the azalea capital of Florida and even held an azalea festival every March. The azalea woman was president of her city's garden club and served as director of "Friends of Ravine Gardens State Park" in the middle of town. For most of the year, park visitors admired the spectacular ravine. In the spring, azaleas took center stage. For six weeks beginning in March they exploded into life in the ravine and along the 1.8-mile park road. Eventually the fragile blossoms fluttered to the ground in pink death.

Miss Joan, 64, had buried her husband a decade ago. Her own personal winter lasted almost two years. Then the widow began to bloom again.

The bass were bedding in the shallows of the St. Johns River. Sometimes Miss Joan saw a bald eagle overhead, clutching a bream intended

Nobody knows azaleas like Joan Turnage. (Photo by Maurice Rivenbark.)

for the chicks waiting in the nest. The swallow-tailed kites had arrived, and one of these days the indigo buntings were bound to show up at the bird feeder.

In North Florida, spring packed a wallop. When Miss Joan heard a Yankee transplant complain about Florida's lack of seasons, she was fit to be tied. She told newcomers to pay attention to the sky and the water. And for heaven's sake, she added, watch the azaleas. Nature, like grits, was part of her sense of place.

She had grown up in a town where her daddy operated a drive-in restaurant that featured 19-cent hamburgers and a 13-year-old carhop named Joan; at home she got her hands dirty helping Mama grow peas and beans, okra and tomatoes. They raised chickens and hogs and reeled in bass.

Miss Joan avoided pigpens in her later years, but she remained the queen of dirty hands. She grew roses and lilies at her Mosely Avenue kingdom and nursed cabbage palms and crepe myrtle, wisteria, iris, and magnolia. She composted with last night's leftovers and quenched the thirst of her fig trees with rainwater collected in buckets.

She thought about Paul as she worked. High school sweethearts, they had married when they were 24. He was career Air Force; they lived everywhere, even Alaska, where they camped with their two children among the brown bears and she learned to shoot a .357 pistol just in case. They also lived in Europe, which is why she speaks a smattering of Italian, German, and French flavored with a Florida cracker accent.

After they retired they returned to Florida and made their plans. They were going to camp—not in a trailer, but in an old-fashioned tent. They'd bring fishing poles and bird guides and bicycles. And when they were home, they'd work side by side in the backyard, maybe have a little vegetable garden. In the spring, they'd take long walks through Ravine Gardens State Park and swoon at the overwhelming sight of 100,000 azaleas in bloom.

In September 2001, only days after terrorists had attacked the United States, a more personal tragedy came calling. Suddenly Paul couldn't remember things. One night he even got lost coming home. Doctors wondered if he'd suffered a stroke.

Tests revealed an inoperable brain tumor. He died on October 19. They had been married 31 years and two days. Miss Joan was 55 years old. "I'd never been alone. Suddenly I was alone. It wasn't easy."

After the shock and the grief she grew numb, going to bed early and sleeping late. Then she found a job working with preschool kids, which meant she had to rise from bed at a decent hour. The nights were still lonely, so she became a cashier at Corky Bell's Seafood at suppertime. It felt good to be around people.

She bought a kayak from which she admired alligators and ospreys. She weaved the fronds from cabbage palms into Christmas wreaths. She made plum jelly. She painted flowers on ornaments and sold them to raise money for charity. One night she flipped a penny onto a map. The penny landed on Bowling Green, Kentucky. She drove to Bowling Green for an adventure, which turned out to be exploring a cave. She knew the worst was over when she felt like visiting her favorite place again. At Ravine Gardens State Park, she noticed the goldenrod, ironweed, winged sumac, morning glory, Indian pipe. She yanked the awful potato vines away from the Formosa, flame, and pink azaleas.

In the spring of 2011 she once again was as much a park fixture as the azaleas. Sometimes she ambled along the road and kept her shoes clean; sometimes she waded into the thick azaleas with a joyful gleam in her eye.

She wasn't afraid of the bees, which darted by the thousands, if not millions, from azalea flower to azalea flower, drinking nectar, transferring pollen, making sure that life would go on.

Spring 2011.

African American Museum

Over at the tiny African American Museum, gray-haired folks grew nostalgic when they talked about Cora Lee Smalley's southern cooking. Mrs. Smalley cooked for generations of black children at the segregated Lake County Training School in Central Florida. Although she passed away years ago, former students still remembered her heavenly ham and her food-for-the-gods fried chicken.

Clifford Smalley, 73, had been looking for his mama's recipes for banana pudding and sweet potato pie. Maybe he would hang them on the wall of the museum at 220 Mike Street. Hang them right next to the picture of Dr. Martin Luther King Jr. and the painting of the Tuskegee Airmen. His mama was part of history, too.

So were a lot of ordinary black Leesburg citizens. Clifford Smalley told me about the day he saw the Ku Klux Klan parade down Pine Street. Smalley's memories—and old yearbooks and photographs he had assembled—were part of the modest new museum's growing collection.

Soon I met Ed Lynum, 78, who had used his woodworking skills to renovate the museum's walls and ceilings. As he hammered, as he sawed, he recalled a long career in law enforcement and the times when black policemen had to buy coffee at a restaurant's back door because only whites were permitted inside.

Celestine Strawder-Wright, who admitted she would blow out 70 candles on her next birthday cake, remembered drinking out of "colored only" water fountains for decades. As a museum volunteer, she greeted visitors and coaxed them to sign the register.

Joyce Jones, who managed the museum in her spare time, dreamt of the day she might hire a full-time curator. She was 63 and grew up in poverty. But thanks to the ferocious great-grandmother who raised her, she never felt poor in spirit.

So yes, Dr. King and the Tuskegee Airmen are giants in the world of black history. But in Leesburg and in other small Florida towns, so were many ordinary older folks who had endured the indignities and terror of racial oppression without surrendering to despair. At the Leesburg African American Museum, they were heroes.

About a mile away, at the corner of 111 South Sixth Street, stood the Leesburg Heritage Museum. Older and better funded than the black museum, it celebrated picture-postcard Leesburg, a Norman Rockwell sort of town where grinning white men haul lunker bass out of Lake Harris, pretty white teenage girls squeal in delight at the prospect of being crowned "watermelon queen," and God-fearing Baptist women in billowing white dresses sit on front porches and sip lemonade.

All those things went on—and still go on—in Leesburg, a charming place.

Of course, the museum did not reflect, nor did it try to reflect, history as older African Americans experienced it—not only in Leesburg but in much of small-town Florida. "I don't know much about black life here," declared the manager, Gloriann Fahs, who moved to Leesburg from Virginia. "But I know it's the South and there was a lot of racial prejudice."

So there was nothing about lynchings or the Klan at the Leesburg Heritage Museum. There was no corner in the museum devoted to Sheriff Willis V. McCall, who served Lake County from 1944 to 1972 and had a reputation—fair or otherwise—for brutal racism.

At the African American Museum, Willis Virgil McCall was accorded his own wall. "We have nothing against the other museum," Joyce Jones told me. "But the truth is, nobody can tell our history like we can."

Sheriff McCall once arrested Clifford Smalley when he was a young man home on leave from the Air Force. Smalley had gone to a dance and there was a fight. As patrons filed out, the sheriff and his deputies began rounding up young black men. Clifford Smalley, caught in the sweep, remembered telling the sheriff, "I wasn't part of that fight." But he was arrested and carted off to jail with the others.

In 1950 Florida, bad things sometimes happened to black people in the sheriff's custody. Waiting in jail that night, Smalley anxiously recalled the old, terrifying stories, including the bad one, from 1949.

Two black men had been arrested, convicted of rape, and sentenced to death in Lake County. Two years later the Florida Supreme Court, citing racism at the first trial, ordered another trial. Sheriff McCall was sent to the North Florida prison to bring the inmates back for their trial. During the drive back, McCall somehow fatally shot one suspect and wounded the other, claiming self-defense during an escape attempt. The surviving suspect told authorities that nobody had tried to escape—it was cold-blooded murder. But to nobody's surprise in the black part of town, McCall was exonerated and the surviving prisoner found guilty in his retrial by an all-white jury.

The outraged director of Florida's NAACP, Harry T. Moore, told newspaper reporters that McCall should be indicted for murder. Six weeks later, on Christmas night, a bomb exploded under Moore's house. Moore and his wife were killed. No one was ever arrested.

Now the notorious sheriff swaggered into young Clifford Smalley's jail cell for a talk. "Sheriff, I didn't fight," Smalley told McCall. "And I'm in the Air Force. I'm supposed to be back at the base on Monday. If I'm not, I'll get into trouble."

Smalley got lucky that night. McCall knew Smalley's mother, the famous cook at the all-black school. Smalley was released.

Ed Lynum's boyhood house during the Depression had a cardboard ceiling. "Sometimes corn snakes fell on you when you were asleep," he told me with a wide smile. "We didn't kill the corn snakes because they were up in the ceiling eating the rats."

It could have been worse. "At least we never went hungry. We grew our own greens and made our own syrup from sugar cane. We slaughtered 15 hogs in December and ate everything but the hair during the next year. We caught bream, bass, and specks and ate 'em for supper. We kids gathered Spanish moss all day and sold it to a mattress factory for 75 cents. Then we could go to the movies. Cost 10 cents to go to the movies. Popcorn was a nickel. Our people had to sit in the balcony."

His dad was black, his mother white. Sheriff's deputies routinely stopped their car and asked why the couple was together. To avoid problems, Ed's mother sometimes sat in the back seat while her husband drove—wearing a chauffeur's cap.

In Korea, Ed Lynum served as a military policeman. After fulfilling his duty to his country he joined the police force in a small town near Leesburg called Wildwood, where white residents addressed him as "boy." He retired three decades later as the police chief. Six of his children became

Joyce Jones grew up in Leesburg. (Photo by Willie J. Allen Jr.)

teachers, one is a nurse, one served in the FBI, and one is a lawyer in Leesburg.

Clifford Smalley, who had endured that rough night in jail as a young-ster, moved away as soon as possible. After the Air Force, he became a mail carrier, got married, and lived in New York. Later he moved to perhaps America's most progressive big city, San Francisco, and worked decades with struggling kids at the YMCA.

Eleven years ago he was widowed. He returned to Leesburg because of the fishing and old friendships and found that things had changed for the better. He can plop down at any lunch counter, drink out of any water fountain, and sit wherever he wants at the movies.

"I don't think young black people really comprehend or appreciate what my generation had to go through to make a lot of things possible for them," he told me.

Leesburg's youngsters have seen a black man become the president, and chances are they will never witness a Klan rally as Smalley did in 1944. "That happened when Roosevelt ran for president for the last time.

The Klan paraded through the black part of town, on Pine Street. It was their way of telling us to stay home and not vote."

At the time of the Klan march, Smalley was a second-grader. He idolized a neighborhood hero, a young soldier named Julius West, a combat veteran. In Leesburg, home on military leave in 1944, Nick's Restaurant refused to seat him.

Sometimes—and this is hard to explain—Joyce Jones misses the bad old days. Not the racism, of course, or the fear of violence. What she misses, she told me, was the close-knit black community that seemed to unravel after integration.

"Back in the old days we had our own stores, our own restaurants, our own schools," she said. "Everybody knew everybody else. You couldn't misbehave. If you did, somebody else on the block would report you or discipline you. I kind of miss that part."

When Joyce's mother was struggling and when her father disappeared, her great-grandmother, Rebecca Sarah Ann Elizabeth Louisa Rhodes Richardson, gave her a home. "She was of medium build, very black, with African features," Joyce said. "Born, I think, in 1887. She was not one of those 'Come over here and give Grandma a hug' kind of grandmothers. She was very stern. She had high standards for me. She expected me to do well in school, go to church on Sunday, and to help with chores.

"She did menial jobs in the white community but had a lot of dignity. She always told me, 'Just because you're poor doesn't mean you're not as good as anybody else.'

"My grandmother was strict. I wasn't allowed to listen to radio because I might hear what she called 'the devil's music.' Only when I was a teenager and moved back with my mother did I hear Sam Cooke and Chuck Berry on the radio."

Joyce's friend Celestine Strawder-Wright grew up in a more traditional household. Her dad managed a crew of black men who picked watermelon and her mother cleaned for a white family. Celestine still remembers her first doll, a hand-me-down from her mother's employer, which had a soft body and a white face. "I never had a black doll," Celestine said with a sigh.

"I did," said Joyce Jones, listening. "You'd pick a weed. Let it dry out a little. Then you'd stuff it, green-side down, into a pop bottle, with the dry roots sticking out. You braided the roots like they were black hair. I loved my weed dolls."

The African American Museum, a former church parsonage, is next to a beauty parlor and a barbershop. The smell of barbecue floats through the air around noon. Across the street, a pit bull on a chain barked menacingly as we gathered on the sidewalk.

The old friends—Joyce, Celestine, Ed, and Clifford—took me inside the museum. In one corner, they showed me an ironing board and one of those impossibly heavy old-fashioned irons used by generations of black women who worked as laundresses or maids in white Leesburg. Nearby were rusty farm tools of the sort employed by black men who toiled in the orange groves and the watermelon fields and lived in terror that they might, for some reason, attract the attention of the sheriff.

Willis V. McCall died in 1994. At the museum, newspaper stories about him hang from the wall. Many young black Floridians know nothing about the sheriff. After they visit the museum, they do.

Spring 2010.

Quilt Museum

The Florida quilt deficit was something that concerned Winnelle Horne. If all of us slept under a comforting quilt, preferably the kind made by a loving hand, Florida surely would be a kinder, slower place. But that wasn't the case. Most of us, city folks especially, had grown up without quilts. For us a quilt was something quaint, like a hot dog roasted on a stick or an old episode of *Little House on the Prairie*. We clutched our smartphones, chatted on Facebook, sped down the interstate, tapped our feet impatiently at the counter while we waited for fast food. Miss Winnelle, as everyone called her, believed a quilt was slow food for the soul.

"Sure, drive on up," Winnelle Horne told me over the phone. "I am always happy to talk about quilts." A little while later she appeared at the screen door of an airy building in northwest Florida, not far from the Suwannee River, and said, "Come on in, honey. Bless you for coming. Welcome to the Levy County Quilt Museum."

Miss Winnelle turned out to be a high-energy, straight-talking, God-fearing country gal who somehow happened to be 87 years old. She was the Queen of the Quilt Museum. It was her dream, her reason for being. "But I give the credit to the Lord," she still told people.

She was something like a quilt, warm and practical. She had learned how to quilt by watching her mama, who had learned from her mama. In fact, Miss Winnelle could trace her Florida quiltmaking lineage to a time when settlers kept their muzzle-loaders handy as Seminole Indians slipped like shadows through nearby pines.

"Now I was born right here in Levy County in 1924," she told me. "The midwife who delivered me told Mama, 'She's right puny. You'll probably never get to raise her unless you can get her strong. You need to feed her mare's milk.' That's right, honey. I was raised on milk from a horse, and it made me strong." She needed her strength. Most homes lacked electricity, running water, or window screens to keep out the malarial mosquitoes. There were few doctors; people died before their time. It was miserably hot in the summer and cold in the winter unless your mama had made you a quilt out of old clothes. Children worked, in the house and in the fields, alongside the grownups. Rural Florida could be a harsh place.

She remembered an uncle, known as "the meanest man in Levy County," whose two wives had died under mysterious circumstances and who whipped his 10 children. Daddy, meanwhile, no prize, "got run out of the county for touching little girls." In 1928, he and Mama moved to Clearwater to manage an orange grove. Mama and her quilts were Winnelle's only comfort. Daddy continued his bad habits.

"I got out when I could. I ended up marrying this handsome boy when I was 14. I had my first child when I was 15 and my fourth when I was 21. My husband, he wasn't no good. He was a drinker and had an eye for the ladies. I did my best. I made quilts for our kids, tried to hang on, but when I was 30 I said, 'That's it. I'm a-going.' People didn't get divorced much back then, but I did. Honey, I had to work hard to support my kids. My ex-husband wasn't no help. He drank himself to death. So I was a carhop at the Bay Drive-In and worked 15 years at Howard Johnson's waiting on tables and cooking and doing whatever they needed me to do. I raised my kids on my wages."

In 1972 she married a kindly truck driver, Harry Horne, who had been a childhood friend and later the dashing guitar player in the honky-tonking Blue-Diamond Boys. "After we married I'd go on the road with him when he was making deliveries in his truck. I'd sit with him high above the road and see America. Sometimes we saw more than we were supposed to. 'Cover your eyes, Pumpkin,' he'd say, when we passed a car where a man and a woman were . . . well, you know."

In 1983 they moved back to Levy County, where the whip-poor-wills called at night from the pastures and women still got together and quilted during the afternoon at the Baptist church. With her great friend Mary Brookins, Miss Winnelle started the Log Cabin Quilters and began hatching plans to build a clubhouse. "After Mary died, the Lord woke me one night at 3 o'clock in the morning" is how Winnelle always told the story. "He said, 'Don't build a little old cabin. Build you a museum. You

Miss Winnelle.

should have porches on at least three sides, a nice big yard where people can park, and you need to make the building 100 feet long by 50 feet wide."

Miss Winnelle followed the Lord's instructions to the letter. "We raised money by bake sales, quilt auctions, and donations. We had inmates from Lancaster Correctional Institute over in Trenton helping with construction. We had people coming from all over. It was something to see."

Miss Winnelle, of course, was at the center of it all, issuing orders, making sandwiches, serving ice cream, planting flowers, hanging birdhouses on the porch, arranging quilts, and keeping careful records of who helped and when. She wrote a regular column about it all for the *Chiefland Citizen*. Florida's only quilt museum opened in 2000.

Miss Winnelle led me on a whirlwind tour, stopping at almost every quilt in the museum. They hung from walls and racks or were stacked neatly on tables. Some looked like checkerboards; others featured every color in a Florida sunset. One quilt was made recently by a teenager; another, acquired from a Levy County family, went back to 1857.

"This here one is what I call a feathered square quilt," Miss Winnelle said as I obediently followed. "This quilt here has the double wedding pattern, two rings interlocked. Over here we got a crazy quilt—look at those colors. This quilt on the table tells the story of the Bible. This one with all the watermelons—it's real special—celebrates the agriculture history of this area."

Every Thursday, when the Log Cabin Quilters met at the museum and stitched, Miss Winnelle allowed no swearing or gossiping and discouraged discussions about politics. She also ran the annual Christmas show at the museum in late November, supervised a chicken-and-dumplings supper, and talked, talked, talked about quilts. "They're family things," she always said. "They can give comfort. They're history."

Miss Winnelle enjoyed talking about quilts and her second husband, who became ill in 1990. Prostate cancer, the doctors said. As his time grew short he told his wife: "Bury me in my red necktie. But use the other 49 ties in a quilt." Harry's quilt had a special place in the museum, close to her. She lived in the museum, opened the doors at 8 a.m. and locked them at 5 p.m. Sometimes she worked on a quilt; sometimes she just looked at them. At night she read her Bible, thought about Mama, and forbade herself to think about Daddy. She had found it in her heart to forgive her late first husband, the drunkard. She thought about Harry, of course, and looked forward to their reunion one day.

"Oh, I'm not ready to go yet," she told me. "I'm still pretty healthy. I think it's because I still move around, keep my mind busy, eat good food, and never take prescription medicines.

"If I have a worry in this world, it's about what will happen to the museum when I'm gone. Out of my four children I only have one left and he's not going to take over. I know that.

"I have two ladies who are interested, but my goodness they're smokers. Honey, you can't smoke cigarettes in a museum full of quilts. You just can't. The smell will ruin them. So it's a problem. I pray all the time about this problem. 'Lord,' I pray, 'send me somebody who can take care of the museum and love the quilts.'"

It was late in the afternoon when Miss Winnelle led me to the door. "Anyway, that's my story," she said. "Thank you for coming to the Levy County Quilt Museum. Please come back."

November 2011.

University of Florida
Special Collections

The cockroaches scuttle out during the wee hours mad with hunger. They creep along the shelves, antennae waving, until they find a rare book as juicy as a porterhouse or, better yet, a one-of-a-kind manuscript as delectable as key lime pie. Mandibles dripping, the cockroach army marches ever closer . . .

Oh, the nightmares of John Freund. Other sleep-disturbing dreams involved book-eating beetles, exploding water pipes, mildew, fire, acidy paper, and spaghetti sauce sprinkled across the title page of a first-edition Mark Twain.

It wasn't easy being the conservator for the University of Florida's massive library system—home to 4 million books and dozens of important manuscripts. In Florida's book-unfriendly environment, Freund was probably the best friend a book, or something made from paper, ever had.

He spent hours patrolling shelves in nine campus libraries to identify the sickest books. If broken he fixed them, using ancient and modern techniques in a kind of book hospital that was something like a monastery. There was no moat deep within the library, but he locked the door to discourage visitors. He was a busy man. Five minutes spent socializing with the curious was five minutes he could better spend repairing the leather cover on Mark Twain's *The Innocents Abroad* (1869) or protecting in plastic architect Frank Lloyd Wright's 1954 blueprint for the Zeta Beta Tau fraternity house that was never built. He says he is a year behind in his work, perhaps more. In his mind, of course, he heard the drip, drip, drip of a leaky water pipe on a 16th-century volume or crunching mandibles on the shelf that contained Marjorie Kinnan Rawlings' priceless manuscripts.

He may have been the only person in library history to welcome the disturbing sight of a leggy and prehistoric beast crouched ominously in a ceiling corner—a saucer-sized huntsman spider. "They eat roaches," he explained. He wanted to think his arachnid friend was still lurking in his library, doing God's work.

It was not his library, of course. But he had worked there a quarter of a century, quietly and often alone, and sometimes felt that in some small way the library was home. He was 62 at the time of my visit, slender, quiet, dressed in black, wearing artsy glasses, with a shaved head. He told me he never played the radio to pass time or stole a minute to read what he was repairing. He focused on what Florida's harsh environment—or perhaps a Floridian—had wrought on the poor written word.

Marjorie Kinnan Rawlings, for example. She had arrived in North Central Florida to write gothic romances in 1928. Instead, the Yankee city girl fell in love with Florida, especially the native rural people who eked out a living among the pines and the palmettos near Ocala. She wrote a wonderful memoir, *Cross Creek*, but her masterpiece was a novel, *The Yearling*.

Her old Cracker house, hidden in an orange grove, initially lacked electricity and indoor plumbing, but had no shortage of paper-destroying humidity, roaches, and mice. A former newspaper reporter, Rawlings pounded out stories on a manual typewriter so violently the hammers sometimes poked holes through the inexpensive pulp paper she favored. After her death in 1953, UF acquired her life's work. For decades it rested, damaged and brittle, in boxes. Freund joined the library in 1987. Protecting and restoring the manuscripts, letters, and notes—4,100 items in all—became his mission.

He had allergies to dust, mold, and mildew. He sneezed, his eyes watered. He pulled on a mask and went to work. He washed pages to remove mildew. Then he dried the pages in a vacuum machine that sucked out the moisture. When pages curled he flattened them out under a 19th-century manual press. Afterward, he treated the flattened pages with a solution to preserve the paper. Finally, using a machine called an ultrasonic encapsulator, he sealed each page inside a see-through polyester envelope.

The Zora Neale Hurston manuscripts broke his heart. Raised in Florida, the prolific African American author wrote many of her finest stories and novels, including *Their Eyes Were Watching God*, on fragile paper she stored carelessly. Hurston is often considered a literary genius in the twenty-first century, but she died in poverty in Fort Pierce in 1960. Her body was hardly cold when nursing home employees tossed her belongings—including books and manuscripts—onto a bonfire. A friend arrived, grabbed a garden hose and extinguished the flames.

Hurston's work arrived at the library. Freund and others repaired the water stains, though many pages even now resemble meat seared on a barbecue grill. Still, scholars who study the plastic-covered pages get at the very least an insight into Hurston's creativity and the harshness of her last years.

Finished with his work, Freund turns materials over to another librarian, Flo Turcotte, who was 53 when I met her. Her job was making the library's prizes available to the public. Her domain was a 5,000-square-foot windowless room something like a giant vault.

Entering requires passing through a series of locked doors monitored by cameras. Inside, the temperature is kept at a paper-friendly 60 degrees and 30 percent humidity. Should temperatures rise for any reason, alarms go off at security desks and in Turcotte's bedroom. The collection—more than 100,000 rare books and manuscripts—is valued beyond any price and is considered uninsurable. "It's up to us to keep it safe," she told me.

Only a few librarians were allowed inside. A visitor who wished to see a one-of-a-kind volume had to go to the high-security "Research Room" on the second floor, wait to be buzzed through a bolted door, and listen carefully to the instructions. No coats, briefcases, or boxes were allowed. No food or drink. Pencils only. A librarian placed the prized material on a table and lurked nearby. Security cameras all the while recorded the action.

Turcotte, like Rawlings, moved to Florida from Washington, D.C. Like Rawlings, Turcotte fell in love with her new home state: the birds, the flowers, the culture, the literary possibilities. Photos of Rawlings and Hurston hang from her office walls next to a bumper sticker that warns "Archivists Make It Last Longer." Turcotte taught a course about Hurston. She also was president of the national Marjorie Kinnan Rawlings Society and joked that "one of my skills is my ability to read Mrs. Rawlings' bad handwriting."

Modern authors usually self-edit, rewriting as they work on computer. Their often sterile manuscripts leave scholars little to study.

John Freund at work. (Photo by Maurice Rivenbark.)

Rawlings edited her work by pencil, often scrawling intriguing notes in the margins. She originally called her greatest novel *The Flutter-Mill*, after a water toy built by the youthful character, Jody Baxter. Rawlings thought better of it, scratched out the title, and penciled in *The Yearling*, which better captured the essence of her story about a nineteenth-century Florida boy and his ill-fated pet deer.

"A column of smoke rose from the cabin chimney," was her typewritten opening. Later, in pencil, she added the words "thin and straight" to describe the smoke more vividly. As she wrote, the cigarette between her lips dripped burning ashes on the manuscript. Other pages were stained by coffee and whiskey.

"When you look at her manuscripts you can see the hard work," Turcotte told me. "You can see her struggles and you can see when her writing is flowing."

Rawlings kept everything, even notes scrawled on envelopes and napkins, about her work in progress, upcoming parties, recipes, and wages she intended to pay orange grove workers. She kept correspondence from her editor Maxwell Perkins and from peers who included Ernest Hemingway, F. Scott Fitzgerald, Margaret Mitchell, and Robert Frost.

John Freund preserved *The Yearling* manuscript. (Photo by Maurice Rivenbark.)

She kept fan letters from soldiers who carried special editions of her books into World War II battles. Rawlings, who battled depression and alcoholism, was married twice. She kept love letters, some happy, some heartbreaking.

Tormented, a flesh-and-blood artist, Rawlings lives on in the manuscripts restored by Freund.

A pipe burst in 1995. Water poured into the library. Sure enough, one of the rarest volumes in the UF collection, *Novus Orbis Regionum*, an atlas of the world as Latin scholars knew it in 1555, was apparently ruined. Worth $225,000. A catastrophe.

Freund took apart the enormous book page by page, fixing water damage as he went along, drying each page, then flattening it in the press. During the next four months he sewed the volume back together. Finally, he repaired the warped cover. "It was the most extensive job I ever had to do," he told people.

He grew up in Minnesota, fell in love with the written word, and studied journalism. He couldn't find a newspaper job. He moved to California and worked for a food corporation. He found it boring. On a lark he took a San Francisco State college course to learn the basics of book preservation. In Florida, Rawlings beckoned.

He told me that he likes reading Rawlings novels and visiting the Marjorie Kinnan Rawlings State Historic Site at Cross Creek. He likes to stand on her porch where she wrote her stories and can almost see her sitting at her typewriter and working on *The Yearling*. "Knowing I played a small part in preserving this material for the future," he wrote me in an e-mail, "is the most rewarding part of my job."

On weekends he enjoyed kayaking North Florida's rivers and hiking North Florida's forests with his wife. He sometimes volunteered at the Museum of Natural History's paleontology wing and once dug up mysterious bones new to science. Professional paleontologists named the 18-million-year-old weasel after him. *Zodiolestes freundi*.

He collected old books, old maps, old prints. When he visited friends, he always looked at their books. Were they taking proper care of them? Any sign of cockroach damage? Perhaps a friend's library needed a hungry huntsman spider. Freund, of course, allowed no insect-attracting food, eating, or drinking in his library work room. That was the purpose of the cafeteria.

Some vintage material arrived at the library almost ready for public display. Other stuff showed up looking like props from an Edgar Allan Poe movie. Freund would stoically don mask and gloves and begin investigating the old, decrepit boxes on the table.

In 2010, he faced what he often thinks was his greatest challenge. Thirty, 40, 50 heaping boxes of material gathered over more than a half-century by the Tallahassee chapter of the Florida League of Women voters were brought to him, boxes containing documents that might turn out to be important one day to historians trying to better understand the workings of state government.

The boxes had been stored for decades in a damp building that eventually was condemned. Freund anxiously opened the first box.

Waving pincers, a scorpion crawled out into the light. Hopping out next was a black widow spider. They apparently had been eating the roaches eating the valuable papers inside the boxes.

Freund knows Florida. It's a nasty place for books. But he knew what to do. He stacked the vermin-infested boxes in the big blast freezer in the back of the room. Switched it on. Froze everything to 50 degrees below zero. Let everything thaw. Blasted it again. Let it thaw. For good measure he blasted the boxes once more, until all the roaches and spiders and scorpions and their eggs were history.

Then he started repairing those old papers. "They might be important," he said. "Somebody might want to study them one day."

Winter 2012.

Bradley's Country Store

Frank Bradley credited his long life to hard work, homemade sausage, and buttered grits. At 84, he was still willowy, still a tough old cob with a bone-crushing handshake. Sometimes, just to keep his cardiologist happy, he ate Cheerios for breakfast. But not every day. He was a Florida boy.

One day he planned to tell his doctor all about grits—the food that fueled rural Florida. "Lot of folks today don't even know what real grits taste like," he lamented. In the woods above Tallahassee, only 6 miles from the Georgia border, Bradley operated one of Florida's last gristmills. He bought corn from a neighbor and ground it in a mill older than he was.

Unlike the bland stuff available in supermarkets and city restaurants, stone-ground grits have real corn taste. Grit is going to get caught in your teeth even if you chew thoroughly. A Florida boy eats his grits with fried eggs and sausage. It helps if the Florida boy knows how to make sausage.

In Frank Bradley's family, grits and sausage went together. In 1910, his grandmother, Mary Bradley, started selling sausage from her kitchen window among the oaks and hickories about 10 miles north of Tallahassee. In 1920, her son, L.E., added a gristmill to his property. In 1927, he opened Bradley's Country Store.

The ramshackle store was still going strong in 2009. Bradleys were still grinding sausage, using Mary Bradley's secret recipe, and they were still milling grits. Cholesterol—and Publix—be damned.

Once, every southern community had a gristmill, powered by water, steam, or an internal combustion engine. In the twenty-first century, they were museum pieces like mule-drawn plows or cane-syrup kettles. But at Moccasin Gap, named after the venomous snake common in nearby creeks, Frank Bradley carried on tradition.

Mister Frank, as everybody knew him, was officially retired. But his daughter, Jan Bradley Parker, who managed their store, told me: "There's not a lot of 'sit' in Daddy." He woke before the sun, ate something that stuck to his ribs, went out to check his cows, walked 2 miles to please his cardiologist, then drove his pickup to the store.

He was always happy when sacks of corn awaited him. "I'll grind you some grits right now," he told me when I arrived. We headed for a shed his daddy had built after the end of World War I. Once it was a sturdy building; now it was held together more by sawdust and grill powder than boards and nails. Mister Frank kept the walls propped up with a pole. A breeze rushed through gaps in the wall and the floor.

He attached an end of a long rubber belt to a pulley on his 1955 Ford tractor. He attached the other end to a pulley on a small machine inside the shed. He ambled outside and cranked up the tractor. The rubber belt, rotating, turned the pulley that moved the heavy stones inside the mill. Back inside the shack, he poured dried corn into the hopper and twiddled a knob. If he rotates the knob to the right, he makes meal for corn bread. To the left, he gets coarse grits. He wanted grits.

Years go by, but nothing changes.

Mister Frank. (Photo by Maurice Rivenbark.)

The tractor roared and spewed diesel fumes into the summer air. Inside the shed, the milling machine sputtered and coughed until corn dust floated through beams of sunlight. Corn dust covered Mister Frank's arm. It covered his face. He breathed in corn dust, but he was a tough old cob. It hadn't killed him yet.

In good years he milled 10 tons of grits, selling it to grizzled old men in overalls and pretty Tallahassee women with painted nails and gold jewelry. He sold most of his grits by mail to folks with long memories or a yearning to try something new that was actually old.

"When I was a boy, back in the '20s, people was so poor. But they didn't go hungry," he said. "We ate grits with everything. We'd kill a hog, shoot a turkey, get some fish. Eat them with grits. Every Saturday morning folks would ride through the woods in their buggies and carry corn to Daddy's mill. Dad'd grind their corn. Nobody had money, so it was all in trade. They'd give him maybe some of their corn, or three-quarters of a hog, or eggs."

They ate grits with squirrel. In the Keys they ate grits with an easy-to-catch panfish known as grunt. In west-central Florida, poor folks filled their bellies with mullet and grits.

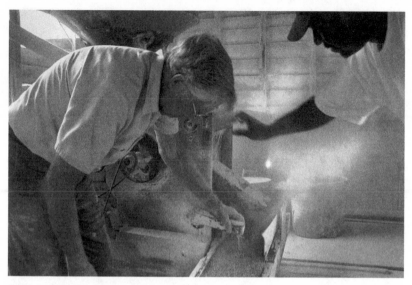

Frank Bradley grinds corn into grits. (Photo by Maurice Rivenbark.)

The Depression ended. World War II veterans who moved to Florida often didn't know what to make of grits. Maybe they tried them once or twice. Maybe not. In twenty-first century Florida, where more folks drank orange juice concentrate than fresh-squeezed, grits were no longer a staple. Fewer people fished, gardened, or hunted. Mister Frank's Florida was about gone.

He makes politically incorrect sausage once a week. Some factory-type operations import boxes of meat for grinding, but Mister Frank didn't. He wanted to meet the farmers, look into their eyes, shake their hands, examine their pigs. He bought robust animals, not too big but not too small either, about 125 pounds.

At dusk, he led them into the slaughterhouse out back. Within 15 minutes they were ground to bits. He added Grandma Mary's secret 99-year-old spice recipe just before the ground meat was squeezed into gut casings. From there, sausages were hung like thick ropes in a dog-proof smokehouse.

Mister Frank lit the green hickory. Smoke—he wanted it 148 degrees—poured in. Four hours later he had Bradley's Sausage. He sold 150,000 pounds a year. He ate some himself, but no need to tell his cardiologist.

Bradley's Country Store has hardly changed over the last century. That's because Mister Frank's daddy built it to last with hard yellow pine and shiny tin that still shed water like a boar's back.

Shaded by enormous oaks, the store is 80 feet long, 30 feet wide, and dimly lit. In its four aisles customers shopped for B.C. Headache Powder, Honey Bee Snuff, Moon Pies, and Yoo-hoo. The Bradleys sold overalls, suspenders, cane poles, and wart remover.

"In the old days, nobody had to pay for their goods until the first of the month," Mister Frank's daughter Jan told me. "My granddaddy would keep track by pencil in a ledger."

Miss Jan, as she was called by locals, grew up sweeping floors starting when she was 3. She went away and worked for a big company in Atlanta but moved back to help her family in 1987.

Miss Jan had three daughters. One was a nurse, one a college student, the other in high school. The great big world was calling them, but who knows what will happen? One day they might want to run a store and sell sausage and grits and keep the modern world at bay a little while longer.

"The people, they always appreciated Bradley's," Mister Frank was telling someone at the front door. "I'd hate for it to end. We've had ordinary folks and important folks buy from us. Lawton Chiles loved my grits. He'd come out to the gristmill and watch me grind corn for his grits. He ate grits in the governor's mansion. He was sweet on my grits."

Summer 2009.

34

The Fort Gates Ferry

Crossing the river would be an ordeal without the help of a blue-eyed, taciturn man named Dale Jones. When he took a day off, certain unhappy northeast Florida motorists had to drive their cars an extra 50 miles to get from one side of the St. Johns River to the other. They had to drive to Palatka across Old Memorial Bridge or head south an hour to pass above the river at Astor.

But for $10, Jones was happy to transport two vehicles and their passengers across the river on the oldest ferry in the state. Since 1853, the Fort Gates Ferry had carried farmers, soldiers, livestock, wagons, and now motor vehicles from the Salt Springs area of the Ocala National Forest to the little community of Fruitland to the east.

In pioneer Florida the ferry pilot employed a long pole to push the little barge and cargo across the wide river. After the Civil War, a steam-driven boat nudged the barge from bank to bank. Now Jones perched at the wheel of a little tugboat powered by an internal combustion engine. The tug and barge, by the way, were almost a century old.

"If things work, why replace them?" was the ferry pilot's philosophy. Jones had nothing against modernity, nothing against bridges. He drove his pickup across them from time to time. But bridges were sadly imperfect, he had found. Sometimes the draw in a modern bridge got stuck in the "up" position during a power outage. Sometimes a traffic accident blocked the lanes.

Then even modern Florida needed a ferry.

Jones, 50 when I interviewed him, owned the ferry with a relative, Dick Hackett, who was 75. They also owned the Fort Gates Fish Camp next to the ferry terminus on the Fruitland side of the river. They rented boat slips and cabins. They said "nice fish" when somebody came in with a stringer of bass. Sometimes they took a photo of the triumphant angler and posted it on a bulletin board for visitors to admire.

Dale Jones prepares to take another vehicle across the St. Johns River. (Photo by Maurice Rivenbark.)

Before it was a fish camp, before the ferry began operating, Fort Gates was a federal encampment during the longest Indian uprising in U.S. history, the Second Seminole War, which lasted from 1835 to 1842. During the Civil War the ferry transported Confederate troops. Today Fort Gates is a place where anglers in orange jumpsuits launch their expensive boats to go after bass. One of these days Jones was going to start fishing for bass.

"I bought me a license last October," he said. "But I still haven't wet a line. Too much work. I got me a ferry to run."

Once there were dozens of Florida ferries, including one that crossed Tampa Bay. Now only a few remain. The Mayport Ferry, founded in 1948, which crossed the St. Johns near Jacksonville, is the biggest, managing 40 vehicles and 200 passengers at a time.

The Fort Gates Ferry transports about 1,500 vehicles a year across one of the most remote sections of the St. Johns. "This part of the river ain't got tore up like some of those places around the bend," Jones told me. In his opinion, development was a double-edged sword. It could bring customers to a business but change the relaxed way of life.

The Fort Gates Fish Camp and Ferry had a new neighbor, a residential development that included a paved airplane runway and hangars instead of garages. Maybe one day, Jones feared, the wealthy homeowners would demand a new bridge.

For now, the ferry operates as needed between 8 a.m. and 5:30 p.m. every day except Tuesday. At the fish camp, a customer can knock on the office door to find Jones. From the Ocala National Forest side, customers have three options to alert the ferry pilot. They can call on their cell phones if they have the number. Or they can blow their vehicle horns and hope the wind blows the sound toward Jones. The time-honored way is to drive to the river bank and turn on the vehicle's headlights.

There is no paved road leading to the ferry on either side of the river. On the fish camp side, the 1-mile-long dirt road is always passable and close to civilization in an emergency. On the Ocala side, though, a motorist requires a sense of adventure to enjoy the experience.

The sand road to the river weaves through wilderness for 7 miles. The road is known as National Forest Road 43, Salt Springs Road, Fort Gates Road, and Florida Bear Scenic Highway. Motorists who break down are more likely to see a bear than a tow truck.

In dry weather, a Honda Civic can make it. In rainy weather, when streams of water flow across the road like a stream, a pickup truck is better. In a frog-strangling downpour, parts of the road simply wash away.

Switch on your lights.

For a long time, nothing happens. Then, if you're lucky, a dot will appear on the river. The dot eventually will turn into a 40-foot barge pushed by a 20-foot launch with Dale Jones at the helm. It takes 10 minutes to make the 1-mile crossing.

He lands, ties up to the dock, keeps his mouth shut. He spins a wheel that raises the ramp to the level of my tires and gestures "come on" with both hands. I drive slowly onto the barge. He gestures "a little more," and I inch forward. Now he holds up his hands in the "stop" position. He unties from the dock; without a word he boards the tug, turns the barge around, and heads for the other side of the St. Johns River.

Ten minutes later, at the fish camp, he is slightly more talkative. Two customers today, he says. But on a good day there can be 30. Maybe more if there's an accident on the bridge at Palatka.

I ask about his customers.

They are deer hunters with rifles in the windows of their pickups and families with kids and tubes heading from the coast to a day in an Ocala National Forest spring. They are foreigners who want to ride on every ferry in the United States. They are a lawn man with a truck and trailer who has accounts on the other side. They are motorcyclists. Twenty Harleys can fit on the trailer. They are cyclists. Jones can fit 45 and their riders on the barge.

Sometimes he's bored, but those feelings always pass. "It's pretty here. It's peaceful. People are nice and friendly." He sees eagles and ospreys. He sees big alligators. One time he saw a bear swimming across the river.

Another time a lightning bolt struck a marker a hundred yards from the barge. "I won't pick you up in a storm," he warns customers. "Not worth 10 bucks. You'll have to wait."

In 1972, Paul Newman visited the Fort Gates Fish Camp to film a commercial for a car company. The guy who ran the ferry let Paul Newman take the wheel for a few minutes. In the stuffy fish camp office, where wasps fly just below the ceiling, Dale Jones has a scrapbook full of clips about the Paul Newman visit.

The owners of the ferry at the time, Fred and Connie Ludolff, had the gumption to invite the famous movie star to supper. At the ferry landing—even now—even close-mouthed Dale Jones likes to tell the story about what happened next.

"Connie," Paul Newman had said, "I'm awfully hard to please. I want bass, corn on the cob, with watermelon for dessert."

He left with a full stomach.

Summer 2009.

35

COPELAND

Fakahatchee Strand

Rick Cruz never stepped into the Fakahatchee Strand swamp without first imagining his own tender flesh sliding through the digestive tract of something large and toothy. Explorers who waded in what he calls the "Amazon of North America" didn't have to be rocket scientists. But they had to be smarter than the resident dragons. Sprawled on his belly, Cruz peeked cautiously into a culvert next to the forested swamp. "You have to be real careful out here," he told me. "I mean, you can't just march into the water. Alligators have a brain about the size of a pea. But want to know something? They're smart enough to feed themselves. They hide in the culverts and ambush whatever happens to pass by."

No gator lurked in the culvert. Now Cruz pushed his way into the black water, but only inches at a time, and only after poking the bottom with a stout stick. I copied him exactly. Alligators, he had learned from hair-raising experience, often lay on the bottom, awaiting a chance to surprise something with meat on its bones, usually a wading bird or snake but sometimes something higher up on the food chain—a swamp man. Cruz, a dedicated swamp man for much of his life, had managed to keep body parts out of the jaws of hungry reptiles, though it hadn't been easy.

He made his living selling Everglades photographs and leading nature tours in the Big Cypress National Preserve. But his volunteer work in southwest Florida's Fakahatchee Strand Preserve State Park, perhaps the most inhospitable wilderness on the continent, could be especially wild and wet. He was documenting the presence of some of the world's rarest plants, including one found almost nowhere else but southwest Florida, the famous ghost orchid.

A ghost orchid in bloom is delicate and white and shaped like a fairy in a child's picture book. Ghost orchids cling to fragile existence from the branches of pond apple and pop ash trees guarded by alligators and

Photographer Rick Cruz, comfortable in the Fakahatchee Strand. (Photo courtesy of Rick Cruz.)

venomous snakes patrolling the black water beneath. A visitor is more likely to see a resident Florida panther or black bear than a ghost orchid, the rarest of the rare.

They blossom only in the heat and the humidity of summer, when the mosquitoes, deer flies, snakes and gators are most obnoxious. Someone who wishes to see a ghost orchid really has to want to see a ghost orchid. Luck is also a necessity. Up ahead, Cruz slipped on a submerged log, brushed a deer fly from his chin, and asked an unpleasant question. "You know what poison ivy looks like, right?"

I did. Poison ivy is as common in the swamp as St. Augustine grass is in Florida's suburbs. "You have to be careful where you put your hands," Cruz continued. "You got your poison ivy, right? You got the cotton-mouths coiled up on tree stumps. And you got to be careful if you lose your balance and lean against a tree. Fish-eating spiders like to perch on the trunks just above the water's surface. They're not venomous, but they're big and they'll bite." From the thicket on the left something croaked ominously. I asked if I were hearing an alligator.

"No," said the swamp man. "Just a pig frog."

Cruz was something like a ghost orchid himself. He was a swamp man who blossomed when the ghost orchids were doing the same, in the heat and the humidity when the mosquitoes and deer flies were biting and when the cottonmouths and alligators were most active. He preferred swamps to the Starbucks in Naples. He didn't belong in the twenty-first century.

He was tall and gangly and needed a shave. He had black hair long enough to wear in a ponytail. Born in Cuba in 1969, he came to Miami about a year later. He told me he remembered looking out the car window as a child during Sunday drives across the Everglades and longing to explore the swamp beyond the road. He dropped out of high school to cut lawns and carry luggage at a Miami Beach hotel. He slung fast-food burgers and washed dogs at an animal hospital. Along the way somebody gave him a camera. He took pictures of water and gators. He sold those pictures. Eventually, he met the famous landscape photographer Clyde Butcher, who became a mentor and displayed Rick Cruz photos in his gallery in the Big Cypress. Butcher told him, "You aren't a misfit. You're a swamp man. Go ahead. Wade right in. Take beautiful pictures. But watch out for alligators."

As we waded through the swamp Cruz slipped and almost fell before regaining his balance. Swamp men always stay on high alert. Ghost orchid season occurs during alligator mating season. Male alligators are especially territorial and sensitive to intrusions. Once in a while, a male will bellow if Cruz gets too close. A few times, a big alligator has leapt into the water from a nearby fallen tree and vanished in the dark water close by. Catching his breath on those reptilian occasions, Cruz watches for bubbles and taps the bottom ahead with his hiking stick, a cypress branch onto which he has attached a feather for good luck.

Ghost orchids in triplicate. (Photo by Rick Cruz.)

He is never without his walking stick. He is never without a compass, sometimes two. "It's very easy to get turned around out here," he said. He twirled in place to demonstrate. "I'm like a kid in a candy store when I'm out here," he said with a grin. "Wherever I look I see something I want to examine."

Whisk fern, a plant that hasn't evolved in 60 million years. Butterfly orchid. Jingle bell orchid.

"Okay, so I see a fish-eating spider over here. That's interesting. Then I want to see what's up ahead. Maybe I'll see an otter or an Everglades mink, you know? And, like, next thing you know you're not sure of the way back out."

Wherever I go in Florida I meet people who assure me that authentic Florida is gone. Florida's population is 19 million, after all. Another

40 million tourists visit for the theme parks, beaches, shopping malls, and fast-food restaurants. Busy roads throughout the state all look alike. They want to know what I think.

I tell them about the woman who recently became lost in the Faka-hatchee Strand. She wasn't the first and won't be the last. She had been trying out a new camera and felt confident enough to step off the road into the water.

The 75,000-acre Fakahatchee Strand is a claustrophobic 20 miles long and about 5 miles wide. The flowing water is deeper in the strand than in the neighboring Big Cypress National Preserve. Two nights and three days later park biologist Mike Owen found the lost woman, scared, bug-bitten, and dehydrated. Welcome to authentic Florida.

Cruz helps Owen keep track of the ghost orchids. Cruz makes pictures and measures the distance between host trees taking GPS readings all the while. Owen and Cruz know the exact location of 375 ghost orchids in the Fakahatchee Strand.

In the 1960s, orchid fanciers from Miami stripped the trees of what was rare and valuable. Finally, laws were passed to protect the rare plants. It didn't completely stop the stealing. In 1994, park rangers arrested a man with a bagful of rarities, including three ghosts.

Susan Orlean wrote a good book about the case, *The Orchid Thief*. An entertaining movie, *Adaptation*, based on the book and starring Meryl Streep, still shows up on cable.

Another five ghost orchids were stolen between 2006 and 2008. Cruz and Owen never take strangers to see ghost orchids. They don't believe that all men are worthy of trust.

In the swamp's Venusian humidity, his long-sleeved shirt stuck to his back. A red-shouldered hawk cried from the top of a cypress. In the distance, a branch cracked. Cruz told me he had seen 12 panthers in the Fakahatchee Strand and 17 black bears. They never made him nervous. He felt blessed to be sharing the swamp with them. Close by, something plopped into the water. Cruz once saw a 5-foot cottonmouth, as thick around as his leg, watching him from a pile of mud. It opened its snow-white jaws and showed him fangs. An alligator bellowed.

"Keep your eyes open," Cruz said.

In May, Cruz was looking for orchids by himself. The water was deep, reaching mid-thigh. Vines and stumps below the water's surface slowed his progress. Going slow in the Fakahatchee Strand, that day, was a good thing.

The water was black like Coca-Cola. When the alligator, hidden on the bottom, suddenly opened its jaws, Cruz saw the white maw and stopped moving. The alligator never lunged. It stayed under the water waiting for his foot like a bear trap. He pivoted and backed away. His heart pounded for minutes.

"It was 6 feet, not particularly big. I don't think he could have drowned me. But it could have bitten me in a place where I would have bled to death. I was 6 miles from the nearest human being."

Rabbit's foot's fern. Resurrection fern.

He and park biologist Mike Owen call it "Cruz Slough." It is on no map. But it is where Cruz discovered the mother lode of ghost orchids in 2005.

Ghost roots look like spaghetti strands entwined around the branches of pop ash trees. In May a bud forms. In June the bud blossoms. Ghost orchids need tropical humidity and shade. They need a pollinator. At night, giant sphinx moths flit through the swamp looking for ghost orchids. The moth has a proboscis 6 inches long—just long enough to reach the pollen deep within the flower. The moth is the only known pollinator of the ghost orchid.

"Start looking," Cruz told me. I failed to find a ghost orchid.

"There's a ghost orchid in bloom very close to you," he teased. "See if you can find it." Cruz had to point it out. It was hanging from a pop ash limb about 15 feet above the water, dangling like a paper-doll ballet dancer.

A little while later, Florida's indefatigable Swamp Man stepped out of the Fakahatchee. Trying to keep him, the mud sucked at his boots. A pileated woodpecker stopped hammering a royal palm, and the pig frogs in the bromeliads oinked their goodbyes.

Spring 2010.

Southernmost Point

Whenever I visit Key West, where I lived for a glorious summer as a boy, I always head for a quiet residential neighborhood far from the boozy hubbub of Duval. At the corner of South and Whitehead streets I like to stand on the seawall and look at the green water. I watch the pelicans dive on the minnows and the blue crabs joust on the underwater rocks. Mostly I like to watch people.

A stranger hands me his camera and asks if I will take a family portrait. He and his wife and their kids pose next to a red, black, and yellow concrete buoy on the sidewalk. The buoy, at 24 degrees 33 minutes north latitude and 81 degrees 45 minutes west longitude, marks the location of the southernmost point in the continental United States.

Key West is a town where people like to argue, and some argue that the southernmost point is actually blocks away from the official sign. Folks who insist on factual information are likely to die unhappy in Key West. The chamber of commerce directs tourists to the buoy at the corner of South and Whitehead.

By Florida's tourist attraction standards, the place seems as dull as a St. Augustine lawn in January. There are no thrill rides or shops selling "I was drunk in Key West" T-shirts, no loquacious parrots or cavorting dolphins, no Jimmy Buffett wannabe warbling "Margaritaville" at 10 a.m. But we tourists like it anyway. The alleged southernmost point may not be Old Faithful or Broadway, but it's ours. It's a place to plant your feet and to dream.

U.S. 1 begins at Fort Kent, Maine, 2,000 miles away, and ends here in the tropics, in the Lower 48's southernmost city, at the end of the line. Of course, the end of the line can also be the beginning of the line. Key West's brightest literary lights, Ernest Hemingway and Tennessee Williams, came here to find their muse. When they did, they went else-

The end of the line.

where. For noted hypochondriac B. P. Roberts, Key West was the last stop. "I told you I was sick," is her famous epitaph.

Nobody keeps records, but I have always guessed that the southernmost point is probably the most photographed place in the Keys. Even in the summer off-season, we tourists show up with cameras and strike our best poses, some of us in bathing suits, others adorned in cargo shorts, tropical shirts, and flip-flops.

One day I walked over to chat with Sally Lewis, who has lived across the street for 32 years and seen Amish farmers, Buddhist monks, and drunken stumblebums smiling at cameras. "It's a constant stream of humanity," she told me. Her neighbor, Ritva Castillo, remembered the night a group of stunning Asian women, all wearing evening dresses, spilled out of a limousine. "You don't see many limousines in Key West, trust me," Castillo said.

In other parts of skin-the-tourist Key West, a hamburger at a mediocre restaurant induces sticker shock. But on the quiet part of town, at the southernmost point, the price is always right. Free.

"I wanted to say I made it here," Oliver Dettmar, a 40-year-old visitor from Germany, informed me at high noon. He had driven three hours from Miami for lunch and a photograph. "I think it's fascinating to be this far south in the United States."

Cuba is about 90 miles away.

"Which direction exactly?" he asked. I pointed, but he didn't believe me and asked Ritva Castillo, who was standing in her yard with her chihuahua, Lolita. She also pointed in Fidel's general direction.

"I can't see anything but ocean," complained her inquisitor.

"To see Cuba you would have to have vision better than 20/20" was her well-rehearsed reply.

My parents lived in Key West during the summer of 1954. It was a different Key West, a Navy town, a brass-knuckles town, a straw-hat-and-fried-fish town. My dad had a gig playing boogie-woogie piano at a waterfront tavern for high-spirited revelers who included shrimpers just back from the Dry Tortugas. "I had to duck flying beer bottles," he liked to joke.

He'd go to bed about 4 a.m. and wake at noon to go fishing. I was 5, eager to accompany him. At the seawall near the southernmost point, we fished with cheap rods and reels next to locals, usually black and Hispanic men, who used nylon hand lines. We all caught the tasty pan-sized fish known as grunts. Later, at our rented apartment around the corner from the Margaret Truman Launderette—it's still there—my dad dressed the fish after my mother took snapshots with her Brownie. Then she'd fry them up.

By the time I started traveling to Key West as a young man, Julian "Yankee" Kee and grandson Albert were fixtures at the southernmost, selling fried fish and rubbery meat from conch shells. Albert sometimes drilled a hole in the conch shell and blew into it as if he were Gabriel playing a trumpet. You could hear him honk blocks away.

After Albert's death, the city posted a "Southernmost Point" sign on the corner, but it was quickly stolen. Generations of other replacement signs vanished as quickly as they went up. In 1982 the city solved its problem by installing the current concrete southernmost point buoy on the corner. Theft-proof, it weighs several tons.

In 2005, Hurricane Wilma swept across South Florida and battered Key West, knocking down gumbo-limbo trees and torturing roofs. "A car graveyard" is how the local newspaper described the flooded city. When the storm tides subsided, the concrete buoy at the southernmost point remained standing, its horizontal lines resembling a devilish grin.

Gary and Becki Love told me they'd just gotten married. The young Tampa couple was honeymooning in Key West. "Make out, dudes," called a friend with a camera. At the end of the line they toasted their beginning by locking lips.

When they were finished, a young dark-haired man stepped forward. "I live in Miami now, but I'm from Lithuania," explained Mantas Kudrinas. "I come down to this spot every year. The marker looks the same in all my pictures, but I look older."

He had brought along three young friends, from Bulgaria, Kazakhstan, and Ukraine. As their cameras clicked, they conversed in Russian. This being Key West, the palm trees swayed while a rooster crowed in the distance.

Fall 2009.

Gone

The Gator Hook Lodge

It's gone now, what was Florida's roughest tavern on what still is a rugged I-hope-my-car-doesn't-break-down byway. For two decades the Gator Hook Lodge stood bristling with Gladesman culture on the notoriously unfriendly Loop Road in the Big Cypress Swamp. Inhabitants included hunters and fishers, froggers and gator poachers, moonshiners and misanthropes. There was at least one amazing musician who played fiddle like an angel.

In the Gator Hook, named after a poaching tool employed to yank reluctant alligators from their dens, folks fought, bled, and drank themselves silly. "No Guns or Knives Inside," warned the sign above the door. On Saturday nights, almost everybody in the place carried a dagger or a pistol.

An hour away, Frank Sinatra and the Rat Pack ruled glamorous Miami Beach. Out in the Big Cypress, out in the Everglades, the Gator Hook served as a rip-snorting relic of an earlier Florida where law and order were of little consequence.

The Gator Hook sat only a few miles from the Miami-Dade County border on the Florida mainland. Actually, it was located in Monroe County, where Key West was the seat of government. The nearest sheriff's office, in Key Largo, was 92 miles away. A deputy who made the miserable drive from the Keys to Gator Hook was likely to be met by hard stares. Trouble? What trouble? In the swamp, Gladesmen preferred to take care of their own problems. Their material and spiritual sustenance came from the gators and the birds and a harsh and unforgiving lifestyle. Gladesmen would have eaten the Hatfields and McCoys, with grits, for breakfast.

The paved road from Tampa to Miami, the Tamiami Trail, was completed in 1928. A dreamer named James Jaudon looped a 27-mile gravel road off the trail in hopes of attracting tourist dollars to his new enterprise, the Chevalier Corp. But in time the only people to use the Loop Road were the loggers and roughnecks who loathed the rotten-egg odor of civilization.

Pinecrest, a settlement of about 200 grizzled Floridians who tolerated the lack of electricity, running water, and telephone service—not to mention mosquitoes and the occasional cottonmouth bite—was what passed for civilization on the Loop. It had two restaurants, a gas station, and what folks later claimed was a brothel owned by gangster Al Capone.

I was a timid and pimply faced city boy who liked to catch bass and the occasional water snake when I first discovered the Gator Hook. Thinking back on my teenage years, I can hardly believe I ever ventured inside. I was never bold enough to visit at night; daytime was scary enough. It was the first place I ever saw a grown man lying drunk on the floor. At noon.

"Where were you today?" my dad asked one Saturday.

"Bass fishing," I answered. "We caught a couple of water snakes and let them go. Then we had a snack at the Gator Hook. Dad, you should have seen the guys on the floor . . ."

He turned pale. "Not for you," he said. He had read something in the paper about unsavory swamp behavior. I would like to say I was always an obedient son. But we all know that teenage boys like to do stupid things that might get them hurt or killed. So in the spirit of adventure I visited a few more times.

Entering the Gator Hook was like taking a time-machine trip into the 19th century. Maybe I wouldn't take my little brother along, and certainly not a girlfriend, assuming I'd had one. But if you were brave enough, and maybe foolish enough, what you got was an amazing peek at a vanishing culture that was colorful and unsettling.

Nobody ever claimed the Confederate flag behind the bar stood for anything but an angry warning to unwelcome outsiders. In George Wallace country, African Americans, Hispanics, Miccosukee Indians, liberals, tourists in foreign cars, and college boys were persona non grata. While perched at the bar to eat a Red Smith pickled sausage, after a rigorous morning of snaking, I was always careful to tuck my long hair under a ball cap.

Even now, when I travel to Miami, I like to leave the Tamiami Trail in Collier County at an abandoned building called Monroe Station and take the turn onto the Loop Road. I look for snakes and alligators and always

Leave your guns and knives in the truck. (Photo courtesy of Charles Knight.)

hope I might see a bear or a panther. Near what remains of the Pinecrest settlement, I try to remember the Gator Hook. But what can I say? It's been 45 years. My memories are vague. I can't even remember where it was.

One day not long ago, when I was supposed to be working on a story, I began poking around Facebook, the social network that connects millions of people and their interests. Out of curiosity I typed "Gator Hook" into the browser. A page dedicated to the old roadhouse popped up. It was maintained by a guy named Charles Knight. Nobody alive, it turns out, knows more about the Gator Hook.

His brother, Eley Jack Knight Jr., started the Gator Hook in 1958. His sister Joyce ran it for few years before handing over the keys to their daddy, Jack Knight, the ferocious former police chief of Miami's rough-and-tumble Sweetwater community. With his sawed-off 12-gauge under the counter and billy club in his back pocket, he oversaw the Gator Hook.

Charles, 54 now, lives in a small house in Brevard County. I drove across the state to meet him. We had a great talk about childhood that included hunting, frogging, and playing with dynamite. "Everybody had dynamite because the ground is so hard out there," Charles says. "You needed it to dig a pond, dig a hole for a fence post, or blow up enough fish for a fish fry."

He illegally hunted gators, illegally drove an airboat, illegally drove a swamp buggy, illegally drove a car, and illegally drank moonshine—all before he was 16. In the Gator Hook, he learned to use his fists. "Beers in cans, never in glass bottles at the Gator Hook," Charles tells people. "And plastic ashtrays, not glass. Glass could be lethal in a fight."

When drunk and riled, Gladesmen liked to mix it up. But if your airboat broke down, they'd stop and help. If you ran out of shotgun shells, they'd loan you one. Many could quote from the Bible.

Charles remembers playing with snakes, skinny-dipping, and the night he was alone in the Gator Hook and heard something splashing outside. He froze when he saw a monstrous shadow looming at the window, followed by an unspeakable odor far worse than snake musk. Grabbing his dad's shotgun, he yelled, "I'm going to shoot." The figure outside the window melted into the gloom.

Outside, he took a brave look around. Whatever he'd seen had been huge. The window ledge measured 7 feet above the swamp. To this day, Charles Knight swears what he saw was Florida's bigfoot—the notorious, smelly skunk ape.

Charles Knight has friends who drink on Saturday night at Chili's. Sometimes they get a little crazy at a World of Beer or a Jimmy Buffett–styled bar out on the beach. He tries not to look bored. Instead he tells them what it was like at the Gator Hook.

Say around 1970. About noon.

Charles Knight is a kid then. He sweeps the dusty plywood floor while Loretta, Tammy, Hank, and Patsy warble from the generator-powered Rock-Ola. He hears the pop-hiss of a beer can opening and the clacking of pool balls. A dozen gator skulls gaze down from the wall.

Charles greets the first visitor, the legendary poacher Gator Bill. Next he waves to Johnny Y, who has walked with a terrible limp since the day

Charles Knight with his late brother's gator-skinning knife.

mobsters in Miami cut both Achilles tendons. The swamp woman Nell, all 225 pounds of her, comes in for an RC Cola. Everybody knows she's having an affair with a slender swamp man named Bob. There are rumors that she has arranged for her husband's murder.

A fearless long-haired young guy from Canada, Emile, strolls in for a hard-boiled egg and some eight-ball. He's taunted by a pair of Gladesmen until Jack Knight, watching from behind the counter, has heard enough. Plopping his 12-gauge on the counter, he asks the usual question.

"You boys looking for trouble?" This time they're not.

The boy Charles Knight steps outside and sits on the front stoop for a smoke. A while later he hears a crash inside followed by his daddy's hushed voice at the screen door. "Charles, move aside." Charles

The great Ervin Rouse, at home on the Loop Road. (Photo courtesy of Charles Knight.)

automatically shuffles aside so his father can drag the unconscious battler into the parking lot.

Same day. A few hours later. About dusk.

A kid named Lucky—Lucky lives on the Loop to this day—is tired after a day of deer hunting. Lucky is a large, gray-haired man now. Back then he was a strapping guy who never ran from a fight. On this afternoon, he's brought along a 14-year-old buddy. Lucky is sure they will be served illegal beer in the Gator Hook. "They don't check IDs," he assures his pal. "All they care about is being paid."

Lucky parks his pickup—his deer rifle in the back window—out on the road. Cocky as a turkey gobbler, he struts up to the Gator Hook front porch and immediately notices an enormous drunk, dressed in camouflage, leaning against the porch beam.

"WHAT YOU BOYS WANT?" he shouts, ejecting a stream of chewing tobacco at Lucky's boots. Lucky tries not to make eye contact, but notices a string of tobacco-colored phlegm dripping from the Gladesman's red beard.

"We just want to go in, sir," Lucky pipes up.

"YOU BOYS ARMED?" roars Gargantua.

"No, sir," Lucky says, hoping he has provided the right answer. He hasn't.

"YOU NEED TO GET YOU A GUN OR KNIFE!"

Lucky and his silent pal retreat to the truck, climb in, and get the hell out of there.

Same day. About two hours later.

The swamp opera has commenced, with parts performed by barred owls, whip-poor-wills, and katydids. Pig frogs, thousands of them, join in. A bull alligator bellows. A black bear growls. Somewhere in the distance a bobcat screams.

Inside the Gator Hook, gripping his fiddle like it's a good woman's soft hand, a white-haired fellow puts down his beer and stands away from the counter. His name is Ervin Rouse and he is the Loop Road's only celebrity and resident eccentric.

He was born in North Carolina, one of a passel of Rouses who all played musical instruments. In 1938, he and his brother Gordon were staying at a fleabag hotel up north, feeling homesick, when they pulled out their fiddles. By the time they'd checked out next morning, they'd written a new tune about the railroad train that ran between New York, Tampa, and Miami, "The Orange Blossom Special." In some quarters, it's still known as "the fiddler's national anthem."

Once or twice a year Ervin Rouse receives a fat royalty check, drives to Miami, and returns with a new Cadillac he proceeds to run into the ground. He impulsively buys airboats, gives away money, and buys drinks for everybody who walks into the bar. One time another musician notices an uncashed royalty check in Ervin's briefcase—for $25,000.

"He was the greatest guy in the world," Charles Knight tells people now. "He was also insane and the drinkingest son-of-a-bitch I ever knew. He never bathed, always smelled bad, always had two dogs with him, Butter and Bean. But he was so kind he'd give you the shirt off his back."

Ten minutes later at the Gator Hook. On the stage.

Tuning up, Ervin Rouse is going to be accompanied by Jack Knight's lovely daughter, Joyce, on bass. Charles, though he's a kid, gets to play drums. Nobody seems to know the new guitar player; the old one disappeared a few weeks ago after somebody accused him of making a sexual overture to a Gladesman's young son. Nobody was arrested, of course, but the alleged pedophile vanished from the face of the earth, no questions asked. Ervin Rouse's bow caresses the strings. He sings in a hoarse and a surprisingly high voice:

Hey, look a-yonder comin'
Comin' down that railroad track.
It's the Orange Blossom Special
Bringin' my baby back.

And couples, dozens of them, rush the floor, men in overalls with hair slicked back and shoes polished, partnered with barefooted Honky Tonk angels in cotton dresses. They're dancing—clogging, actually—at the Gator Hook, celebrating Saturday night on the Loop Road in the mighty Big Cypress. About midnight, when things have quieted down a little, an inebriated Gladesman wades into the swamp and hangs a dynamite stick from the limb of a pond apple tree. From the back porch, a couple of other high-spirited Gladesmen open fire with their .22s.

KABOOM!

The marksman whose bullet ignites the dynamite wins a free beer.

Today, part of the Loop Road is paved. Most of it is gravel, though it's usually passable even in a Prius. During the day, tourists from Germany and England and Miami admire the swamp through open car windows. If they have a problem, or a question, a nice park service ranger in a station wagon will stop and help. At night, it's still lonely and spooky and loud from the frogs and insects. My cell phone can never pick up a decent signal.

In 1974, the federal government declared the Big Cypress a 700,000-acre national preserve, protecting it from development that threatened from all directions. Environmentalists were thrilled, but dismayed Gladesmen knew that life was about to change in the swamp.

In 1977, Jack Knight closed the Gator Hook, disillusioned with the federal government's presence in the Big Cypress. The Loop Road and the

Gator Hook were Gladesmen habitat, was how he saw it, not a place for city folks in VW Beetles come to look at the pretty birds and butterflies and snails. So he locked his door, went home to Miami, died of throat cancer.

His oldest son, the Gladesman, Eley Jack Knight Jr., the bar's original owner, gator poacher, and wildest heart, drove out to the swamp a few years later with a can of gasoline. No way he was going to let the park service knock down the abandoned old bar. He burned it to the ground instead.

More than three decades have passed. You won't read much about the Gator Hook in the history books, though it remains alive in Randy Wayne White's novel *The Man Who Invented Florida* and in Tim Dorsey's *Electric Barracuda*. Peter Matthiessen set a terrifying scene inside the bar—a gator poacher menaces a college professor—in his National Book Award–winning novel, *Shadow Country*.

Ervin Rouse is dead. His bass player, the gentle Joyce Knight, has passed away. Eley Jack Knight Jr. may or may not be resting in peace: in 2000 he died from pernicious anemia after a troubled life that included three years in a penitentiary for arms trafficking. Charles keeps his brother's intimidating gator-skinning Bowie knife in a cardboard box. It's a prized possession.

Charles? He's had his downs and his ups. Today he is a rock musician, manages restaurants, and plans to write a novel based on his wild youth on the Loop Road. He has wonderful children and a beautiful fiancée to whom he enjoys retelling the legend of the Gator Hook.

"I didn't appreciate it enough when it was there," he says. "I wish I could go back to that time. It was a wonderful life."

Charles never tells anyone exactly where to find what's left of the bar because "I don't want it desecrated by some idiot." I guess he trusted me; he told me where to look. Even with directions I couldn't find it. I had to stop at my friend Lucky Cole's house on the Loop Road and ask for help. Lucky climbed into his truck and told me to follow him.

"It's in there," Lucky said a few miles later. "I'm wearing shorts, so I'm not going in because of the poison ivy."

Wearing jeans and boots, I kicked my way through the poison ivy and weaved through the red maple, sweetbay magnolia, cocoplum, and sword fern all the while looking for cottonmouth snakes.

My hair is gray. I take Lipitor.

The broken steps of the Gator Hook, weeds sprouting from cracks, lay before me like a monument. Beyond the steps in the shallow swamp water stood the two dozen or so concrete blocks on which Eley Jack Knight Jr. placed his Gator Hook Lodge in 1958. I saw no cottonmouths or gators, bears or skunk apes. I heard the distant cry of a great blue heron, but not Ervin Rouse playing "The Orange Blossom Special."

Lucky called out from the road.

"I'll come back in a week," he yelled. "If your truck is still out here, I'll send a rescue party."

Winter 2012.

Wendy Johnson

Wendy Johnson is on the telephone. Want to meet a bunch of us for dinner? Wendy has picked the restaurant, picked the time. She knows the menu and the price and where to park. At the table, when the waiter arrives, everybody orders promptly. Otherwise she may order for us all. Just kidding. But that's how she thinks about dawdlers. As long as I've known Wendy she has been a take-charge woman.

Years ago, when a guy had a heart attack and drowned while swimming in a public pool, the Wendy factor came into play: "Why doesn't this pool have a defibrillator?" she asked. She took charge of the campaign and now the pool has a defibrillator.

If, say, Wendy sees somebody, say, walking their dog, say, on the beach, Wendy will tell that person, a perfect stranger, burly, with tattoos and earrings, kind of scary looking: "Hey, you! Nobody wants to step in your dog's shit. Get him off the beach right now!"

Let's say Wendy is on a bike ride. Let's say a doofus in an SUV has sped past her and made an immediate and dangerous right in front of her. She has to brake, skids, comes close to going over the handlebars. The Wendy Factor: she upshifts and pedals furiously after Doofus, who has to stop at the light ahead. Wendy glides up, taps on the glass, says with fury: "Hey, buddy. You almost killed me back there! What were you thinking?"

Let's say a friend of Wendy's is sick. Wendy phones, sends an e-mail, brings food.

Let's say the kids at Sunday school are restless. Wendy puts the fear of God in them. Let's say a young woman, a little wild, engages in self-destructive behavior. Wendy, who turned 50 on her last birthday, remembers what it was like to be young. She becomes the young woman's mentor.

Wendy's old friend, Rose, loses her kindly husband, Buzz. Wendy lets everyone know about Buzz. She makes sure Rose knows she is there for her. A friend's teenage daughter, Emily, is diagnosed with leukemia. Wendy helps the young woman achieve something important on her bucket list: a bone-marrow education drive. After Emily dies, Wendy is there to grieve with everyone.

February 2009. Phone rings. It's Wendy's friend, Dianne. "Wendy had a seizure," Dianne says.

So Wendy's friends Gary and Bill go to the hospital. Wendy is breathing through some kind of device. Anyway, she can't talk. Gary makes a joke about Wendy's inability to speak—something that never happens, requiring Wendy to extend her middle finger in Gary's direction.

Wendy was born in Chattanooga, Tennessee, and grew up in Birmingham, Alabama. She is bossy like some New Yorkers but with a southern accent. She worked her way through high school and the University of Alabama as a lifeguard. She planned on becoming an accountant but instead made a lot of money selling computer software in Pittsburgh and Atlanta. Her sales credo: "Never take no for an answer."

In 1997, Wendy vacations in Florida, where her sister, Carol, helps set up a blind date with this handsome guy, Al Johnson, an engineer at GE. Wendy is an endurance athlete and so is Al. Wendy is bossy. Al dislikes being bossed. Somehow they hit it off. In 1998 they marry.

Al has done well in business. Anyway, he has enough money to retire. Now he can exercise as long and as hard as he wants. Fat chance. Wendy suggests they start a new business. They start Motion Sports Management. They put on athletic events, mostly running races such as the Bay-to-Bay and the St. Pete Beach Classic.

After the seizure, Wendy's doctors order a series of tests.

Still February 2009. Phone rings.

Mary Ann on the line. "Wendy has brain cancer," Mary Ann says. All her friends know Wendy is going to fight. Of course she will. That's what Wendy does.

Surgery. Radiation. Nausea. She loses her thick, auburn hair.

Wendy starts a blog, read by thousands of friends and strangers, writing about the ups, the downs, about her moods, about how she can hardly stand to be inactive with her cancer. Time passes and her strength returns. Soon she is swimming 1,500 meters at the pool, biking 15 miles, running 3, ordering friends around, trying to boss Al. "Bullshit, Wendy!" says a husband who is no pushover.

The damn cancer. Months later it comes back.

Wendy. (Photo by Al Johnson.)

So she returns to the hospital, where her doctors treat her disease aggressively. The cancer fades, but she begins losing her sight. It has to do with swollen optical nerves. Now the job of writing the blog falls to Al and her sister, Carol.

The Wendy factor: She figures a way to endure. Talks about getting books on compact disc. Somebody buys her *It's Not About the Bike*, Lance Armstrong's account of his battle with cancer. She listens to *True Compass: A Memoir*, Ted Kennedy's autobiography. Ted is fighting brain cancer, he's a ferocious liberal, and he's long been an advocate of universal health care, just like Wendy.

Blind, she rides a stationary bicycle. Blind, she does yoga. She wants to stay strong for Al. For all of us.

April 13, 2010. Phone rings. It's Mary Ann. "Wendy has taken a turn for the worst." Wendy can't keep food down. Well, maybe applesauce. She sleeps most of the time. She's in and out of consciousness. Everybody hopes for a miracle. But we want her to know it's okay to leave us.

On April 14, we all gather in the living room: Mary Ann Renfrow and her sister Virginia Adcock, Linda Borgia, Dr. Roland Lajoie and his wife, Diane. On the way are Diane and Peter Sector, Karin Kmetz, Bill and Sue Castleman, Susan Harmeling, Wendy's sister Carol Wells, and her mother, Sarah Fechter.

Wendy's husband, Al, says, "I can't get my arms around this." Nobody tries to hold back the tears.

The hospice nurse arrives. I go upstairs. Wendy looks tiny on the bed, bald as a baby mockingbird. I hold her hand and she opens eyes that can no longer see. I read to her.

April 20. Phone rings. I don't want to answer, but I do. "Wendy died tonight at 9:05 p.m."

Diane Sector, Karin Kmetz, and Mary Ann Renfrow wash her. They slip her favorite summer dress, blue with a floral pattern, over her motionless body.

Diane Lajoie finds Wendy's makeup. Diane applies lipstick. Then she puts some red into those pale cheeks.

When the undertaker comes to get her a while later, Wendy looks like a million bucks.

Spring 2010.

A Golfer

Under the trees at Dunedin Country Club, Chris Long poured his dad into a golf shoe. At the 10th hole he sprinkled the ashes next to the sand trap. "Dad was always good around the green," Long said. For a half century, Jim Long was a fanatical golfer who played every day if he could. He was especially good with short irons from the rough or sand trap.

"We called him Houdini," one of his oldest friends, Phil Desreaux, said from the lip of the green. "If he got into trouble, he could always escape."

Almost always. On September 7, 2008, as he got ready to putt for a birdie, Jim Long dropped dead. He was 70.

A few days later, his family and hundreds of friends gathered to say goodbye at the golf course. They told stories about how he drew faces on his golf balls and always carried a bottle of Jim Beam in his bag. They wept, laughed, and toasted his memory. A few spoke in reverent tones about his new set of Adams golf clubs with the graphite shafts.

"He didn't tell me he bought them," his wife, Joann, told me. "I just noticed them one day. He'd put them on the Master Charge. Kind of sneaky." In the endless chess game called marriage, she considered running over to Macy's and buying herself a new outfit.

They had met in 1984. A Canadian, Jim was on a Florida golf vacation. He was divorced. So was she. At a nightclub he asked for a dance. They married four months later. He owned an architectural hardware consulting business in Canada but was happy to move to Florida and its year-round golfing climate. She was okay with her role as golf widow.

Jim was funny, and he was good to her, but he wasn't perfect. Joann fussed at him whenever he reached for a Marlboro. Riding a golf cart was his primary source of exercise. He ate too much Breyers vanilla ice cream and watched too much TV. On the night before he died, she fixed him his favorite meal: grilled chicken and fresh corn cut from the cob. Even after one heart attack and a pacemaker, he feared no pat of butter.

On September 7, a Sunday, he drove his personal golf cart from the house to the golf course two blocks away to meet Whitey Williams and Billy Turner, the other members of his regular threesome. Jim double-bogeyed the first and second holes. He usually shot in the low 80s, but today his game was off. On the seventh, he told his companions his latest story:

"A long-married couple are fighting because hubby has forgotten their anniversary. Wifey tells him there had better be something waiting in the driveway tomorrow morning—something that can go 0 to 200 in six seconds.

"Next morning, she sees a package on the driveway. Must be the keys to a new sports car. She can't wait. With shaking hands she opens the package and discovers—a bathroom scale."

Jim bogeyed the 364-yard, par-four ninth. He was starting to play better, but he complained about an aching back and a cold sweat. His friends suggested a cool drink and a rest. Jim didn't want to miss any golf.

His drive exceeded 220 yards on the par 5, 477-yard 10th hole. His second shot, with a 3-wood, floated to the edge of the green. Now a graceful 9-iron left him 8 feet from the pin—and a birdie. He grabbed his putter and climbed onto the green.

He fell right next to the hole. In life, he never believed in mulligans; Billy Turner's attempts to revive him failed.

Last Friday at dusk, while the memorial was still going strong in the clubhouse, Jim's family and closest friends headed quietly for the 10th green. A slight breeze rustled the Spanish moss hanging from the oaks. The cicadas sang a requiem.

Jim's son, Chris, sprinkled more ashes from his dad's size 10 Foot-Joys. "There's still plenty of Dad left to go around," Chris said, handing off the shoes to Tom Shores and Phil Desreaux. Shores, Jim's son-in-law, lifted the flag. Desreaux, Jim's old friend from Canada, poured in the ashes.

Hole in one.

Summer 2008.

Baseball Betty

Betty Leone, the most devoted baseball fan I ever knew, was especially passionate about her hometown major league team, the Tampa Bay Rays, whose games she attended as often as possible in St. Petersburg. When she moved to North Carolina to live with her family a while later, she missed going to Tropicana Field, but she watched them on television no matter what.

In the fall of 2008, with the Rays engaged in their first pennant race ever, Betty never missed a televised inning. "They're going to win it all," she told me by long-distance telephone during our last talk. Lying in her sick bed, surrounded by her collection of Rays caps, Rays jerseys, Rays coffee mugs, Rays bats, Rays balls, and Rays bobble head dolls, she told me she was confident her team was going to win the divisional playoffs, American League championship, and the World Series—not for money and glory—but for her, Baseball Betty Leone.

Everyone who loved Betty wanted that to happen. But it didn't look like Betty, who was 86 during the pennant race, would last long enough to see it come to pass. Betty being Betty, she was confident she'd be around for the last out.

It begins early, if you're lucky, when a loved one, perhaps your mom or dad or grandparent, invites you to a baseball game. You don't understand the rules, but your loved one patiently explains things until you do. One day, if you're lucky, you become a baseball fan.

It happened that way for Betty. Her dad, William Burns, loved baseball and taught her the game, even how to keep a scorecard. In the 1950s Betty married Fred Leone after a long courtship. A minor league pitcher, he had to get his baseball dreams out of his system before he could say, "I do."

They moved to St. Petersburg, partly to attend as many spring training games as possible with their children, Joann and Becky. During the

Baseball Betty never gave up. (Photo courtesy of Rebecca Leone.)

regular season, it was a family tradition to watch the Saturday game of the week on television. Later, she discovered the Braves on cable and became a Dale Murphy fan. Betty's husband died in 1993, but she didn't give up baseball.

Then the Rays came to town. She attended their first game ever in 1998. The lopsided loss to the Tigers did not discourage her. Through many losing seasons, she visited Tropicana Field regularly with family, church groups, and friends until arthritis made it painful to climb stadium steps. So she watched on TV, keeping a special eye on a player named Rocco Baldelli, an Italian like her late husband. Rocco even had Fred's nose.

When her daughter suggested that she join the family in North Carolina, Betty negotiated with Joann. "I have three demands. First, I need an Internet connection for my e-mail. Second, I want to watch my favorite soap opera, *The Young and the Restless*, every day. Third, you have to get me some kind of cable hookup so I can watch the Rays."

Done, done, and done.

For most of the 1998 dream season, Betty had the time of her life. Sometimes she telephoned an old St. Petersburg friend in the first inning and they'd watch together, 600 miles apart, chatting as if they were sitting in the cheap seats side by side, until the final out. The pastor at her former St. Petersburg church clipped all the Rays stories out of the paper and mailed a daily package Betty's way.

In July, Betty started feeling ill, and not just because of the awful losing streak right before the All-Star game. It took a while for doctors to figure things out. On August 15, they diagnosed her with cancer of the liver. On September 1, the teetotaler was told she had a month at best to live.

But there was baseball to watch, so she hung on, sometimes refusing to swallow her powerful pain pills because she wanted to stay awake for the whole game. If Rocco Baldelli homered, she intended to be an alert witness.

On the day the Rays clinched a playoff spot, Betty arranged to have a special photograph e-mailed to old friends. In the picture, Betty looked glamorous in her new hairdo, which had become popular during the season with the Rays players, a Mohawk. Betty's Mohawk created a sensation among her shocked, church-going friends. She let them worry a few days before coming clean: she'd doctored the photo.

The season continued and Betty clung to life. When the Rays beat the White Sox in their first playoff game ever, Betty watched through her pain. But it had been worth it.

The Rays eliminated the White Sox from the playoffs; Betty lost her appetite and her ability to walk.

The Rays took on the hated Red Sox; her daughters pointed their mother's bed at the big-screen television and rooted along with her. Baseball was keeping their mother alive, though she thought she was keeping the Rays alive.

The Rays eliminated the Red Sox; they had won the pennant. Next stop, the World Series.

The Rays played their first World Series game at their home park, Tropicana Field, against the Phillies. As Betty watched from her bed in North Carolina, her granddaughter, Veronica Carroll, suddenly popped up on the television screen, holding up a sign in the stands. "Win for Baseball Betty," said the sign. A second later Betty's photograph, the one with her wearing a fake Mohawk, flashed on the jumbo scoreboard. Maybe it was coincidence, but the Rays beat the Phillies that night.

Betty, of course, would have preferred seeing at least three more victories and the World Series championship. That's how she planned it, anyway. But the Phillies, let it be said, won the World Series. At least Betty didn't have to see it. She died on October 28, before the last out.

Betty being Betty, she had planned her own funeral. She wanted her ashes mixed with her late husband's. Their ashes were placed in a little box Betty had picked out, a box with the Rays logo on the top. Her daughters buried the baseball box in a church cemetery, about 20 minutes from the stadium where Betty's beloved Rays continue to play.

Fall 2008.

Conrad Yankee

Conrad Yankee was an old salt, one of those fishing fools so common on the Florida waterfront, grizzled guys with scales in their hair and stinking guts under their fingernails. He fished every day when he could, usually from the *Miss Pass-a-Grille*, a party boat that departed every morning from the island's Merry Pier. He had a favorite place to stand, had a favorite fishing rod, had a favorite bait.

He was generous with his tackle, with his beer, and especially with his advice. "Don't cast over my line," he'd bark at his best friend, Catherine Dow, who would bark right back.

"Captain," he'd call to the guy behind the wheel, Mike Gunther, "when are you going to put us onto some real fish? Isn't that your job?" Sometimes Gunther and Dow got so irritated they wanted to toss Conrad overboard. But even when they wanted to kill him they loved him.

He died in 2004. Bleeding in the brain. He was 76. Friends and family scattered his ashes in Conrad's favorite fishing hole, the Gulf of Mexico. Ex-wife Mary Susie Yankee ordered a bench built in his honor, complete with a plaque featuring Conrad's name.

The Rolls-Royce of benches cost $1,500 and was constructed from recycled plastic. The green bench was 6 feet wide and 3 feet high and weighed 185 pounds. Moving it required two or three burly fishermen, a lot of grunting, and the usual hair-raising foul language.

They put the Conrad Yankee Memorial Bench next to the jetty at Pass-a-Grille. They aimed the bench at the Gulf, where Conrad had spent so many hours of his life thinking about fish, talking about fish and, when he was lucky, catching them.

Friends and family enjoyed sitting on the Conrad Yankee Memorial Bench during visits to the jetty. They could talk to him and finally have the last word. In August, when the bench disappeared from the jetty,

Conrad Yankee after a good day in the Gulf. (Photo courtesy of Catherine Dow.)

friends and family were mystified. But even more they were distraught. Now Conrad really was gone.

The missing bench especially bothered Catherine Dow, his 78-year-old friend and teasing adversary. "Did a wave wash it off the jetty?" she asked friends.

Unlikely. St. Pete Beach experienced no major storms that summer.

"Drunken kids? Maybe they pushed it off the jetty."

That made more sense, provided the kids had eaten their Wheaties. She looked into the dark green water next to the jetty. Maybe the bench lay on the bottom among the rocks and sand and toadfish. She wasn't about to dive in and find out. She tried to put the bench out of her mind.

But how could she forget Conrad, whom she had met on the stern of a fishing boat in 1985? Anglers are territorial and superstitious; she and Conrad wanted to occupy the same prime fishing spot near the stern. She won. Grumbling, the tall man with black hair camped next to her and offered unwanted advice. So went their chess game for the next two decades.

Sometimes he irked her, sometimes he made her laugh. They were like the competitive couple in one of those madcap Tracy-Hepburn movies, but without the romance. He was married. She valued her independence. Even if he'd been free, even if he had courted her, she would have turned him down.

"I would have killed him with a frying pan after two days if we'd been married," she liked to joke.

Tourists who had sat on the bench at the jetty naturally wondered: "Who was Conrad Yankee, and what did he do to merit a memorial bench? Was he in *Scarface* with Al Pacino?"

No, he had been a guy who loved fishing. He was born into a Catholic Connecticut family in 1929; in the Yankee clan, man and boy were expected to catch something for the meatless Friday supper, namely, fish. For a while, Conrad attended seminary, destined to become the priest in the family. But he was too much the charmer and there were girls. Sometimes he even persuaded his little sister, Flo, to iron his shirts before he went out on the town. Eventually he married a recent high school graduate, Barbara. They had six children in their three decades together.

He supported his family by inventing things. His golf course rake is still working in the twenty-first century. So is a squeegee used to remove water from athletic fields. He came up with technology to generate steam for toy electric train locomotives. He patented a design for making modern beer cans.

When he wasn't inventing, he was fishing. Or watching James Bond movies on television. Or reading Tolkien novels. Or growing zucchini, squash, and tomatoes in the rich soil of the garden. At night, he dug up worms in the compost so he would have fresh bait in the morning.

His mind raced in many directions at once. He took medicine to slow his thoughts. His wife, another strong personality, helped keep him focused. When she died of lupus before her 50th year, he fell into a deep funk.

He rallied after discovering St. Pete Beach, warm weather, and salt-water fishing. He loved going out on the boats and catching grouper and snapper. He enjoyed the company of new friends. He bought them beer, loaned them money, invited them to dinner. They loved his cooking, especially his baked fish, which he stuffed with crabmeat.

He married for a second time, but it was over so fast that even friends have only the vaguest memories.

He exchanged wedding vows a third time. His new bride, Mary Susie Yankee, liked fishing enough to help him make lures in the garage. His friends? She liked some more than others. Encouraged them to shower before visiting.

The union lasted 10 up-and-down years. After the divorce, Conrad once again was thrown for a loop. Contributing to his misery was a chronic blood disorder and weakness of the heart. At least he had fishing to inspire him—and the occasional grand idea that terrified friends and family.

He wanted to buy an apartment building and fill it with his favorite folks. "Uh-oh," thought Catherine Dow. Had Conrad stopped taking his medication? Another idea: he wanted to take friends to the Keys and charter a boat. Destination: the Dry Tortugas. Las Vegas is to gamblers what the Dry Tortugas are to certain Gulf anglers. The Tortugas, about 70 miles from Key West, are a series of islands accessible only by boat or seaplane. The water is clear and full of fish. An angler who lowers a bait may hook into a pan-sized mangrove snapper one minute and in the next instant something gargantuan that escapes with every inch of line. Years before, Conrad and Catherine and a lot of other hard-core anglers had taken a fishing trip to the Dry Tortugas. He dreamed about returning, talked about it all the time.

A trip to the Dry Tortugas? With all his friends? Sounded nutty to Catherine. But it could also be the tonic that might lift his flagging spirits.

In early 2004 he was deathly ill. A daughter, Susan Yankee, brought him to Louisiana to care for him. On one of his good days she took him to Walmart so he could buy fishing tackle for himself and his newest pals. Later, she listened to him get on the telephone and book a fishing charter out of Key West, destination Dry Tortugas.

Conrad's bench.

In the spring he was admitted to the hospital to get a pacemaker. He fell one night on his way to the bathroom. He died from a hemorrhage in his brain on June 8, 2004.

He had two funerals. In Connecticut, old friends who attended the service donated money to the Milford Children's Trout Derby, in care of the Milford Striped Bass Club, in Conrad's name. In St. Pete Beach, his old captain and sometimes nemesis Mike Gunther cranked up the *Miss Pass-a-Grille* and headed into the Gulf. Conrad's family and Catherine scattered ashes.

As the months passed, everybody talked about Conrad. Remember the time he did this? What about the day he said that? What was the secret to his bisque? Was it because he made his stock with flounder bones?

At the jetty, they sat on the bench among the sea oats and missed him terribly. And then the bench disappeared.

Conrad Yankee fished for pleasure and for the occasional meal. In bad weather he stayed home. Paul Doyon, Robert Callahan, and Eric McKay are commercial fishermen who dock on Madeira Beach near St. Petersburg. They go out, no matter what, for 12 days at a time in the Gulf of Mexico in a boat called the *Michelle Marie*. She's 44 feet long, though in harsh weather she feels smaller.

Doyon, 40, is captain. He's a wiry guy with a tattoo on his neck. He and his crew set long lines bearing thousands of hooks. They look for water 180 to 240 feet deep. The bottom of the Gulf is mostly sand; they look for a rocky bottom because that's where the grouper and snapper are.

Commercial fishermen like to work near the Dry Tortugas. In November, they were north of the Dry Tortugas when the fishing got red hot. They landed red grouper and black grouper, red snapper and delicious scamp.

One night after Thanksgiving, while they were cleaning the deck of the fish blood and fish slime, somebody noticed something white in the water about 50 feet on starboard side. It was a gull perched on something in the high seas.

Doyon spun the wheel for a better look. In his light's beam he saw some kind of floating structure. Got closer. The Gulf washed through the slats of a bench. Doyon and his crew were tired and the bench looked heavy.

"We can't leave it out here," Doyon told his workers. "This would smash the hull of any boat that hit it." They maneuvered the bench to the stern. The three of them leaned over and tried to haul it aboard. Too heavy. They waited for an incoming wave to provide momentum. They yanked it aboard without breaking their boat or their bones. The bench had grown algae like hair. The bottom was covered with tiny barnacles.

"This bench is going to look good in my yard," a crewman announced.

"Wait a minute," Doyon said. "There seems to be a plaque here. What's it say? Hmm. I wonder who he was?"

Late in his life, Conrad Yankee wanted to go to the Dry Tortugas one last time. He didn't make it.

His bench nearly did.

Back on land, the owner of the *Michelle Marie*, Jim Bonnell, turned on his computer and typed the name "Conrad Yankee" into the browser. Turned out a Conrad Yankee lived in New Port Richey; Bonnell telephoned him. Like so many others, the son of the late fisherman had wondered what had become of his dad's bench. Bonnell provided the answer.

In the first month of 2010, the bench was back in St. Pete Beach, on the Merry Pier, about a block from where Conrad had lived on Pass-a-Grille. Despite the barnacles and dried algae, the bench seemed as sturdy as ever. Tourists sat on it during the day. In the evening, the yellow-crowned night herons used it as a perch.

Catherine Dow liked seeing the bench whenever she visited the pier. She walked past it to the end of the pier and boarded the *Miss Pass-a-Grille*, where she claimed her usual spot on the stern. She could almost feel Conrad's presence next to her. She could almost hear his unwanted advice.

"Don't cast over my line."

Winter 2010.

Richard Coleman the Lionhearted

First the river was a river, long and meandering, with alligators and ducks and bass and bream. Then, in the name of efficiency and flood control, the river was turned into a canal, wide and deep and polluted, lacking much animal life except the vultures that floated above on the afternoon thermals, watching, always watching.

My old friend Richard Coleman loved the Kissimmee River and hated Canal 38. As a boy, he caught bass and hunted ducks on the river. As a man, he did everything he could to persuade the U.S. Army Corps of Engineers to change sterile C 38 back into the river nature had intended.

"What the canal needs is an enema," Richard told me in disgust the first time we met, in 1992. He thought a couple of sticks of dynamite, strategically placed, might do the trick. A minute later he stopped the airboat and pointed at one of the rare nice spots, a place where a sandbar or a floating log had blocked the current and created a little alcove that looked natural.

"A river is a cauldron of birth, death, and diversity," he declared. "It's life itself."

That was Richard Coleman: roaring about enemas one moment and in the next breath sounding like Walt Whitman. He was the Lion of the Kissimmee River, and I am sad he isn't around to see the good things happening to his river nearly two decades later.

Paul Gray, an old friend of Richard's, wanted to show me the new good things. Gray is the biologist who studies the Everglades on behalf of the National Audubon Society. On a cold morning, he cranked the engine of the airboat and went looking for Richard's river.

"You can't fix the Everglades," he told me, "without fixing the Kissimmee River first." That's what Richard always said. And that's what is more or less happening as the Comprehensive Everglades Restoration Plan creaks along. Parts of the river are starting to look like a river again.

Somewhere in the netherworld, Richard has to be smiling. He spent most of his life lobbying on behalf of the Kissimmee. Even when the corps first began turning the river into a canal in 1962, his was the dissenting voice. When it was finished in 1971 he was apoplectic. In 1983, Governor Bob Graham called the C 38 canal "an insult to nature," but it took another decade for the words to become action.

Of course, nobody set out to deliberately despoil the river or the Everglades. The intention was to control flooding, to move water quickly from Central Florida to Lake Okeechobee, where the excess could be pumped through canals into the Atlantic Ocean and the Gulf of Mexico, with the agriculture area south of the lake receiving just a taste. The intention was to make Florida a safer and drier place for progress.

The result was catastrophic to nature—and ominous for people who like to drink clean water. The meandering, 103-mile-long river had filtered pollutants out of its slow-moving stream since pioneer days. After the corps straightened the river into a 56-mile, 300-foot-wide, 30-foot-deep canal, polluted water rushed into Lake Okeechobee as if flushed by a toilet.

That filthy water? Well, Lake Okeechobee and the Everglades recharge the Biscayne Aquifer, South Florida's drinking supply. Water is also the lifeblood of Everglades National Park at the state's tip. The park began dying of thirst, and smart Floridians began worrying about water to drink.

Over thousands of years, the meandering Kissimmee had created 50,000 acres of marsh, home to millions of living things. When the marsh vanished, the wildlife went with it.

Richard Coleman called C 38 "the Ditch."

He was one of those larger-than-life folks of myth—only he was real. The Paul Bunyan of the environment loved adventure, food, cowboy hats, smelly cigars. When I traveled with him in his speeding boat, I tried to stay upwind so the cigar ash wouldn't set my hat on fire.

He was born in New Jersey but evolved into a Floridian as a boy. He lived for a stretch in Clearwater; he and his teenage buddies rowed to Caladesi Island to live like Huck Finn during summer, mosquitoes be damned. As an adult, he invited friends on camping trips; only when they were trapped on board did they learn of Richard's plans to "live off the land."

He studied chemistry at Florida Atlantic University in South Florida and discovered the Kissimmee and the Everglades. One time he wrapped an unhappy 4-foot mud snake around his waist, strolled into the college library, and asked the most attractive women to critique his belt. They answered with shrieks.

As a U.S. Department of Agriculture chemist, he had to behave. But deep down he was incorrigible. He patched together a career that included property management, plant growing, commercial photography, and leading Caribbean tours by sailboat. He established the state's first Sierra Club chapter, but he was an environmentalist who also liked to eat wild ducks and bass.

He loved fast boats. Even atheists who climbed aboard were likely to utter prayers before long.

Paul Gray stepped on the gas and the airboat leaped to life. The cold wind made our eyes water. Orlando was about an hour north, Lake Okeechobee about 30 miles south. We were on C 38, in the middle of nowhere, in the Ditch.

It looked as bad as I remembered from my tour with Richard in 1992. Straight, wide, deep. No alligators on the bank. No deer sipping from the river shallows. Nothing but vultures in the sky.

A mile later, we saw the flags. It was the beginning of the construction site. The corps has been filling in the canal to make it as shallow and narrow as the river used to be. The corps has blown up one dam and has plans to blow up another.

The canal remembers how to be a river. The river is happening. Eventually the corps hopes to restore about 40 percent of the current waterway. "The wildlife is coming back much faster than we ever expected," Gray said.

He stopped the airboat. We looked at ducks, a lot of them, flying over the river into the marsh beyond. Gray, 52 on that day, was a waterfowl guy. At the University of Florida, he studied mottled ducks and earned a doctorate. He can tell you everything about them, including how they taste. He likes to get out on the river with his shotgun and his retriever in the fall.

The river started meandering. Gray had to slow the airboat to get around the corners. In places, sandbars had climbed out of the water. On one bank, a huge oak tree was about to topple into the drink.

"And that's a good thing," Gray told me. "There shouldn't be oak trees growing on the flood plain. They should be MILES away. But when the canal was here, and the marsh dried up, we got oak trees."

In August, Tropical Storm Fay had crept into Florida and stayed a week. Some areas in Central Florida received 2 feet of water. Towns flooded. Oak trees toppled. The new parts of the Kissimmee River rejoiced.

"It was the most exciting thing I've seen," said Gray, who has worked in South Florida for more than a dozen years. "The river overflowed and covered the old flood plain for four miles. FOUR MILES."

Richard Coleman would have lit a cigar and sipped a tumbler of cognac.

"The ducks are coming back now," Gray said. "Look. I see some teal over there and that looks like a merganser. For years there was no duck hunting because there were no ducks. Now there is a population of ducks large enough to support hunting again."

A great blue heron abandoned a branch, pumped its wings, and croaked at us in utter disgust. A flock of glossy ibis whipped overhead. In the distance sandhill cranes flapped majestically. "It's easy to be worried about Florida," Gray said, "and I do worry about Florida all the time. That said, if you give nature half a chance it will try to heal."

We heard no cars, no sirens, no loud stereos on the marsh. My cell phone didn't ring or beep. Civilization was out of range. Sorry, Facebook friends.

A marsh wren hollered. A Northern harrier, a beautiful hawk, soared inches above the millet. We saw a pair of wood storks. We heard a limpkin squawking. A raccoon and her young swam across the creek in front of us. An otter poked its head up, glanced our way, and vanished as quickly. Alligators tried to get warm on the bank.

I thought about Richard and his "cauldron of birth, death, diversity" accidental poetry.

It was time to go home. Paul Gray cranked the engine and drove the airboat across the shallow marsh. I was lost. Paul carried a GPS, but he knew where we were. The marsh led to a creek and the creek led to the river, and we followed the river slowly around one curve and then another, being careful all the way, because on a wild river anything can happen.

On July 18, 2003, when he was 59, Richard Coleman launched his airboat on C 38 not far from his home in Winter Haven. He wanted to show friends a good part.

His boat and another boat collided on a curve.

Serious injuries all around. Everybody recovered but Richard. He died in a tributary of the Kissimmee called "Dead River."

But I'll tell you something. He lives. His spirit inhabits the river that once was a canal that once was a river. When you hear the frogs croaking and the herons crying, you are hearing Richard Coleman, the Lion of the Kissimmee.

Winter 2009.

43

Wes Skiles

At the moment of his death Wes Skiles must have felt completely alive. He was doing what he loved doing more than anything. Wearing diving equipment, carrying a camera, he was in the process of capturing a hidden world. He was a Florida boy who was also a twenty-first century Viking, an explorer without peer.

He explored deep water and underwater caves mostly in Florida but in other places, too. He sought danger all over the globe, though not in a deliberately macho way. He wanted to know what was down there. He wanted to see what few other human beings had ever seen and then show his pictures to folks who would otherwise never understand or sufficiently value their planet.

He was 52 years old when he died in Palm Beach County on July 21, 2010. For most of us, a half century sounds all too short. But for someone like Wes, who lived life on the edge, five decades might have constituted a ripe old age.

The most famous diver in history was the late Jacques Cousteau. The second most famous diver was probably Wesley Cofer Skiles. Many of us have seen his photographs in magazines such as *National Geographic*. Many more people have seen his documentary films on television or at the movies. *Water's Journey—The Hidden Rivers of Florida*, his look at the Florida beneath Florida, is among his best known. Another is *Ice Island*, which he filmed in Antarctica under and inside the ice. "One hundred and fifty years after the advent of photography," Gainesville landscape photographer John Moran once told me, "after we thought we had seen everything, he showed us a whole new world."

He started diving as a kid in Jacksonville. Soon he was an expert, the go-to guy for advice at northeast Florida dive shops. And he was only 16. Among other things, he was beginning to explore the underwater caves near Gainesville, arguably among the most dangerous places on Earth for the careless. In the decade or so before 1970, for example, at least 26 divers drowned exploring the main cave at Ginnie Springs.

"They'd go in with 7-Eleven flashlights and ski rope," said Mark Wray, who owns the Ginnie Springs attraction now. Wes helped install a gate across the cave mouth to keep out the death-seeking rookies. It's still in place, next to an underwater sign featuring a skull and crossbones.

Wes, the guy who loved life, recovered the bodies of dozens of drowned divers during his half century, including friends. "He lived with the idea of mortality," said Jill Heinerth, who produced his movies and lived close to Wes in High Springs, blocks away from Ginnie Springs. Yet he never obsessed about it. Why bother? Diving deep, exploring dangerous caves, getting close to dangerous animals was what he did. What was he going to do for kicks? Play golf? Watch reality TV?

In Africa, he modified a shark cage to allow better access to the Indian Ocean for his high-definition camera and his own mortal self. As the 14-foot great white approached, Wes leaned completely out of the cage with his camera. The shark kept coming. Wes continued filming. The shark kept coming. Wes retreated into the cage. The shark kept coming. Chasing Wes, the shark burrowed into the cage's open door. In a corner, Wes assumed the fetal position and prepared to be eaten. Thrusting its powerful tail, the shark propelled the cage toward the bottom, out of sight of the boat. On deck, friends began weeping. Wes popped to the surface.

"I got amazing video!" he shouted.

He liked to laugh. He liked to sing at the top of his voice. He taught himself to play guitar and harmonica. Friends told me, "Wes runs with scissors." He loved fireworks. Sometimes he got in bottle rocket fights with friends. When he talked to school kids, he wore an Indiana Jones–style hat as a joke. After a talk, he'd go to the cafeteria and have lunch, not with the principal, but with the kids.

He was an underwater astronaut. He was an ambassador for Florida's springs and for clean water. He came up with new ways to film in caverns. He developed new techniques for cave exploration that involved lights, ropes, air, and common sense. He helped map out some of the longest underwater caves on Earth, including awesome Wakulla Springs near Tallahassee. He mapped a cave for about a mile.

He was married for three decades to Terri Skiles, a brave and patient woman. They had two children, Nathan and Tessa, who shared their dad's sense of adventure. Often, Dad brought friends home. In the Skiles

The late Wes Skiles. (Photo by Luis Lamar, courtesy of the Skiles family.)

household, strangers often slept on the couch, drank coffee, told stories, listened to even better stories, laughed until they cried.

He enjoyed practical jokes. Sometimes, deep in a cave, he'd pick up a prehistoric skull, hold it over his face and tap on the back of an already nervous companion. A prized possession was a novelty store set of plastic, yellowed, rotten teeth. Many people who visited High Springs wanted to meet the town's only celebrity. "I'll introduce you to Wes," a friend might say to the eager fan, "but for the love of God don't look at his teeth. He's really self-conscious." The pilgrim would shake hands and stare at the ground so as not to embarrass the famous diver with the yellow teeth.

Wes would spit out the teeth in laughter.

The day before he died, he visited his old friend Spencer Slate in Key Largo. They had met when they were young and foolish and thought they were immortal. Spencer runs a dive boat in the Keys. They traveled into the Atlantic with a couple of folks from *National Geographic*. Wes wanted to photograph toothy barracuda as they fed. Easy enough. He also wanted to take video of frenetic mahi-mahis as they fed in the Gulf

Stream where the water is infinitely deep and forbidding. Everything went swimmingly.

The next morning, after Wes and Spencer said their goodbyes, the expedition headed north to Palm Beach County and another trip into the Atlantic. Two miles east of the Boynton Inlet, three divers slipped over the side of the boat. On the bottom, Wes signaled the other divers with his hands that he had run out of film and was returning to the boat. The other divers signaled their understanding and continued on. Nobody ever saw Wes alive again.

They found him lying on his back in 75 feet of water. We can only guess what went through his mind as he drew his last breath. Did he conjure up the faces of his wife and children? Did he think, "What's wrong with my equipment?" Perhaps he thought, "After everything I've done in my life, I can't believe I'm going to die in open water only 75 feet down. What a laugh."

A week after his death, friends celebrated his life and mourned his death at his favorite place on the planet, Ginnie Springs. As gray clouds billowed above the Santa Fe River, and thunder rumbled over the trees, they gathered to say goodbye. His friends included dozens of people who had never ventured into a cave and a colleague who two weeks before had survived a tussle with a 12-foot alligator at Silver Springs.

There were prayers and many Wes stories, tears, laughter, barbecue, beer, angel food cakes, hymns, and more laughter and tears. There was music, of course—John Prine's recording of "It's a Big Old Goofy World" seemed sadly appropriate—followed, inevitably, by a fireworks show Wes would have enjoyed.

As the night went on, and the mosquitoes started whining, and the frogs began croaking, someone brought out an 8-foot model of a Viking ship. Nathan, Wes's 22-year-old, swam with the ship out to the middle of Ginnie Springs and set it on fire. It burned for hours, the flames licking the low branches of the oaks and the cypress trees.

A twenty-first century Viking had received a perfect sendoff.

Summer 2010.

44

Bill Haast

Snakes were Bill Haast's business and his calling. When they bit him—poisonous snakes bit him more than 170 times—he never blamed them, never vowed to give them up, almost never went to the doctor. The painful encounters only made snakes more interesting to him.

He died last week in Punta Gorda, where he was quietly operating a lucrative business collecting venom for snakebite medicines. The cobras, mambas, or rattlers didn't do him in. "Death by natural causes," the doctor announced. Bill Haast, who could have been a character in a Carl Hiaasen novel, was 100 years and almost six months old.

"The snake bit the mouse. The mouse died. I found it intriguing," is how he once explained his fascination. He was the most interesting Floridian I ever knew. In fact, when I was a boy, he was my idol. He ran a place in Miami called the Serpentarium, which he had started as a roadside tourist attraction in 1947. I started going to the Serpentarium in the 1950s when Florida theme parks tended to be small anything-can-happen family businesses. My dad also took me to the Monkey Jungle, the Parrot Jungle, Coral Castle, and the Seminole Indian Village at Musa Isle, but it was my many visits to the Serpentarium that fired my interest in natural history and Florida culture.

Haast was a terrific showman who dressed in white as if he were a distinguished scientist. He was actually a former carnival worker who had once roomed with a moonshiner at a speakeasy. Yet he conducted more research than many university-trained scientists, using his own body in unprecedented experiments.

Over the years he built up his immunities by injecting himself daily with a cocktail of various snake venoms. Bites that might have killed or crippled ordinary people usually only made him ill or eroded his flesh. Sometimes he refused to go to the hospital and instead took careful note of his symptoms while resting at home.

Bill Haast with his king cobra. (Photo courtesy of the Florida Memory Project.)

Haast enjoyed performing for tourists, but he earned most of his money selling venom to companies that manufactured snakebite medicines. At least 10 victims of deadly snake bites who were allergic to antivenin medicines received transfusions of Haast's immunized blood and survived.

The best day to go to the Serpentarium was always Sunday, when Haast released a 14-foot king cobra on a roped-off section of the lawn—no worries about liability insurance back then. When it inevitably slithered toward the audience, Haast jerked it back by the tail.

King cobra venom can kill an elephant. In fact, the cobra had twice almost claimed Haast's life, despite his immunities, paralyzing him and shutting down his lungs. A breathing machine had kept him alive while his body fought off the venom.

On the Serpentarium lawn, the great snake's head rose several feet above the ground. Puffing up, it gazed into the eyes of Haast, who was kneeling within easy striking distance. They were old antagonists. As Haast weaved left, the hissing cobra followed the movement as if hypnotized. The snake always struck sooner or later. Like an agile mongoose, Haast sprung backwards.

"Be careful, Bill! Don't use your hands! Use a stick to catch him, Bill!"

Haast's second wife, Clarita, was supposed to be narrating the show. On Sundays, her angst touched the heart of every tourist. One time as I watched, the cobra attacked. Its fangs tore open Haast's white pants at the knee and venom streamed down his leg like an egg yolk. Clarita began weeping. "Did he get you? Oh, Bill, did he get you? Tell me, Bill!"

He didn't answer, merely focused on the cobra. Next time it struck and missed, he was able to grab it behind the head. A minute later it donated another load of venom, this time into a glass vial. Nobody was surprised when Clarita divorced Bill.

He closed the Serpentarium after a six-year-old child fell into a pit and was drowned by a 12-foot Nile crocodile in 1977. Haast jumped onto the croc but failed to save the boy. The next day he shot the crocodile with a pistol.

The Serpentarium limped along until he retired to Utah in 1984. But his love for snakes called him back in 1990. He settled in southwest Florida, opened the Miami Serpentarium Laboratories, and focused on snake-venom production for pharmaceutical companies.

In 1995, he invited me for a visit. I was expecting to see a bent-over old guy. Surely I would find him sitting in a chair from which he could watch his young assistants conduct the deadly work. But when I arrived, Haast was milking a cottonmouth, a common Florida water snake known for its painful and destructive bite. "I'll never quit," he told me. "What else am I going to do?"

Except for his mangled hands, which had taken the brunt of his snakebites over the decades, he looked at least three decades younger than his 85 years. His gray hair was flecked with black and he still moved gracefully like Rikki-Tikki-Tavi in the Rudyard Kipling tale. He claimed the daily injections of snakebite venom kept him young.

I immediately noticed the missing fingertip. A year earlier, a cottonmouth had bitten his pinkie. The poison had eaten away his flesh and turned what was left of the finger black. Haast avoided doctors. Eventually, he asked his young third wife, Nancy, to perform the surgery.

She snipped off the dead digit with rose clippers.

Summer 2011.

45

Elmo Boone

Elmo Boone handed me a fruit jar. The offering contained no preserved pears, peaches, or cane syrup but a clear liquid that burned my throat on the way down. The potent gift served as an introduction to both moonshine and perhaps the most amazing Floridian I ever knew. Elmo, who died recently at the age of 90, was one of those vanishing species of men who was completely self-reliant and comfortable in the ways of Florida. I knew him for a quarter of a century.

He was a country boy who was born in Miami when Miami was country. In fact, he remembered spending the worst of the horrific, historic 1928 hurricane under his daddy's tomato truck. Moonshine making was among the least of his skills and experiences.

Elmo could build a house, without help, from floor to roof. He could fix a balky outboard engine. He knew how to plow a field behind a mule. He could look at an ailing plant and tell immediately what was needed to restore health. If the answer was as simple as "more water," he could find you a well—using a dowsing stick. Don't tell me he couldn't. Lots of people over the years watched him do it.

For most of his adult life he made a living as a nurseryman. Elmo planted many of the trees at Walt Disney World. Many St. Petersburg backyards, for that matter, are graced by cabbage palms and oaks he lovingly installed. He knew how to grow the best tomatoes, okra, and field peas. He made wine from the plums of his backyard trees. He could throw a cast net with the best of them and was famous for his smoked mullet. He knew how to gig a bullfrog from a moving airboat. He ran his own stone crab traps and shucked oysters like lightning—an important skill when surrounded by a crowd of hungry men. A talented angler, he had an uncanny ability to lure giant bass—"lunkers" is how he described them—to the end of his line.

After his family moved to St. Petersburg in the 1930s, he hunted deer and turkey close to where you'll find a Starbucks today. Of course he knew how to dress a deer. Of course he knew how to butcher a hog. He hunted raccoons with the famous beachcomber and semi-hermit, Silas Dent, on mangrove islands near today's Sunshine Skyway Bridge. An amazing southern cook, Elmo could make almost anything palatable. This is a family newspaper, so I can't fully describe the power of his lima bean soup on the human digestive system. Maybe later.

I can tell stories, but I'm an amateur compared to Elmo. Over the years he regaled me with tales of being lost at sea, snake-bit, or encountering the skunk ape or a UFO during a routine outdoor excursion. He even had one about a widow who answered to "Ma" and toted a machine gun. I always liked to believe every story was gospel truth.

The best place to know Elmo Boone was at his hunting camp in northwest Florida, not far from the city of Perry and the Aucilla River. I never hunted, but I loved being in the woods with Elmo, and so I would drive into the woods, at least for a night, so I could enjoy one of his suppers and storytelling jags.

He was a big fellow with a bone-crushing handshake, bald when I knew him, with great big white teeth and a magnificent set of mutton-chop sideburns. In his youth he was handsome like Marlon Brando in *The Wild Ones*—in fact, in his youth, he had paraded around town on a motorcycle.

One time, as we sat at the campfire and sipped his coveted Plum Crazy wine, he told me about how he had learned how to hunt squirrels and catch bream when his family lived in Ocala National Forest. It was the Depression and everybody was poor, and Elmo's mother suggested that Elmo share the bounty with the folks down the road in Oklawaha.

"The Barkers. Now Mrs. Barker was a real nice lady, just about as nice as my Mama. You'd have never thought different until the FBI showed up one day." Agents snuck up on Ma Barker's home. She and other members of the notorious Ma Barker gang perished in a hail of bullets.

Elmo had more lives than a bobcat. In one hunting story, he was thrown by his horse onto an angry wild hog and saved from the tusks by his ferocious bulldogs. Reaching for a fish at the end of his line in another story, he was bitten by a venomous cottonmouth moccasin. Another time he was pinned under a tractor that turned over in a ditch. His World War II ship, the USS *Laramie*, was torpedoed by a German U-boat

Elmo Boone and one of his lunkers. (Photo courtesy of Denise Boone Antonewitz.)

in the North Atlantic. Clinging to wreckage, he was rescued hours later having barely survived hypothermia.

Elmo once told me about hooking a huge bass in Pinellas County's Walsingham Reservoir in 1951. I thought the story had to end with the landing of a stupendous 14-pound lunker. But, no, this was an Elmo story: "There was this houseboat out there on the lake with blue lights. Only it wasn't a houseboat. All of a sudden it took off, without a sound, and flew over the beach."

Elmo also was certain that Florida's wilderness was home to a storied, apelike creature with enormous feet. "One time I waded across some water to this island. There was this little tree, bent down and stripped of leaves, like a bear will do to trees sometimes. But whatever done this was no bear. The tracks were huge, like nothing I've ever seen, big kind of human tracks except with a spike mark down at the heel. And there was two huge piles of droppings. Animals aren't so neat about where they make their droppings, but this one was."

I can just imagine Elmo talking Florida's Bigfoot, the Skunk Ape, to death.

He was married 63 years to his beloved Billie Jean. After her death from pneumonia in 2009, Elmo lost a step. Although he had moved to Citrus County, on a bass-infested lake, he stopped fishing. He stopped hunting and driving around the woods in his 1986 red pickup. He couldn't bear to sleep in his marital bed without Billie, so he'd watch television until he nodded off in a living room chair with Margarita, his Chihuahua, in his lap.

His body began to fail, his legs, his back, his kidneys, his brain. He passed on December 13, 2011, at Citrus Memorial Hospital in Inverness. His brother James and his two daughters, Dona Boone of Hernando and Denise Boone Antonewitz of St. Petersburg, held a memorial at the Florida National Cemetery in Bushnell. From there they drove back to Elmo's house, to scatter his ashes in Lake Tsala Apopka and tell Elmo stories.

I will hang onto my hunting-camp memories of Elmo frying fish in a pan next to his famous "wampus" bread, a concoction made from cornmeal, diced potatoes, onions, milk, eggs, and stewed tomatoes that tasted better than any hush puppy. I will remember him sitting at the campfire, his feet resting on a log, telling a story that becomes another story that becomes another story that ought to be true even if it wasn't.

Finally, I will remember the hours before dawn when the camp awoke and Elmo and fellow hunters emerged from tents dressed in camouflage with Elmo talking, talking, talking. Marching into the dark woods, they carried their deer rifles and, just as important, heaping rolls of toilet paper, because they had eaten Elmo's celebrated lima bean soup the night before.

Winter 2012.

46

Stetson Kennedy

Florida lost a true icon in 2011. Stetson Kennedy, folklorist, author, and civil rights activist, died in a hospital near Jacksonville. He was 94. "He was a giant," said Peggy Bulger, a friend, protégé, and director of American Folklife for the Library of Congress. "He never quit working. Last time I talked to him he was still full of piss and vinegar."

He was Florida's Homer, a talking history book, a troublemaker, a scamp, a radical, and a shameless promoter of everything Stetson. I got to know him late in his life. Now and again I visited him at the North Florida home he called Beluthahatchee—"Heaven" in the Seminole Indian language. His little paradise, sort of a rickety cabin on stilts perched over a swamp near the St. Johns River, will become a museum one day.

He grew up down the road in Jacksonville, left home for the University of Florida, enrolled in a writing class taught by an up-and-coming author named Marjorie Kinnan Rawlings, quit college, took the train to Key West, drank rum, chased women, married his first wife, and wrote down everything he found interesting, which was quite a lot.

He made his mark during the Depression as a writer and editor of *Florida: A Guide to the Southernmost State*, which was part of Franklin D. Roosevelt's New Deal project to provide work to unemployed writers. Helping him gather information in the Florida hinterlands was another pauper, the African American author Zora Neale Hurston, who had recently published her novel *Their Eyes Were Watching God*.

Kennedy could have ended his career at that moment. The guide, considered an important historic document today, secured his legacy. But he had mixed feelings about a book intended to be carried in the glove compartment of a typical tourist's car. "I thought it was a chamber of commerce kind of thing," he once told me. "The idea was to get people to come to Florida and spend money and help the economy. There was

Stetson Kennedy shows Jeff Klinkenberg his collection of Woody Guthrie lyrics.

excellent information in that book, but it hardly told the real story of Florida."

Kennedy was more proud of *Palmetto Country*, published in 1942. Driving through the state with a coffee table–sized tape recorder, he collected the stories of orange pickers, spongers, cigar makers, mullet fishermen, gandy dancers, and turpentine gatherers. Kennedy called his favorite book "sort of a barefoot social history of Florida," but it was also a shocking exposé of southern violence and racism.

Later he fictionalized his investigation of the nation's best-known hate group and called the book *I Rode with the Ku Klux Klan*. Accused of Communist sympathies, threatened with death, he fled to France. In Europe, he wrote the *Jim Crow Guide* about how "separate and equal" actually worked for African Americans, but timid American publishers turned it down. In Paris, the existentialist philosopher Jean Paul Sartre not only published the book but arranged for its distribution in the United States.

Another friend was folk singer Woody Guthrie, whose "This Land Is Your Land" was a poor man's sarcastic reply to Irving Berlin's patriotic "God Bless America." Guthrie often wintered in Florida with Kennedy, slept in his hammock, skinny dipped in the pond, and wrote poetry on the back porch. In 1950, Guthrie wrote one he called "Stetson Kennedy." In 1997, a band called Wilco and a rocker named Billy Bragg put the poem to music. You can hear it: "Stetson Kennedy" is on iTunes.

"He knew everybody," said Tina Bucuvalas, the former director of Florida Folklife who now leads a similar program in Tarpon Springs. "What a life!"

It was an astonishingly messy one. A Don Juan, he enjoyed romances with many women, some who turned out to be married to other people, including friends. Between paramours he still managed to marry seven times, though he admitted to having tied the knot on a mere five occasions.

He feuded with other writers, sometimes about who deserved what credit or how much money. Sometimes he needlessly exaggerated his own already considerable accomplishments.

In 2005, his Klan investigations were praised in *Freakonomics*, a block-buster best seller. But the following year the authors Steven Levitt and Stephen Dubner backed away from their praise. The authors somehow had mistaken Kennedy's steamy Klan novel—full of sexy dames and gats hidden under the pillow—for a work of serious scholarship. Kennedy, who enjoyed seeing his name in print, had not bothered to set them straight. Still, there was never doubt about his courage.

"Let's be honest about understanding Stetson Kennedy's life," said Gary Mormino, the co-director of the Florida Studies program at the University of South Florida. "He held passionate and unpopular opinions about race relations, the Klan, and the nobility of plain folk when such beliefs were wildly unpopular."

Kennedy made some money during his life, but was better at spending it and chronically lived on the edge of poverty, often depending on the charity of friends and fans who'd show up, often unannounced, at his door. Sometimes it was a widow with a casserole or an Audubon bird-watcher who hoped to photograph the osprey nesting in the swamp.

On one of my visits, the nearly deaf Kennedy handed me his telephone when he couldn't hear the caller. On the line was his old friend from Chicago, Studs Terkel, the oral historian who had won a Pulitzer Prize for a book about World War II. Terkel, a fellow veteran of the New Deal project, had written something he wanted to share with his friend. I took dictation.

"Tell him I'm on death's door," Kennedy shouted. He wasn't joking. Pale and fragile, he walked with difficulty, stopping often to gulp air from a breathing tube. But after a short nap—while I looked at his scrapbooks in the den—he emerged strangely energized. He told me he planned an autobiography, a "Stetson Kennedy Reader" for college students, and a book about old Key West. At the time he was 89.

He never finished writing his own story or the anthology. But *Grits & Grunts*, a delightful collection of his Key West memories from the Depression, came out in 2008. It contains stories and songs that would otherwise be lost to antiquity, sketches of characters he knew as Copper Lips, Black Caesar, and Monkey Man.

Like Stetson Kennedy, they're gone but won't be forgotten.

Summer 2011.

47

Moby Dick

In 1977, when I was new in town, I saw a giant on the downtown pier. He lurched out of the dark toward the bait house like Frankenstein's tormented monster. At first I thought he was 8 feet tall. On second glance he seemed only slightly smaller. Towering over the pier railing, he hurled a spear into Tampa Bay with a mighty grunt.

An instant later he tore a flopping fish from the prongs of the spear as if he intended to devour it raw. Instead he tossed the plate-sized prey into a shopping cart that carried his meager belongings. He seemed more feral than human and walked with a horrific limp. As he vanished into the night, a chill ran up my spine.

"Who's that?" I asked the bait monger.

"Slim," he whispered from the doorway.

"Slim who?"

"Just Slim."

The bait monger didn't know his real name. Nobody I talked with in the following weeks did either, even though Slim had been a waterfront icon for generations. But they had stories. Slim is a nice enough guy, someone told me, but he has a bad side. He is the best fisherman on the pier, more than one person said. He might be a murderer. He's insane. Slim is a bum who sleeps under the pier, Slim has no friends, Slim limps because of an old bullet wound in the hip, Slim hates tourists—watch out, he's quick with a knife. Everyone seemed to have stories about Slim without really knowing him. From anecdotes and hearsay they had constructed a life history.

A few weeks later, I had another chance to talk to the giant himself.

I saw him on the pier around twilight, pushing his shopping cart with his left hand while carrying his spear in his right. He leaned over the water, let fly, and roped in a corpulent striped fish, a sheepshead.

My notebook and I stepped into his path.

"Excuse me," I said, beginning an introduction.

"I'm not going to talk to you," he hissed. "Get the fuck out of my way."

I gazed into his tortured eyes, looked at the long fish-gutting knife on his belt and the 10-foot spear at his side. I noticed his huge hands, the humongous black orthopedic shoe, and his crazed flattop. I got out of his way. There are other fish in the sea, I told myself. Write their stories instead.

For three decades, I have. But I never stopped thinking about Slim. Every time I walk on the pier, or ride my bike on the pier, or go for a meal on the pier, or eat an ice cream cone on the pier, I think about him. Slim has always been the one that got away. Slim is my Moby Dick.

Call me Ahab. When I heard about the city's plans to knock down Slim's old haunt and build a new pier in 2010, my old obsession took hold. I hadn't seen Slim in decades. Most likely he was dead. Maybe he was living in a nursing home or with a beloved son or daughter. If I had a name I could find him.

Ahab had his memories, his wooden leg, his sextant, and his maps. I tracked down people named Mastry.

In St. Petersburg, Mastrys are realtors, doctors, lawyers, barkeeps, and business folks. But they're almost all fishermen, and they go way back. I started my hunt at Mastry's Bait and Tackle, which opened in 1976, when Slim was still an everyday St. Petersburg sight.

"He was a commercial fisherman," Dale Mastry, 59, told me. "He sold his fish all over downtown. We cashed his checks. He was so big he had to duck when he came through the doorway."

What was his name?

"I don't remember his name. He was only Slim and I knew him for years. When I was a kid, I was scared to death of him. All the kids were. I think kids must have made fun of his height and his limp—he just didn't like kids. But he was always a gentleman when he started coming into Mastry's. He repaired cast nets for us. I stocked his favorite wine, Taylor's Port, but I don't know if he was an alcoholic.

"Hey, you should talk to my cousin."

Jay Mastry owns his dad's old tavern, where stuffed tarpon and photographs of long-dead anglers hang from nicotine-stained walls. Jay is a fishing guide when he isn't pouring beer. Mastry's Bar and Grill once was a regular stop on the Slim circuit.

The legendary giant known as "Slim" (*right*) with an unknown angler.
(Photo courtesy of Mary Copechal.)

"He was a damn scary guy," said Jay, now 57. "Always had that knife on his belt. You'd see him every day on Central Avenue, dragging a stringer of sheepshead behind him. It didn't matter if it was a Tuesday morning and the street was empty or it was the Festival of States Parade day and the street was packed. He'd take the same route, wouldn't look left, wouldn't look right, look just straight ahead. There was something really creepy about that.

"But he could throw a cast net like God. It's a real art and he could do it, make the net open just right every time. One time my dad and I, we took Slim in our boat out to Skyway bridge. It was before a fishing tournament, and my dad thought Slim could catch us some great bait in that cast net of his.

"For some reason Slim seemed nervous. When he threw his net, something went wrong. The net caught on something on the back of the boat and didn't open right, just kind of collapsed in the water. Slim put his head in his hands and muttered to himself—almost cried. I was just a kid, so I mouthed off about how he was carrying on, and he slowly turned and looked at me with those eyes.

"He said, 'I wish you were my kid just now.'"

Ahab and his doomed crew, far from home, encountered other whaling ships. "Hast seen the white whale?" Ahab would ask. "Hast seen Moby Dick?"

I kept asking around, too. Finally I put a squib in the paper soliciting information from readers. The telephone started ringing.

"One time I asked him his name," Mary Ann Blank, now 71, told me. "He said, 'It doesn't matter. I'm just a fisherman.' I was only 16, but I learned quickly not to ask questions."

I asked Mary Ann for a description.

"He had blonde hair and had a light complexion like he was Scandinavian or something," said Mary Ann, who worked three decades at St. Anthony's Hospital before retirement. "He was good-looking but in kind of a rough way. And he was rough.

"One time, this tourist approached Slim and asked how much Slim charged for a couple of sheepshead. His price was two for a dollar. The tourist laughed in Slim's face and said he wouldn't pay a dollar for those silly-looking fish. So Slim—I've never forgotten this—picked up a fish and slapped the tourist across the face with it."

Telephoning from North Carolina, Walt Hillyer, 55, remembered Slim grunting when asked a question. He remembered how Slim hid under the pier and sometimes stole fish from stringers hanging into the water.

Now 67, Judge John C. Lenderman of the 6th Judicial Court in St. Petersburg recalled the time he and boyhood friends were exploring under the pier. "Slim came out of the dark, shouting at us and waving his arms, like the bogeyman. We took off like a shot. Years later, when I was a young lawyer, my secretary poked her head into my office and said, 'You ought to see what's in the waiting room.' So she showed in this giant. It was the bogeyman.

"Turned out he was a perfectly nice, well-spoken fellow who wanted me to do some legal work for him. As I recall, he'd found this submerged barge full of valuable copper and wanted to explore his options. I don't think it amounted to anything."

His name? "I just don't remember."

Barbara Meyer had grown up in St. Petersburg, too. Her dad, Les Trafton, was dockmaster at the city marina for 26 years, starting after World War II. "My dad let Slim sleep in his skiff—I remember it as a little green boat—under the dock," Meyer, who was 58, told me. "When I was a little girl, I'd go to the marina after school. Slim often was there. I was never afraid of him. He was very sweet to me. He'd tell me stories about all kinds of things, and he sang me songs. He liked to sing 'Frankie and Johnny.'

"He made me a cane pole for fishing. I'd sit on the dock and catch pinfish for hours on that pole. One time, he came rowing toward the marina in his rowboat from the pier. 'Babs, Babs'—that's what he called me—'I need another pole. The mackerel are running. Throw your pole to me.' He was frantic to borrow my pole!

"I said, 'It's my pole. I'm not giving it to you.' Suddenly, he kind of blew up. He got very angry. He started shouting at me. Shouted, 'You're never going to catch another fish on that pole!' Want to know something? I didn't. Slim put a hex on my pole."

Decades later, when Barbara took a creative writing course, she fashioned a story about her most memorable character.

A man called Slim.

As a rough-and-tumble young guy, Jimmy Kelley caught shrimp at night and huge tarpon during the day. He's 76 now, more or less retired, and full of waterfront memories. As soon as Jimmy learned to walk, he began helping his daddy, whom everyone called Pappy, at the bait house on the pier. Slim, like the pelicans, was a daily sight. "To tell the truth, Slim was usually not a nice man," Jimmy told me. "He was mean as can be. He always carried this slingshot in his back pocket. I saw him shoot pebbles at pelicans when they'd dive on the bait fish. He considered the pelicans competitors for the fish.

"But a minute later he could be nice. My dad sometimes let him sleep in the bait house at night when he was nice. Then Slim would act up and my dad would kick him out. Sometimes Slim slept under the stairwell at the pier. One time I went to wake him and saw he was covered by cockroaches. They were crawling even on his lips. He slept right through the roaches. I don't know if he was drunk or not.

"He liked fishing under the pier in his little skiff with a hand line. He was after the sheepshead. Sheepshead, you know, they have this delicate little bite. You almost can't feel them take the bait. One time I saw Slim take his knife and make little slits in the creases of his fingers where he laid the line. He wanted to make sure he'd feel the fish bite.

"Another night he was catching shrimp in a net under a light on the pier. This girl, a tourist I guess, got in his way. He told her to move. She pointed out that he didn't own the pier. He didn't say nothing. He just threw her in the bay. Her boyfriend came running up to defend her and he threw the boyfriend's ass in the bay, too. Slim got arrested for that.

"One time I'm standing out on the pier with him when we hear a car honking. Teenagers. They got their bare asses sticking out the window. They're mooning Slim. In one motion, he kind of leans over and slings his spear at the car underhand. He throws it so hard it sticks in the door for a minute, quivering. The teenagers got out of there. They weren't going to mess with Slim."

And his name? Oh, never mind, you probably don't—"Sure I do," said Jimmy. "It was Doudna. Arno Doudna."

Once I had a harpoon in him, I began to learn things about my white whale. Arno Doudna was born in Wisconsin on October 8, 1922. His parents, Leland and Gertrude, moved their family to the Tarpon Springs area in 1928. He had one sister and two brothers. His baby brother, Alan, got hit by a car and died in 1934.

When the family moved to St. Petersburg in 1945, the pier became Arno's second home. Old newspaper clippings mention Arno "Slim"

Doudna's fishing prowess, though one article reports his arrest for assault and battery without going into details.

On June 7, 1990, he died at Bayfront Medical Center. The brief obit, which listed no cause of death, mentioned two survivors, a brother in Citrus County and a sister in St. Petersburg. I started looking for Slim's kin. His brother, it turned out, died in 2005. When I read the obituary, I wondered if violence ran in the family. John Doudna shot himself to death after killing Trudy, his terminally ill wife.

That left a sister. I couldn't find her in public records or on the Internet. I mentioned my frustration to Jack Belich, a former colleague, now a private investigator who has his own sources for information. A while later he e-mailed me an address and phone number.

Around Christmastime, I knocked on the door of a little St. Petersburg bungalow.

"Come on in, honey," Mary Copechal called through the screen. "I'll tell you what I can about my brother."

She sat in a favorite chair and looked across the room at her little Christmas tree. "I loved him," Mary, now 79, told me. "But I was deathly afraid of him. He was 7 feet and he had this terrible, terrible temper. I always wondered if he had, what do you call it, a dual personality. I wouldn't be surprised if he killed somebody at one time or another."

Mary's eyes welled up. "I say that, yet he was beautiful. In his own way he was precious. He had such a hard, hard life. Like out of the horror stories."

I asked for details. "When Slim was 6, he was playing on a car. He was sliding off the back of the car, like kids will do, for fun, only his skin—it must have been wet or something—stuck on the metal. He didn't slide, he fell off the car real hard and broke his hip. The bone got infected, got abscessed. The doctors had to remove the hip joint. He was in horrible pain his whole life. That's why he had to wear that special shoe.

"We had a bad father, a roustabout. He'd be home, then he'd go away, then he'd come home, then he'd go away, running up bills. Finally my mother divorced him. My mother kept us going, making dresses, curtains, and bedspreads to barter for goods we needed.

"We had a cow and chickens and a little garden. My brothers caught fish and hunted rabbits in the pines. Slim had a little dog he called Dash. He loved Dash more than anything in the world. On a hunting trip, Dash ran into the woods and started squealing. What happened is a rattlesnake got Dash. Slim never, ever got over losing Dash. Oh, my goodness, honey."

I was getting the picture: a boy trying to grow up without a good male role model, who is crippled, traumatized by the death of his brother, and who loses his best friend, his dog Dash.

"He had a beautiful singing voice. He had a photographic memory. If he heard a song once, he could sing it—all the words. He played a nice harmonica. He was really smart. He liked to read. Math books and history especially. He went to school but got so big he couldn't sit in a normal desk. The kids were always making fun of him. So one day he quit going to school.

"We were so, so poor. Our roof leaked. We'd sleep under newspaper to stay dry. The house was falling apart. The house always somehow seemed evil to me. I always thought the only thing that could cure the evil house was fire. I don't know what caused it, but one day the house caught fire and burned up and we left."

Mary married and had a family. For decades she operated a day care business in St. Petersburg. Slim and his bad temper weren't allowed to visit. Slim never married, his sister told me, but he had at least one great romance during his lifetime.

"Irene her name was. I think they lived together. I don't remember her last name. I do know Slim loved Irene to pieces. When she died, he was all broken up. He never got over Irene's death."

I wondered about the end of Slim's tragic life.

"I think he had cancer for a long time. To tell the truth, I never went to the hospital to see him. Even in the hospital I was afraid of him. One time, I was talking to him on the phone, and he was so full of anger and pain he told me he wanted to kill the nurse."

Mary started weeping. As I held her hands, I felt like weeping myself.

"After he died, I inherited his belongings in a cardboard box. In the box were all these papers filled with his writing. He had written a lot of things down about his life. One night I started reading. I ended up burning just about everything in the box. LIES! LIES! LIES! He told lies about our family and about our mother."

Mary's angry explosion took me by surprise. A minute passed before I asked if she would mind talking about Slim's lies about the family. She did mind. "They were lies! I'd never repeat them. Lies! He just wasn't right in his head."

For the longest moment we both sat in total silence. I looked around the room. I looked at her Christmas tree. Then I noticed some yellowed notepaper on a table next to Mary. Someone had written on the paper with pencil.

"This is what I have of his," Mary finally said. "Slim wrote poetry."

It was a poem about what apparently sustained him for much of his 67 years on earth. Slim wrote poems about fish, stanza after stanza about blue runners and sea robins, redfish and trout, tuna and sharks.

Of all the fishes in the gulf,
Mangrove snappers are most wise.
The balloon fish is a puffer,
He'll grow before your eyes.

Slim was part Frankenstein and part bogeyman, part Boo Radley and, I guess, part Moby Dick. He was a complicated and tormented man. We know a lot of stories about him. But we will never know what it was like to stand inside his 15EEEE shoes.

Winter 2011.

The Last Hamburger Joint

I was there the day Louis' Lunch, a greasy spoon that survived the Great Depression, World War II, the civil rights movement, the arrival of fast food, and even a fatal shooting, closed for good.

As Tommy Pennisi grilled his last burger, hovering above the dilapidated stove, I am sure I saw the ghost of his father, Louis, who founded what the family believes was the state's first hamburger joint in 1928.

Now it was 82 years later. "One Louis burger!" shouted waitress Emily Cheves, Tommy's daughter, jotting the order on cardboard. Tommy didn't glance up. He just threw a patty on the grill for the very last time.

"I hate that I have to close," said Tommy, 75. "But this recession has killed me."

If only every day had been like the last one, when the ancient white building on Louis Pennisi Street was packed with customers wanting burgers, fries, and milk shakes. Every rickety table and every stool along the ancient counter was taken, and as the phone rang with order after order, another car drove up to the takeout window. Louis' Lunch was, among other things, the first known drive-through in the university town.

"I love this place," Margaret Kennard told me. "My momma and daddy started bringing me here in the 1940s. Now I'm 69. I've been coming here at least twice a month all my life. I'm not a McDonald's person, so I'm not sure what I'm going to do."

Louis' Lunch was 12 when the first McDonald's Restaurant opened in California in 1940. In a sleepy Florida town, in a tin-roofed building shaded by oaks, Louis practiced his version of slow food. Born in Sicily in 1896, he immigrated to the United States in 1911 and tried construction, orange picking, and ice-cream mongering before using his mother's meatball recipe for his unusual hamburgers.

Last day at Louis' Lunch.

Louis, whose formal education consisted of exactly three days in school, got by on elbow grease. "I worked 18 hours a day, seven days a week, for 20 years," he once said. "I never went outside, never went to a picture show."

When he was 97, he could still be found behind the grill in his white apron and paper hat. In 1993, his son Freddie was shot dead in a restaurant robbery. Louis, long a widower, went on to help at the eatery until his death at age 106. I saw his photo next to the old menus and knickknacks, calendars and rusting Coke signs.

In segregated Florida, Louis served black folks in a back room that later became a museum for photos of military vets who had been his customers. In integrated Florida, he served all comers at his ketchup-smeared counter. They included working folks in overalls, generations of students, and at least one future governor, Fuller Warren. Louis sold burgers for a nickel, then a dime, then three for a quarter. On the last day of business, they cost $1.90 plain, $2 dressed with tomatoes, lettuce, and onions.

"There was nothing quite like them," Terry Cake, 43, explained to me. He was raised in Gainesville but attended college in Colorado. His favorite Thanksgiving was the one when his Florida friends showed up with a treat. "Louis burgers," Cake said. "They tasted like home."

Tommy Pennisi, Louis's son, gets ready to grill the last hamburger.

Tommy Pennisi, who worked at his father's side for almost six decades, ate a burger a day. "No health problems at all," he said. "Except for my hearing, which didn't have anything to do with hamburgers."

His hearing was good enough to know when the cash register was ringing, but lately it had been quiet. The most seasoned customers had gotten too old to drive or had passed away. When jobs started disappearing during the Great Recession, middle-aged customers spent their money elsewhere. Younger customers preferred the fast-food chains. A downtown construction project that resulted in closed streets was the final blow.

On the last day of business, Tommy flipped the last burger onto the last bun. His daughter carried the last plate to Casey Hamilton, who looked down at his last Louis burger with sadness. An Alachua County sheriff's deputy, he began eating Louis burgers four decades ago when he was a boy. "My mom would bring me here after doctors' appointments as a reward for when I didn't cry," he said.

He took a big bite, and then another, until the last Louis burger was gone.

Fall 2010.

6

Special Folks

49

Rose Man

Despite rumors to the contrary, Willard Campbell, the Rose Man of Lake Placid, actually found time to sleep. Sometimes he got a good five hours before waking at dawn. Sometimes he napped after lunch. His life was all about the cultivation and distribution of roses. For two decades he had grown and given them away by the thousands. He had given them away for free at a time when a good florist was charging anywhere from $20 to $100 for a dozen.

The Rose Man gave them to Central Florida hospital patients and to residents of nursing homes and assisted living facilities. He presented them to bank tellers, waitresses, and dental hygienists. His wife, Opal, received a daily rose, too. In Lake Placid, population 1,700, the Rose Man was regarded as a kind of Santa Claus. His likeness was even on one of the Central Florida city's celebrated murals.

"I don't know anyone who is more beloved in this community," said Eileen May, the Chamber of Commerce director, after receiving her weekly allotment of roses.

"Well," allowed the Rose Man without a smile. "It does give me some pleasure."

The Rose Man, who was 85 at the time of my visit, wasn't much of a talker. He was taciturn by nature, and besides, his hearing was shot. He had spent World War II in a tank, only inches away from blazing artillery. Even with state-of-the-art hearing aids he sounded bewildered from time to time as we spoke. How often did he water his roses? Why would anyone need to water a nose?

In his work as do-gooder, talking and hearing were overrated qualities. The same was true for his olfactories. "I got the sinus problems," he said. Even if he took the time to slow down, he would never be able to smell the roses. The roses in his backyard needed him, though, and he needed them, too. "If I set around doing nothing I'd be a dead man," he muttered. "I got to keep busy."

The Rose Man was less a bloom than a mature blossom. He ambulated through his garden and through his life on artificial knees. Two quadruple bypasses kept his ticker ticking.

Before becoming the Rose Man, he was a coal miner. Born in Kentucky, he sounded to me like Loretta Lynn's daddy in the movie *Coal Miner's Daughter*. "Tired" came out "tarred," not that he ever seemed to be. He called his rose bushes—224 awaited his TLC in his sprawling backyard on Lake June-in-Winter that day—"my fellers."

He had grown up poor but somehow managed to feel rich. His folks had been known for their Jack-in-the-Beanstalk vegetable patch; what food they couldn't grow, Willard supplied with his shotgun. Sometimes even now he had a hankering for fried rabbit. He joined the Army after Pearl Harbor and remained a soldier for 23 years. After a second career as a home builder, he retired to Florida and became the Rose Man.

In Kentucky, his wife Opal—they had been married 65 years at the time of my visit—once had enjoyed growing roses. She stopped when her back went bad. So he took it up. When he took up a hobby, the hobby ceased to be a hobby.

After his first heart attack, his doctor ordered him to give up everything strenuous, especially hunting. He quit hunting and tried fishing. For most people, fishing for speckled perch is a relaxing just-what-the-doctor-ordered kind of activity. Willard Campbell made work of it, customizing his pontoon boat into a speck-catching machine complete with lights and bait wells and comfortable seating.

As for growing roses, nobody would ever reproach him for taking shortcuts.

The Rose Man liked to be up an hour before dawn. If it were light enough to see, it was light enough to take care of his roses. He pulled on his gloves, grabbed his clippers, began working. I was hoping he might talk to his roses, or sing to them, but he didn't. He clipped one rose from this bush, another from a different rose variety. He maintained what had to be the most organized rose garden in the state. The bushes were lined up in ridiculously neat rows. The earth below them was hidden under flawlessly arranged plastic to keep weeds in check.

"This here fella is a Marilyn Monroe," he told me, inspecting his bushes like the master sergeant he once had been. In life, the real Miss

Willard Campbell, the Rose Man, gets ready for a delivery. (Photo by Skip O'Rourke.)

Monroe likely was never called a "fella." The rose variety that carried her name was blonde, however, and bristling with thorns. He fertilized, applied herbicides, fretted about manure, peat, and black mildew. He said, "Thank God we don't get Japanese beetles, though we do have thrips," and gave his roses something to drink. He carried harvested roses into the house, placed them in vases—they were lined up on neat shelves by the hundreds—and then put the vases into the fridge in neat lines.

At 9 a.m. he packed the Rose Mobile, a 2007 Lincoln Town Car, which had a cavernous trunk and long back seat. The Rose Man being the Rose Man, he had designed special carrying crates for his roses. Each crate hauled a dozen vases without spilling water and hurting the roses.

Our first stop was a Wachovia Bank. He carried in the roses like an old-fashioned milkman on a delivery—and placed a vase at each teller window without ever saying a word. At our next stop, the Heartland National Bank, teller Teresa Trujillo tried to make a joke. "It's always a pleasant surprise when a man brings me roses," she said. Roses are serious business; the Rose Man didn't smile. "Where are the vases?" he asked. Over the years he had tried training everybody in town to recycle vases. It irked him when the vases were not ready when he arrived. In the car I asked about his no-nonsense philosophy.

"If I spend too much time talkin', my roses are gonna wilt," he explained.

At Florida Hospital every nurse station received a vase. So did every patient. The ones in the psych ward got plastic vases, just in case. The Rose Man didn't sweep into a patient's room like Errol Flynn, bowing gallantly from the waist and announcing, "Greetings, milady." He didn't seem to have a romantic bone in his body.

At Home and Office Essentials, Jeanne Fortier, standing behind the counter, was thrilled to receive her weekly bouquet. "Here's one of them good-smellin' roses for you," the Rose Man said, in a speech for him.

"Usually he isn't happy with his roses," Fortier whispered to me. "He'll say, 'marginal roses today' or 'wind-blown.'" In the parking lot, a woman pedestrian gazed in rapture at the roses inside the yawning car trunk. "Do you sell them?" she asked.

"I give 'em away."

"How can I get some?"

"Well, you got to be a patient in the hospital."

At home, he washed vases, making sure there was no sign of mildew. Then he prepared equipment for tomorrow. I asked if he worried about mortality, thinking he might tell me, "You know, I'm a little worried about what's going to happen to my roses when I'm gone. I'm sad that the people who depend on my roses won't get them anymore."

He was no sob sister, mister. When life ended, the tradition of the Rose Man would die with him. "This is expensive," he said, calculating aloud. Let's see: he spent about $15,000 a year on his roses, plus equipment and gas and his own valuable time. "Who's going to do that?" he said. "Nobody."

Mail arrived. He gave a rose to his carrier. At the kitchen table, the Rose Man's wife sorted through the day's delivery. Opal opened a letter from a South Florida stranger named Norma Attardi. Norma's aging mother had been a patient in a nursing home and had received flowers from the Rose Man. Opal read Norma's letter aloud. "My Mom passed away a couple of weeks ago. But I can only say thank you for the lovely roses you gave her and the pleasure she got from them."

"Isn't that a lovely letter?" Opal asked her husband.

"Oh, we got boxes of letters like that," he said. Then he hurried off to find some additional vases for tomorrow.

Summer 2007.

50

Boston Bill

This story is about what happened on one remarkable day in St. Petersburg—on Tuesday, February 19, 2008, to be exact. It's about a chance encounter between a couple of Dickensian characters, a crusty one-legged man who lives in the city, and a sad-eyed little boy from Orlando. The amazing coincidence of their meeting changed lives. When the broken man met the broken boy, they began a journey to become whole again.

The crusty one-legged man is Bill Hansbury, though everybody calls him Boston Bill because his roots extend to Fenway Park. Pass the lobstah, please. Boston Bill is 71. He is a hard-nosed bachelor who enjoys swearing, adult stories, and well-toned women. He ran in a dozen Boston Marathons in his younger days and in middle age became an even better cyclist. In the fall of 2007, a jog in the woods changed everything.

His right foot was hot and swollen after the run. A doctor told him he had developed a virulent staph infection commonly called MRSA. Maybe it was related to his diabetes. Maybe not. But he had two choices. Die or undergo an amputation. When he awoke in the recovery room his right leg was gone, removed just below the knee. Bill swore like the old Army guy he once had been. An old friend had vanished, one that had carried him thousands of miles in countless races on foot and on a bike.

Boston Bill became the world's grumpiest patient. He hated the crutches, the walker, even the cane. He longed to get an artificial leg and learn how to walk on it, maybe even ride a bike again. Two days after he got out of the hospital, he showed up at North Shore Pool, the gathering spot for the city's elite cyclists, with a borrowed hand-cranked recumbent. He managed 20 miles.

Once he got his new leg, Bill became even more driven. He sat in bed every night and banged the heel on the floor again and again to train the foot he didn't have to get used to sensations it couldn't feel.

"Most people can't wait to get rid of phantom pain," said Mike Rieth, who had built Bill's prosthesis at St. Petersburg Limb and Brace. "Bill embraced it." After a while Bill insisted he could feel a crack in the sidewalk under his artificial foot.

Impressed by Bill's motivation, Rieth sent him to talk to other people adjusting to their amputations. Boston Bill was the ultimate tough-love guy. One day, at a bicycle race, he noticed an elderly amputee watching from the crowd. Bill had counseled him in the hospital. The elderly man was sitting in a wheelchair, prosthetic leg nowhere in sight.

"Where's your fucking leg?" Bill asked him.

Uh.

"Next time leave your good leg home, too," Bill told him. "Look at your wife. You got her pushing your wheelchair around in this heat? When are you going to get off your ass and take care of yourself?"

Another time, Bill visited the hospital to meet Tom Papaleo, 45, who had lost a leg after an infection. "Maybe I can help you," Bill said. "But if you think this is going to be a goddamn pity party, you're looking at the wrong guy."

When Bill found out Papaleo's insurance didn't cover the cost of a prosthetic, he cajoled Reith into building one for him out of spare parts.

"I consider Boston Bill an angel," Papaleo told people. "But, you know, an angel with rusty wings."

Exit the grumpy angel. Enter the sad-eyed little boy. His name is Jake. He was born on May 11, 2000, to Jodi and Brett Bainter, who live on Lake Mary Jess, near Orlando. Brett is Florida regional director of the national wetlands conservation organization, Ducks Unlimited. Jodi works in marketing at Disney World.

Jodi was 31 at Jake's birth. He did his best to wear her out as he grew, worming across the floor to get his fingers into things. He was walking at 11 months, then running. He loved going outside with his dad to gawk at the lake. Brett, an outdoorsman, looked forward to one day introducing his child to hunting and fishing. Jake's favorite bedtime books were colorful nature guides intended for adults. He knew his fish and ducks like other little kids know their colors.

On April 9, 2004, Jake was a month shy of his fourth birthday. The Bainters are still learning to live with what happened that afternoon.

Jake and other neighborhood toddlers were riding their training bikes

Boston Bill Hansbury meets Jake Bainter for the first time. (Photo courtesy of Jodi Bainter.)

on the big driveway at the Bainter house. Jodi was working and Brett was home.

Their lot is so large Brett needs a riding mower to cut the grass. He mowed the front lawn first, then slipped behind the house. At that very instant, Jake leapt from his bike and sprinted after his daddy, too fast for the babysitter to grab him.

Brett shifted the mower into reverse to cut a patch he had missed. As he backed up, he felt a bump that wasn't supposed to be there. Turning, he saw his little boy's head protruding from under the mower. Brett stopped the engine, jumped from the mower, and like Superman yanked the heavy machine off his child. He scooped up Jake and sprinted to

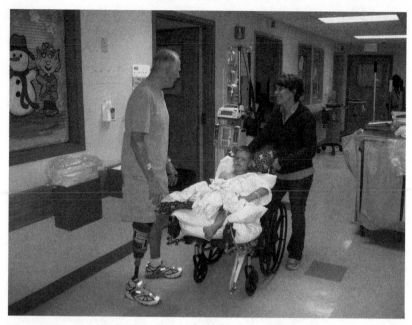

Boston Bill visits Jake and his mom after surgery at All Children's Hospital in St. Petersburg. (Photo courtesy of Jodi Bainter.)

the house next door, where his neighbor, a nurse, stanched the bleeding while they waited for the ambulance.

The small toes on Jake's right foot were gone. Half the big toe was severed. The outer half of Jake's leg, from the ankle to the thigh, had been sliced off by the whirling blade.

The phone rang at Jodi's office. Brett. Crying. "It's not your fault," Jodi said. Brett blamed himself. Couldn't be consoled.

The hospital became Jake's new home, his life now full of pain, morphine, nausea, feeding tubes, catheters, bed sores, and visits from weeping relatives.

Surgery followed surgery, in Orlando and at All Children's in St. Petersburg. Consultation followed consultation in Florida and elsewhere. Brett was so depressed he sometimes wanted to stay in bed. Jodi kept up with the insurance companies, the paperwork, and life outside the hospital.

One year went by. Two years. Jake was old enough to see the difference between him and other kids. Other children ran and jumped and skated and skied on the lake. He watched from the sidelines like Tiny

Tim. He cried, threw the occasional tantrum, sucked his thumb, begged his mom to sleep in his room.

Three years. He endured tissue and bone transplants, more pain and more morphine. He walked with difficulty but couldn't run. Would he ever? Ride a bike? Sit with his dad in a marsh, in a blind, waiting for the pintail ducks to fly in low at dawn?

In the wee hours, Jodi searched the Internet for answers. What about an amputation? Would it be wrong to even consider it? Were they giving up too soon? She and Brett talked constantly about what they should do. They consulted doctors all over the country.

Late in 2007, she and Brett reached an uneasy decision and told Jake. The little guy was braver than they were. Sleepless night followed sleepless night. Brett walked the hallway like a ghost.

On February 19, 2008, the Bainters headed for a St. Petersburg hospital in their Tahoe. At his home in St. Petersburg, Boston Bill strapped on his prosthetic leg and climbed onto his bicycle.

He was on his daily morning ride with 60 cyclists when something strange happened. The cleats on his cycling shoes felt as if they had frozen into place. Cycling shoes clip to the pedals and are supposed to uncouple when a rider pivots his feet. But as Bill prepared to stop at a traffic light on Sixth Avenue S, they didn't come loose.

He braced for a fall and aired a few choice Boston Bill words. Two cyclists quickly flanked him like slices of bread to keep him upright. Others had to pry his shoes from the pedals. He sat on the curb and tried to figure out what had gone wrong. "This is the first time that's ever happened," Bill barked at his friends.

The other cyclists continued on their way, leaving the grumpy white-haired man with his bike, his shoes, his artificial leg, and his fear of appearing helpless.

He was sitting there when a black Chevy Tahoe braked in front of him and a sad-looking man behind the wheel waved.

"Excuse me, sir," said the sad man.

"Yes," Boston Bill said.

"I notice you're a cyclist."

"Yes."

"And you're an amputee?"

"That's right."

The sad man climbed out of the station wagon. "I'm Brett Bainter," he said. "That's my wife, Jodi. We were wondering if you'd talk to our little boy. His name is Jake. We're on our way to All Children's Hospital. This afternoon they're going to amputate his leg."

Boston Bill leaned his expensive specialized racing bicycle against an oak and hugged the boy, whose right leg was bent at a crazy angle at the knee.

"Jake," Bill said as they stood together. "You're going to be fine. Look at me. I'm 70! You're going to be running and biking soon. You've got your whole life ahead of you." He kissed the little boy, 7 going on 8, on the top of his head. Jake even managed a smile. Bill beamed as Jodi snapped a photo of the two of them together.

The Bainters blinked back tears as they told Bill what had happened to Jake and the difficult decision they had made. "Listen," Boston Bill told them. "You're doing the right thing. Don't have second thoughts."

Leaving Bill alone on the street, they headed for the hospital and Jake's amputation.

Men don't cry. At least that's the way Bill grew up in a tough Irish-American family near Boston. He reads action novels featuring manly heroes. He likes Charles Bronson movies. After high school he joined the Army and after his discharge got married, had kids, sold jewelry and cosmetics, ran a flea market, did whatever it took to put food on the table. In St. Petersburg, he even started a little business selling his own Boston Bill line of sunglasses.

He talked too much sometimes, bragged a little, accepted some blame for the end of his marriage. Even good friends thought he was irascible at times—heaven help the dawdling waitress who got on his bad side. Boston Bill wasn't Ebenezer Scrooge, but nobody was going to mistake him for the kindly John Jarndyce from *Bleak House* either. But on February 19, 2008, something changed. At 8:40 a.m., near the traffic light on Third Street S, a new feeling washed over him. There was something about the Bainters that got to him. There was something about how he had met them—that chance encounter—that gave him chills.

What if the Bainters had left earlier that morning? Or even two minutes later? "They would have missed me. And—this is the big one—what if my cycling shoes had worked? More than likely I would have zipped around the corner and been long gone when those heartbroken people drove past."

Bill meets Jake and Jodi once more. (Photo by Maurice Rivenbark.)

Bill climbed on his bike and went on with his ride. His pedals and shoes worked perfectly. They hadn't failed before that day and they haven't failed since.

They cut Jake's leg off that afternoon below the knee. They pumped him with painkillers. Boston Bill showed up the next day. Jodi took another photo of Jake and Bill together. Bill said he would stay in touch.

And he did. Not every day. But he seemed to telephone when the Bainters needed him most. He called after they brought Jake home to Orlando from the hospital and the morphine wore off and the phantom pains began and Jake bolted upright in his bed and started bawling. The little boy couldn't always explain what he was going through, but Bill could, and after a talk the Bainters always felt better.

As months passed, Bill enjoyed hearing about Jake's progress. "Can he ride a bike yet? No? Well, maybe one day? He's running? You ought to join the Challenged Athletes Foundation. I'm a member. It'll be good for Jake. You know, they have races."

The Bainters joined. Jake competed. He didn't run, but he walked a race. "Jake has inspired me," Bill told Jodi over the phone. Bill bought himself a special running prosthesis and started jogging again. He dreamed of running the Boston Marathon.

The cynical lapsed Catholic who preferred the bike saddle to the church pew now believed in miracles. "There are all kinds, you know. It's not like one day you have cancer and the next day you don't. Sometimes there are smaller ones. You have to pay attention to your own life and recognize the miracle when it shows up."

On a spring day in 2009 Bill drove to Orlando to see his young pal, Jake Bainter.

First Jodi took Bill to Pine Castle Christian Academy, where Jake is a second grader and the only amputee in the elementary-through-high school. "How many of you have heard us talk about Boston Bill?" Jodi asked, and every second-grader waved frantically. Bill used his special running prosthesis as the show-and-tell. Bill avoided swearing in front of the children and for a moment his rusty wings turned golden.

Then Bill went to Jake's house. Jake showed Bill his cool room. He showed Bill his guinea pig, Tweek, and his leopard gecko lizard, Lo. "We have our little boy back," Jodi whispered from the doorway. "That artificial leg is hardly a blip in Jake's life."

Brett's depression had lifted. He and his little boy do a lot of fishing together in their backyard lake now. One day they'll go duck hunting. "I can catch all the bass I want, but today I'm going after gar," Jake explained to Bill. "Sometimes I catch great big mudfish. They put a bend in your rod because they're big. You can ask my mom."

Bill took Jake's word for it. Jake dressed in his play clothes and replaced the school shoe on his prosthesis with a rubber foot. He flew out of the house toward Lake Mary Jess with his leg click-clacking like train wheels on rusty track. "He has worn out his leg," Jodi said. Jake will receive a new one soon. Perhaps it will have a super-strong knee for running and jumping.

"Watch this!"

Jake wanted to show Bill how fast he can run now. He was going to run across the yard to the palm tree by the fence, then to the oak, then back to Bill. Jake took off and ran very fast, his artificial leg click-clacking like the little engine that could.

"Way to go, Jake," Boston Bill said. "Way to go."

Summer 2009.

51

Airboat Hero

This is about the night a jumbo jet landed among the pig frogs and alligators, the cottonmouth snakes and yellow-crowned night herons, in the Everglades. Robert L. Marquis—"Bud" to friends—wanted to eat frog legs. He was out there gigging frogs when it happened.

A yellow flash. Boom. Blackness. Silence.

It was closing in on midnight on December 29, 1972. Speeding across the 'glades in his airboat, Bud was the first rescuer on the scene. He saw tangled metal and smelled aviation fuel. He saw mangled bodies and heard the pitiful moans of the dying.

He rescued some terrified folks—he doesn't know how many—before the regular cavalry of official rescuers arrived in helicopters, directed to the carnage by his head lamp. He carried survivors to safety and made them as comfortable as he could.

Then he was pretty much forgotten.

Old and sick, he was living in near poverty on the edge of the Everglades when I looked him up. I had seen his name on a Web site about the anniversary of the tragedy that killed more than 100 passengers and traumatized dozens more. Folks from South Florida's sporting community, mostly hunters, fishers, and airboaters, had heard, many for the first time, about Bud's heroics on the black night. "He's one of us," John Canti, a firefighter, paramedic, and outdoorsman told me. "He's an airboater."

Canti and others began to make pilgrimages to Bud's screened door to hear his story. The ultimate "yes sir, no sir" man, Bud shuffled reluctantly onto the porch, blinking furiously in the sunlight, wondering what was up. He wasn't looking for attention.

"Nobody paid him to go out there and try to rescue people," said Ken Pine, who had fixed Bud's roof during a visit. "He was just a guy out there frogging and minding his own business who knew he had to help people in trouble. In my mind, that makes him a real hero."

Pine told me he wanted to do something nice for Bud, perhaps honor him with a special day, raise cash for Bud's taxes, groceries, and medical bills. Bud? He said he'd be happy if he could go out into the 'glades one more time in his airboat and harvest a mess of frog legs.

We talked on his porch. He told me what he would do if he could be young again. He'd launch his airboat at the Miccosukee Indian Reservation on the Tamiami Trail and race north into the river of grass. On a moonless night, in the beam of his head lamp, the frog eyes would glow like rubies. He'd cruise up on the frog, spear the frog with the 3-pronged gig, knock the frog off the gig into a sack, all the while moving forward in the airboat while getting ready to gig another frog. Mama, heat up the frying pan. We're having legs tonight.

Even at 78, Marquis was an old-fashioned country boy. Born in Arkansas, he had grown up in South Florida when everybody seemed to be poor. His fishing and hunting skills helped put supper on the family table. He liked remembering about those days. He also liked not remembering those days. In his mind, he was still a strapping young fellow with big muscles. The bent, white-haired man he saw in the mirror had a bad heart and breathed from an oxygen machine, hadn't been frogging in a coon's age, and hadn't been in his airboat since, well, he couldn't remember. "It's broken," he told me. "Just like me."

At least he lived near his precious Everglades. At night, when he sat on the porch, he could hear the wup-wup bellows of the pig frogs and the heh-heh-heh chatter of the leopard frogs. Of course, hearing them from the porch wasn't the same as being in the middle of them armed with a gig, taking a long breath of Everglades air, feeling utterly alive.

Back in the day, when he spent so much time in the wilderness, only the airplanes overhead reminded him of civilization. He'd see the lights and hear the roar as the jets climbed into the black night over the swamp or descended toward Miami International Airport.

He wasn't a talker to begin with, unless it was about boats or engines or the 'glades. He had never taken any pleasure in talking about what he saw after Eastern Air Lines Flight 401 went down and how he felt about it. His wife Nancy—they married when she was 15—could always tell when it was on his mind, though. He'd get that look.

Bud Marquis and the rescue airboat.

Before a bad back forced an early retirement, Bud laid carpet, grew avocados, and worked as a game warden in the Everglades. A friend once warned him: "One day you'll work a plane crash out there." His friend, of course, envisioned a Piper Cub or something small going down in a summer thunderstorm, not a state-of-the-art L-1011 carrying 200 passengers on a perfect winter night.

Bud spent his time arresting grizzled gator poachers and rough-cob deer thieves, cane-polers with too many bream on their stringers, and feral teenage boys selling protected Indigo snakes to pet stores.

Sometimes, back when there were no cell phones or GPS electronics to help navigate, he'd get lost at night. He'd stay calm, look at the stars for direction, think things through, then crank up the airboat engine and find his way back to the Tamiami Trail.

At home, waiting sometimes fearfully, was Nancy, a pretty barefoot country girl in a cotton dress. "You didn't have nothing to worry about," he'd tell her, finding a seat on the porch, from where he could hear the barred owls and their singular "who-cooks-for-you" calls, exciting and mournful at once.

Eastern Air Lines Flight 401 traveled from New York to Miami. The jet, a new "Whisperliner," could transport 229 passengers. On December 29, 1972, it carried 178, including crew.

It promised to be an exciting week in Miami, especially for people who had bucks for a meal at Joe's Stone Crabs and a night at the Fontaine-bleau Hotel, where the sexy dancer Ann-Margret was headlining. Rowdy fans of Notre Dame and University of Nebraska, scheduled to play on New Year's Day at the Orange Bowl, were poised to take over the town.

Bud no longer worked as a game warden—his day job was laying carpet. After dark he moonlighted as a commercial frogger. He had promised to show a slight acquaintance, Ray Dickinson, how to gig frogs.

Flight 401 left John F. Kennedy at 9:20 p.m. The trip to Florida, by official accounts, was pleasantly routine. "Welcome to Miami," the pilot announced during the descent at 11:30.

Altitude 900 feet.

Something was wrong with the landing gear or the landing-gear light on the control panel. Anyway, the pilots couldn't tell if the wheels were down. At 11:32, they aborted the landing, climbed to 2,000 feet and swung west over the Everglades to work out the problem.

They turned on the autopilot. At least they thought they had. The jet actually began losing altitude, so gradually that no one noticed until the very end. Nobody, not the pilots nor passengers, knew anything was amiss. A glance out a window, after all, would have shown nothing but the black Everglades below.

"Hey, what's happening here?" the pilot asked at the last second. That was the last transmission before the left wing sliced into the Everglades at 225 mph. The jet bounced once, then hit again. Survivors described a flash or spark that exploded through the cabin as the jet ripped apart.

Bud Marquis had experienced better nights of frogging. But he and his helper had 30 pounds of legs.

"Then," Bud told me, "I saw this great big fireball and the whole 'glades lit up. Then zip, the light was out."

Bud revved up the engine and headed northwest. That section of the Everglades is a tangle of sawgrass, tree islands, canals, and levees. Fortunately, Bud was an expert. With the engine dangerously wide open—the boat slipped over the grass at 35 mph—he maneuvered around all obstacles.

Then wham! Aground. When he stopped the engine to push the boat back into the water, he heard a chorus of terrified human voices, hollering, moaning, shrieking.

He cranked up the engine and moved cautiously toward the sound. He shut down the engine again to listen. "Hey! Hey! Hey!" yelled someone who had seen his frogging light.

In the narrow beam of his head lamp he now saw enormous strips of torn metal. He saw openings in the sawgrass created by sliding chunks of broken airplane. He saw a man standing, shocked, in knee-deep water.

"He was naked. A lot of the people I saw were naked. I guess their clothes got blown off them." Bud helped the man into the airboat and poured him coffee from the thermos.

"Help us!"

Three women on the jetliner's tail, about 20 feet above the water, begged Bud to save them. "Ladies, you're safe up there. You don't want to be in the water with me."

Water saturated by jet fuel was already filling his boots and burning his legs. He felt helpless, hearing what sounded like hundreds of voices coming at him from different directions. He had lost contact with his frogging helper, Ray, too. Forgotten about him, actually. They didn't find each other until morning. They never met again, never talked again, and never will: Ray died years ago in Arcadia.

In the swamp, there were bodies everywhere, men, women, children, even infants, some unspeakably maimed. Bud saw bodies strapped into seats upside down in the water. If he saw legs kicking, he turned the seat over.

He saw a man, sitting in the water with a neck injury, trying to remain upright. "When I tried to prop him up it felt like every bone in his body was broken."

After about an hour, he saw the first helicopter. It seemed to be miles off course. Bud waved his light until the helicopter took notice. When the Coast Guard helicopter attempted a landing, the prop wash threw hunks of debris dangerously around. Bud waved the helicopter toward a nearby levee. That's where the helicopters, one after another, landed that night, and where ambulances arrived to load the dead and injured.

Officially, 103 passengers and crew died. Seventy-five miraculously survived. Bud's heroics were featured prominently a few days later in the *Miami Herald*. He was mentioned in a book, *The Crash of Flight 401*, later made into a B movie, and helped a Hollywood writer with the awful *Ghosts of Flight 401*, about commercial jets haunted by the dead pilots.

Several survivors tracked him down to thank him personally after leaving the hospital. One gave him money. He can't remember anyone's name now.

In 1985, his years as a manual laborer caught up with him. Carpet layers need strong backs. His required surgery. The government considered him totally disabled.

In 1992, Hurricane Andrew blew the roof of the house across the street through his front windows. The other house is gone; his still requires repairs.

"It's 100 degrees in the house today, honey," Nancy said, joining her husband on the porch. Only their bedroom had an air conditioner.

Bud asked his wife to look for his scrapbooks. After five minutes she returned with a musty volume that smelled like a lion's den. Bud and Nancy owned 27 domestic cats, including 15 that lived indoors on sofas, tables, and bookshelves.

Flipping through the pages, Bud smiled for the first time. He was looking at the photo of the primitive camp he had built in the cypress trees so many years ago when he was young and strong and could hunt and gig frogs and look at the stars. "I'd like to go there now," he said.

"Remember what the doctor said," Nancy chimed in. His doctor had warned him not to travel alone, not with his weak heart and lungs and aching back.

Clutching his walking stick, Bud led me past a mango tree into the backyard. The old airboat, the airboat in which he carried injured passengers, waited on a rusty trailer with flat tires. The airboat was 12 feet long and 7 feet across. It had a flat bottom and a high seat and a cobweb-draped engine and propeller. "I could get it running," he said, fighting for breath. "It needs new points and plugs, maybe a new set of rings. It wouldn't take much."

A Web forum, Southern Airboat, which attracts thousands of worldwide participants, planned to take care of the repairs. Organization members also planned to honor Bud and the victims and survivors of Eastern Flight 401 with a service and a barbecue in Miami. Afterward, folks hoped to take the old man into the Everglades, in his own airboat, if he wanted. Bud wanted to. He wanted to show them how to gig frogs.

"You have to keep your eye on the frogs real good when that airboat is moving—I mean not take your eyes away—and be quick with the gig," he told them, in what amounts to the Gettysburg Address for him.

"I think I can still do it. I really do think I can gig some frogs if I had to."

Summer 2007.

52

Alligator Trapper

This is how Julie Harter kept her fragile life together. This is how she coped with her terrifying grief about her late husband, Billy. She caught dragons.

She pinned up her long auburn hair, backed the truck to the trailer, and hit the interstate. She checked her cell phone messages, muttered to herself about the work ahead, and aimed her Ford F-250 four-wheel diesel past the Walmarts and Starbucks of the twenty-first century. She drove through subdivisions where winding streets are named after herons, all the while keeping her eyes on the ponds and the lakes where the dragons dwelled.

"Hello, ma'am," she said to the young mother, child in arms, who answered her knock in West Tampa. "I'm the state alligator trapper for Hillsborough County. I hear you're having a problem. Can I go in your backyard and take a look?"

Every alligator trapper I had known until that day had been a macho man with a baritone voice or missing fingers. Gold bracelets flashing, Florida's only female alligator trapper sounded like Loretta Lynn. "Sweetie, I'm going to get you your gator," Julie told folks who had discovered that Florida, deep down, is Jurassic Park.

Feisty from spring weather, hungry and hormonal, the dragons had been rambunctious all over the state that year. In my county, Pinellas, near St. Petersburg, a different trapper had captured one that had wandered into a suburban kitchen. Julie, a 46-year-old grandmother, had nabbed another gator suspected of biting a ball retriever on a Tampa golf course. She hauled the 8-footer to a Dade City processing plant, fired a bullet into its brain, sold it, and was paid $40 a foot for the hide.

"The dude who got bit on the golf course, he's still telling people I got the wrong gator, that it had to be much bigger than it was," she told me. "I ain't saying he's wrong. But I have to stick up for myself and say that I

Julie Harter, gator trapper, with a big one.

got the one that was in that pond. Sugar, I'm going to tell you something. A lot of men, they can't stand that it's a little old girl who is catching gators."

Even Billy was like that sometimes. Overly macho. He was a handsome country boy; she was a pretty farmer's daughter who knew how to turn a boy's head. She had married for the first time at 18. The marriage went kaput. She was lonely and wanted her kids to have a dad, so she married again, and then again. Strike three.

Along the way she graduated from the University of South Florida with a teaching degree and got a job working with mentally and physically challenged high school kids. She still spent half her day at Lakeland Gibson High, trying to persuade kids not to quit.

She encountered Billy Harter at a rodeo in 1994. He was handsome, a few years older, nice but wild. A month later they were married. He operated heavy equipment at the Tampa shipyard. On the side, he caught Tampa's bad boy alligators. One time he and a tow truck hauled a 13-foot, 11 5/8-inch dragon from a construction pit after it charged out of a canal after a worker. The photo of that gator still shows up on the Internet as an 18 1/2-footer allegedly caught in Orlando. "Ain't so," Julie told me. "I know the girl who has the stuffed head in her living room. Me."

Eventually she learned how to catch dragons, too. She remembered the time Billy sent her out to scout an alligator-infested pond in a Tampa Bay backyard. She didn't scout. She caught. "He 'bout had a cow that I was messing with gators," she said. Another time, when Billy was indisposed, she answered an emergency call. While she stalked her prey, the woman who owned the home stepped into the yard to watch. "She was a pretty girl in a little cotton night dress," Julie told me. "She bent down to pick up her dog and she wasn't wearing panties. Boy, did I give it to Billy. 'No wonder you love this job!'"

Billy, who had never been seriously injured by an alligator, taught her caution. She has been hurt only once, when a sheriff's deputy, worried that a woman could not handle an alligator alone, tried to help. "Dude," she told the lawman. "You do your job and I'll do mine." He panicked and released the catch pole when the alligator started thrashing on the bank, as they usually do when pulled from the water. The catch pole—it has a loop of cable on the end—gashed Harter's hand.

That pain was nothing compared to what she felt for Billy. Grief is one terrible dragon, more terrible than the ones she was supposed to catch in Tampa yards. She hoped one day she could slay the worst dragon of all.

Billy wasn't tall, but he was powerful, with enormous hands. Yet he had a soft side. One time he brought home a frightened beagle puppy that needed a bath. Some men might have dunked the little fellow and been done with it. Not Billy. He got naked and joined the new family pet in the tub. Sometimes, when Julie chaperoned at the prom, Billy would gussy up and be her date, wearing his cowboy hat and string tie. "He was the love of my life," Julie said, weeping in her truck one day. "He was more involved with my two children than their real dad ever was. Billy and Julie. We were like peanut butter and jelly."

Like at least some men, alligators are primitive animals with brains about the size of a walnut. Nobody knows completely what makes them tick. When they get a mind to go somewhere, or to do something peculiar, they'll do it, even if they have to knock down a screen or climb a wall.

In a recent year, 40 licensed state trappers killed 11,000 alligators, mostly in suburbs that once was wilderness. Julie harvested 392. In a perfect world, those gators would have been relocated, unharmed, to a place where alligators are scarce. That Florida no longer exists. "We have a saying around here," Lindsey Hord, the state's nuisance alligator coordinator, once told me. "Any body of freshwater that does not have

Julie and friends haul a huge gator from a Tampa pond.

an alligator will have one soon. For your safety, just assume there's an alligator."

Hunting, legal and illegal, had put *Alligator mississippiensis* on the protected list in 1970. In the twenty-first century more than a million gators shared habitat with 18 million human guests who never thought they'd be on the menu. The state had started keeping track of alligator attacks in 1949; the first fatality didn't happen until 1973. Now fatalities were almost an annual occurrence. Alligators killed three people in 2006. In 2007, there had been one fatality but 17 other attacks.

No wonder people got hurt. Many lacked any idea of what they were dealing with.

"No sir, that's not an alligator," Julie told a guy alarmed by the backyard racket coming from the weeds. "Those are pig frogs." She told a woman, "Ma'am, stop feeding alligators Oreos and they won't come up on your lawn."

Some folks, of course, weren't crying wolf.

"I heard a knock on the door," a man explained over the phone. "I looked out the peephole, but there was nothing out there. I heard the knock again, looked out the peephole, nothing there. So I opened the door . . ."

Julie caught the alligator that had been lounging on his front porch. She caught one in a screened-in swimming pool. She got one that climbed a 4-foot wall and ended up in a rich man's fountain. She hauled one out from under a Nissan at an apartment complex when I was with her one afternoon. "The Crocodile Hunter is a girl!" yelled someone in the crowd.

She had become something of a celebrity in Tampa, her exploits often landing her on the news. "If you're taking a picture," she sometimes advised photographers, "no butt shots." A solidly built woman, Julie had striking blue eyes and a nurturing personality. Sometimes, after she caught a menacing alligator, the grateful homeowner who had just been called "Sugar" developed a crush.

"Yes. Nice to hear from you," I heard her tell someone who had tracked down her cell number. "I'm actually on an emergency call right now and can't talk."

She hung up. "Never catch an alligator for a lesbian," she said.

After Billy's death, friends set her up with a number of interesting dating prospects. "They're men who want to be taken care of," she told me one night. "I don't feel nothing when I'm with them. I'm sorry, but I don't." After one dating disaster, she drove to Lakeland's Socrum Cemetery where Billy is buried, sobbed, and swore at him for leaving her. "Look what you done to me," she told him.

He loved fast cars almost as much as he loved catching alligators. Eventually he joined the Goodson Farms Racing Team. Comfortable with tools, he had befriended the team's owner, a strawberry farmer named Donn Goodson. They were always cutting up together and enjoyed the same boyish jokes.

On October 21, 2003, Billy drove to Goodson's estate and farm in Balm. Goodson planned to give helicopter tours to some visitors; he recruited Billy to shoot video. Goodson, with a passenger at his side, flew in low while Billy stood on the ground, shooting video. Billy's camera captured the tragedy. The helicopter hit him, then crashed into a nearby building. Billy, 46, died instantly, Goodson a few days later.

Goodson, it turned out, lacked a valid pilot's license. A National Transportation Safety Board report blamed the accident on the "pilot's intentional buzzing and his failure to maintain altitude/clearance which resulted in an in-flight collision with a building."

Julie seldom got out of bed for the next four months. She barely ate.

The moment of truth.

One day, someone from the state telephoned and asked if she wanted Billy's old job. She said yes. In a way, Billy could live through her. But first she got rid of his old gator truck. When she got behind the wheel, she could smell his aftershave.

In Carrollwood, a prosperous Tampa suburb, Helena Martensen stood in her patio and looked at her pond. The length of a football field, it happened to be home to three alligators. Martensen told her 7-year-old son, Brenden, "You can't play in the backyard." Yet Martensen loved Florida and alligators. She had won awards from the city for her ideas about saving water. "We just have to weigh common sense with conservation," she confided to her husband. "That gator scares me."

"That" gator was a dragon, twice the size of the others. Julie saw it and tried to coax it to eat an odoriferous beef lung, in which she had hidden a baited hook. Suspicious, the monstrous gator sank under the water.

After a while Julie set out a line and staked it to a pole. "Call me if something happens," she told the homeowner. Martensen called the next morning. "You got one. I don't know which one."

Julie was at her job at school. But when classes were over, she jumped in her truck and drove toward Tampa. Within an hour she was standing in a backyard on Breland Street, among those expensive homes in Florida's Jurassic Park.

The line she had set the day before, a 1,000-pound-test parachute cord, was taut as a piano string and angled deep into the black water. Julie gave it a yank and felt resistance. Next she used her back and shoulder to pull hard.

She started hauling with all her might. Out in the pond, a hundred feet from shore, the dragon thrashed to the surface. He submerged, water exploding like when Godzilla marched out of Tokyo Bay in the old movie. The line hissed through Julie's hand. She played the beast like Hemingway's marlin, tried to tire him out before landing him.

After about five minutes his head popped out next to the shore. A huge, scary head. All of us who were watching instinctively stepped back. Julie inched forward with a long pole and poked a dart into its massive jaw. Attached to the dart was a stout rope. She had him.

Her strapping 28-year-old son, Lee, had come along to help. Foot by foot they began dragging the dragon onto the lawn. Inches away from her hands, it hissed and popped its jaws.

Julie walked behind him, then came forward and sat on his back, the way Billy had taught her. The annoyed dragon hissed a deep hiss from a primeval nightmare. Reaching forward, she leaned against the top of his closed jaws with everything she had. The muscles that open an alligator's jaws are weak. He couldn't open against her weight.

What happened next was hard to watch. She managed to clamp her small, bare right hand around the tip of the huge jaws, holding them closed. If the dragon were to escape her grasp, it occurred to me, it might use its chomping power—2,000 pounds per square inch—to crush her hand to jelly.

With her free hand she encircled the jaws with layers of black electrician's tape. Finally she reached behind her and hog-tied the legs. "I hate it when one of those slippery bastards tries to run away from me," she said, breaking the tension.

Finis. Except for one thing. Tape measure.

Eleven feet, 6 inches. About 500 pounds.

If Billy Harter was out there, he had to be proud of his gator girl, the dragon slayer.

Spring 2008.

Scallop Shucker

Snorkelers who harvest scallops in northwest Florida regarded the tired eyes of Miss Beverlyn Hanson as beautiful jewels. Her summer weariness meant she was awake and ready for honest toil. She was an institution in her Gulf of Mexico fishing town of 1,500. Without her, things fell apart. Miss Beverlyn, which is what everyone called her, was the queen of the scallop shuckers.

Her clients during summer brought her bay scallops by the hundreds, if not the thousands, every day during the state's scallop season. She stayed up all night, if she had to, and the next night if necessary, and sometimes the night after that, to clean their scallops.

In Florida, there must not be a more onerous job. Scallop shucking involves prying open a stubborn palm-sized shell with a special knife, yanking away the slimy guts and then slicing the thumb-sized dollop of edible muscle away from the shell—all in one quick motion. To under-stand the nature of the work, multiply the previous sentence by 1,500 or even 5,000. That was a day in the life of Miss Beverlyn, though I should mention the mosquitoes and the sand gnats that bite constantly as she labors. "If you swat 'em," she once told me, "you get scallop guts all over your face."

Miss Beverlyn might have been baggy-eyed, gut-smeared, and bug-bitten, but she was used to it. During scallop season, which lasts 10 weeks in Florida, her pay worked out to about $50 an hour. In return a customer received about 8 pounds of scallop meat. Eager to remain in her good graces, her clients often brought spaghetti and meatballs, fried mullet, and angel food cake along with their cold cash.

"There are a lot of folks around Steinhatchee who will clean scallops for you," fishing boat captain Jim Henley once told me, "and then there's Miss Beverlyn. She's the best there is. She's been cleaning scallops since Jesus was a child."

For the record, Miss Beverlyn did not count the fisher of men as a peer. Although she was 65 that summer, she had been wielding her scallop knife for a mere three decades in Steinhatchee. On the Fourth of July weekend, when her town was bustling with scallop-laden tourists, heavy ice chests lined her driveway, 100 deep. For 48 hours she shucked scallops between catnaps. When Labor Day approached—her busiest weekend of the year—sleep was like money in the bank.

"Well, I'll tell you," she said, "sometimes I'm so overtired I can't sleep at night. A day or so ago I took an afternoon off and went to Lake City to go to the movies with kin. In the middle of *G-Force* I nodded off."

Miss Beverlyn, who has a thick bun of gray hair, rough hands, and dark, penetrating eyes, was an old-fashioned country gal. Born in North Florida among the oaks and lakes, she learned to hunt and fish from a dad who "taught us kids how to survive under any condition."

Once in a while, her daddy had a hankering to eat saltwater fish and drove with his little girl to Steinhatchee. They'd catch snapper and sea bass and pick up scallops. He taught her how to fillet a fish and how to shuck a bay scallop. A career was born.

Bay scallops, many old-timers have always insisted, are Florida's most delicious gift. They're pink, delicate, and sweet. They are much smaller and tastier than the larger and coarser sea scallops sold at restaurants. When sautéed in butter and garlic, a bay scallop is a melt-in-your-mouth food for the gods.

Bay scallops nearly vanished because of development, foul water, and commercial fishing. But regulation and pollution laws slowly have brought them back, in at least a few places in northwest Florida. Unlike oysters and clams, duller mollusk cousins that rest passively like bumps on the bottom, scallops give a snorkeler a run for his or her money. A bay scallop lies in the shallow-water turtle grass, shell partly open, 30 electric-blue eyes scanning the surroundings for predators, which in Steinhatchee's Deadman Bay included human hands. Bang! Scallop sees you sneaking up and slams shut. Expelling water through its hinge, scallop jets away from harm.

If catching a scallop is challenging fun, cleaning one is slow torture. "All you got to do is clean scallops one time in your life," declared Jim Henley, the garrulous fishing guide. "That's enough for most of us. Then you find yourself a nice lady who has the patience and skill that a man doesn't have and pay her anything she wants."

In the twenty-first century, Steinhatchee's dozen or so scallop shuckers usually were women who set up come-hither cardboard signs all over town. When it rained, the handwritten cardboard signs fell apart. After the downpour, new signs went up. "This is our time of year we can make real money," Susie Grant, who shucks scallops at the River Haven Marina, told me. Grant, 46, cleaned motel rooms in the morning, then headed for the dock in the afternoon to shuck scallops.

Over at Miss Beverlyn's yard on Ninth Street, the heavy action often began about dusk when scallopers showed up in force with buckets and coolers, money and kind words. "I'll do my best," she told one.

"You're an angel," replied the scalloper, who knew what was good for him.

One afternoon Miss Beverlyn sat under a canopy on a just-the-right-height stool next to buckets of scallops, fresh water, empty shells, guts, and just-shucked meat on ice. Sometimes her adult son and daughter helped, and sometimes neighborhood boys lent a hand, but often Miss Beverlyn worked alone, admired by her son's pit bull, Malachi, who looked mean but wasn't.

Sometimes a fisherman, waiting for her to finish shucking his scallops, felt the need to converse. Miss Beverlyn didn't mind listening but never replied. Professional scallop shucking is unsociable work, for the most part, requiring Zen-like concentration.

"I try not to think about what I'm doing," Miss Beverlyn told me one evening during a break. "Like, I don't think about how many scallops I have already done or how many thousands are waiting for me because it will overwhelm me. While I shuck scallops I put myself into a dream state. I transport myself into my garden, where I'm working on my beans and my tomatoes and my okra. Or I'm thinking about my bird feeders and my birdhouses. In my mind I'm getting ready for when the purple martins come in the spring. Or I'm filling my hummingbird feeders with sweet water. Honey, we got a lot of hummingbirds in these parts."

Break over. At dark she switched on a bright light inside the canopy, and moths bounced off the walls like dodge-'em cars. She tugged rubber gloves over majestic hands scarred and gouged but still capable and picked up her knife.

Inside the house her second husband, Donald, 76, watched television in peace; a retired carpenter, he studiously avoided anything having to do with scalloping. Miss Beverlyn, a factory unto herself, forged ahead as she did every day and every night. She poured scallop meat into a Ziploc bag and deposited the bag immediately on ice in a cooler on which she had written a customer's name. Then she began again, her knife clinking against shell like a gold coin on a front tooth.

"I'm a tough old biddy," she told me, "but sometimes on Monday morning I swear I'm so sleepy I can't remember my name."

Summer 2010.

54

Tommy Ward

Tommy Ward stood on his dock and looked out at the green water. He took off his ball cap and ran a huge hand through thinning red hair. He was thinking about oysters. They're fat right now. They're plentiful right now. But business wasn't as good as it should be. The oil had never quite reached Apalachicola Bay the spring before. But some oystermen, who took money from BP to look for the oil that never arrived, stopped fishing anyway.

Seafood businesses such as the one he operated no longer could supply their customers with oysters. Like scows that had lost their anchors, old clients drifted away. "So now we're starting over," Ward told me. "We're going to be smaller. It ain't easy." From the dock he peered across the bay and saw oyster skiffs bobbing on the waves. He watched the oystermen lean over the water and pick up oysters with long wooden tongs. "So we're getting oysters now," Tommy said. "It's pretty good for oysters right now. But listen. It's a hard business. I'm telling you, it's real hard."

Commercial fishers are superstitious souls. When something good happens they automatically want to knock on wood. They are always waiting for the other rubber boot to drop. Luck is too much like the tide, here today and gone tomorrow. Like most commercial fishermen, Tommy Ward knew about hard times. He knew about death and disaster and finding a reason to believe.

He was 50. With his brother Dakie, he ran the business his daddy started more than half a century ago, Buddy Ward and Sons 13 Mile Seafood and Trucking Company. In northwest Florida's Franklin County, population 11,000, Buddy Ward's name was probably better known than the governor's. More than 1,000 residents had oyster licenses. Apalachicola oysters were justly famous all over the world.

Both Ward boys grew up on a salt marsh where Daddy built an oyster processing plant exactly 13 miles from Apalachicola. The Wards have had to repair or replace the building a half dozen times following tropical weather. At present, it was a small white and green structure with a tin roof and guarded by Rufus, a stray pit bull who apparently had never missed a meal.

As boys the Ward brothers found Indian arrowheads in the marsh, jumped rattlesnakes in the palmettos, and played hide-and-go-seek in the slash pines across County Road 30C. Mostly they worked. Their daddy believed that idle hands bred weak boys and that weak boys became weak men.

Buddy's boys swept and hosed, fished and shucked oysters, woke up early and went to bed late. When Tommy got his driver's license, he hauled shrimp in a semi from Daddy's business to customers at night. This was after putting in a full day's work at the oyster processing plant. His daddy once fired him for oversleeping.

A tough old cob, Buddy stood 6 feet 4 and was famous for his powerful handshake and the piercing way he looked people in the eye. Customers who paid for 60 pounds of oysters never needed to double-check the scale. If Buddy said a bag weighed 60 pounds, you could take it as gospel. "Buddy was all about hard work," Martha Pearl Ward, his wife, told me once. They had met at a beach cookout when she was a teen and married before they turned 20. They had five strapping sons.

Tommy was the biggest. The fish scale at the market once recorded his weight at more than 300 pounds, though he's down to a relatively svelte 265 now. Like his daddy before him, he is also 6 feet 4. Even with a bad shoulder he can swing a 60-pound oyster sack onto the dock as if it were a feather pillow.

"You done good today," he told an oysterman named Ricky Long, who had tied his skiff to the dock. Long was 52, though he looked older after spending four decades doing backbreaking work under a broiling sun. "It's a hard way to make a living," Long said.

Oystermen were getting anywhere from $10 to $20 for a 60-pound bag of oysters. A good day might add up to a dozen bags. Of course, most fishers remained in port during bad weather unless they were desperate for money, which often they were. Every year someone who tempted fate got zapped by lightning or drowned in a squall.

Most oystermen build their own skiffs, buy their own gas, and provide their own food. Some lose their teeth. Many smoke or chew and eat badly. Few have medical insurance. Some are functionally illiterate.

Tommy Ward. (Photo by Maurice Rivenbark.)

Like old-time cowboys, they're mostly self-employed, free to come and go and live on the edge of poverty. In Apalachicola, some families have harvested oysters going back to the Civil War. "The thing of it is, it's a free life," Long told me after flinging another bag on a scale. "You're your own boss. You don't have to answer to nobody." If he doesn't work, he doesn't get paid. If he wants tomorrow off, he takes tomorrow off.

For some oystermen, the oil spill in 2010 turned into a bonanza when BP began putting checks, some as big as $5,000, into their calloused palms. Some earned their money by looking for oil in the Gulf on BP's behalf. Others towed oil-stopping booms into vulnerable spots up and down the coast. Some banked the money, some spent it on booze, some bought clothes for their children, and some frittered their cash away on big-screen televisions and WaveRunners.

"It was hard to watch," said Lynn Martina, Tommy's friend and owner of a seafood business down the coast. "We had plenty of oysters to harvest, but we didn't have enough men to harvest them. It was brutal."

Martina's oystermen were mostly working again. But not Tommy Ward's. He no longer bought from oystermen who had left him dangling last summer. "I'm only buying from the men who never stopped fishing," he told me. "I believe in loyalty."

He remembered the oil spill year as one of the worst of his life. Not the worst—a death haunted him still—but plenty bad. Sometimes he broke down and wept with frustration. Some nights, as he tossed and turned, he wondered if he was going to have to close his daddy's business.

Then the experts figured out how to shut down the leaking well.

Tommy almost never took a real vacation. For fun, he sailed the family trawler, *Buddy's Boys*, into the Gulf of Mexico. He relaxed by netting shrimp for the market and thinking about his big brother, Olan, who was the best fisherman in the family. In 1978, Olan died in Apalachicola Bay of exposure after his boat went down in a winter storm. Olan was 23 and left behind a wife and three kids. Tommy sometimes told people, "I wish Olan was here so we could talk over things."

He also wished he could talk to his daddy. They sometimes rubbed each other wrong but loved each other in a rough country way. In 1986, Buddy developed a sore throat that turned out to be cancer.

Between treatments, he was known to sneak Lucky Strikes under the trees outside the hospital. It's the only time anyone can remember him acting in the slightest way dishonest. When Martha Pearl found out about the cigarettes, she wanted to take a switch to him.

But the sick old man fooled them all. He lived another two decades, saw grandchildren come into the world, ate a gazillion oysters, and watched the 2005 hurricane, Dennis, blow away his seafood business for the umpteenth time.

He died nine months later. Apalachicola threw what was considered the biggest funeral in the history of the town in his honor.

His boys rebuilt after the hurricane.

I watched a black snake cross the road near a sign that warned motorists about black bears. Pelicans flew over a tin roof, and laughing gulls pecked at a pile of discarded oyster shells. An old man in overalls carried a flat of plum-sized strawberries into Tommy Ward's office. "Mister Cliff," Tommy said to white-haired Clifford Sanborn, "what do I owe you? They look great."

"Nuthin,'" grunted Mister Cliff. "They ain't worth a damn. Too much rain lately. But I hope you like 'em." Mister Cliff was famous for always being disappointed with the year's eye-popping crop. He always shared his delicious bounty with Tommy.

Folks liked Buddy Ward's boy. Tommy did good things for the community. When the town needed something, Tommy drove to Tallahassee

Tommy Ward still operates his late father's seafood business.

and asked the legislators for help. When someone died, he attended the funeral. When folks up the Apalachicola River dumped sewage that can ruin the oyster beds in Apalachicola Bay, Tommy spoke up. "I know it ain't an easy issue," he explained patiently, "but we're at the end of the river down here. Pollution will put us out of business."

Twice Apalachicola had named him the "King" of its famous annual seafood festival. The Southern Foodways Alliance, a University of Mississippi–based organization that celebrates southern cuisine, once gave him the prestigious "Keeper of the Flame" award for his determination to keep the seafood culture alive in Florida's most important little seafood town.

He liked to eat oysters. He liked them any way he could get them. As a young man, he once finished second in an oyster-eating contest, downing 12 dozen and four more. He didn't get sick. He got a trophy.

He was sick now. About a decade ago, during the period his daddy was battling cancer, he suddenly felt weak all over. "I thought I was ate up with the cancer myself," he told me. It turned out to be something else. Every day he shoots himself with insulin to keep at bay a serious case of diabetes.

Because of his weakened immunity, he had been ordered to avoid eating raw oysters. His daddy's son, he occasionally ignored the doctor's advice and ate them anyway. Sometimes he got away with it, but sometimes he felt woozy after a few.

Tommy told me he had been thinking about slowing down or even flat retiring. Often he thought about what would happen to the family business if he quit. He also thought obsessively about the oil spill. He was no expert, but he wondered if the bottom of the gulf was coated by it. He didn't trust the scientists, he didn't trust the doomsayers, he didn't trust people who told him not to worry. "I've lost my innocence," he said.

He wondered if a bad hurricane might churn up the oil and commence another crisis. If that happened, what would happen to Buddy Ward and Sons 13 Mile Seafood and Trucking Company? His daughter, Sara, a sophomore at the University of Central Florida, was studying hospitality and hoped one day to harvest not oysters but tourists. So Tommy had placed his hopes for a successor in his son, T. J., who was 22.

"T. J. reminds me of me," Tommy told me. T. J. was serious, a straight shooter, stubborn. T. J. had been especially close to his grandfather. A family story: when T. J. was 10, Grandpa Buddy hired him to paint the front porch. Grandpa provided him with a ridiculously small paint brush that made the job last forever.

"Why did Grandpa make it so hard?" T. J. asked his grandmother. Martha Pearl answered, "Honey, he's teaching you character."

Sometimes T. J. and Tommy rubbed each other wrong. T. J. was known to say, "Buddy wouldn't have done it that way" when he disagreed with his father. Tommy pretended to be insulted, but secretly felt proud of his boy's steel backbone.

One afternoon Tommy and I stood on the dock and watched for T. J.'s oyster boat. At 4 o'clock T. J. came in—with the day's biggest harvest, 20 bags of plump Apalachicola oysters. Tommy carefully avoided complimenting his son on his catch. He didn't want a compliment to go to his boy's head. Do good work because work is good.

Tommy knew about work, of course. And he knew better than most of us about hard times. For many years, his company had delivered seafood throughout the South. Now, after the oil crisis and company downsizing, he delivered mostly in northwest Florida. He still had a few trucks, though not as many as he once did.

In 2008, a mentally ill employee who had just lost a fight with a girl-friend stole Tommy's brand-new Peterbilt semi, headed up Highway 98, and crashed into the Apalachicola State Bank in a suicide attempt. The thief survived. Tommy's truck was totaled. So was the bank.

"It was a bad string of luck," Tommy told me in that understated way of his. "First the hurricane flooded out my business, then my daddy died. And somehow my truck destroyed the bank."

The bank was almost ready to reopen its doors. Buddy Ward's son was still standing, too.

Spring 2011.

55

A Gardener

Serafim Da Conceicao, a serious man for serious times, was sweet talking his tomato plants in his amazing backyard in Central Florida when I arrived. Tomato plants are temperamental, he explained. The slightest thing—too much sun, too little sun, too dry, too wet, nematodes in the soil, aphids on the leaves—throws them off. The prima donnas in Florida gardens, he told me, will pitch a tantrum and wilt. He usually rose at dawn, drank his coffee, shook his head at the bad news in the paper.

Then he tended his tomatoes, his cabbages, his kale, his turnips, his grove of fruit trees. As the early-morning traffic rushed past—his home lay in the middle of an industrial neighborhood in the most urban of Florida counties, Pinellas—he closed in on the tomatoes. "Hello, my friends. Grow and be healthy. Listen to me, and I will give you a little more fertilizer."

I helped him measure a tomato plant. We measured his best tomato plant, tied to a fence, at 102 inches. "If we can avoid a freeze, I think we will get him up to 10 feet," he told me. But he knew it was no sure thing. Born in Portugal in 1936, another difficult time in world history, he had learned that life is a struggle, but that if you worked hard in America, hung on to your money, wasted nothing and grew things, everything would be okay. A serious man for serious times, Serafim Da Conceicao knew he would miss no meals even if the world fell apart. It felt like it was falling apart. The experts were calling it a recession, but it seemed worse.

Like so many immigrants, he was grateful to be an American. The garden in the yard and the small garden of dirt beneath his fingernails belonged to him. He ambled through the garden, pointing and chatting in broken English, introducing his trees and plants as if they were his family. "Here is my kale. Here are my turnips. Have you ever seen cabbages like this? Look at this cabbage."

Out came the tape measure again. The cabbage head stretched 20 inches across. Ever sauté cabbage in vinegar and oil? I hadn't. Nor had I eaten cabbage stew. Knowing I had missed something important, I watched him water, weed, and baby his soil. I saw him add a tad of pesticide now and again and fertilize with fresh manure from his chickens and rabbits. He and Arminda—they had been married four decades at the time of my visit—regularly enjoyed fresh eggs and fresh chicken, fried rabbit and rabbit stew.

As far as they were concerned, they lived in Eden. Technically, their homestead lay in an industrial section of town, behind a pawn shop, across a dirt road from a weed-strewn field that once had been home to a mobile home court, near one of the busiest roads in the Tampa Bay area. The world out there was rough and no doubt would become rougher during hard times.

But, no, did I not understand? He and Arminda lived in Eden. So I watched him amble among his 100 trees, oranges and grapefruit mostly, but also avocado, mango and papaya, olive and fig. He had sugar apples from the tropics, and lychee, plums, and peaches. By spring, he predicted, his vines would be loaded with grapes.

He asked me why so few Americans seemed to grow their food. What is the problem? Time? Inclination? Fear of sweat? Many Americans, he said he had noticed, paid others to care for their yards. His was immaculately groomed by his own hand; every blade of grass knew its place. The roses perfumed the air, the grotto to the Virgin Mary was weeded and waiting for Arminda's rosary and bended knee. The house, her province, smelled of mothballs and was as immaculately kept as her husband's yard. Every photograph, every statue, and every prayer card with the Savior's likeness knew where it belonged in the world.

Canned tomatoes—tomatoes they put up last fall—waited on the kitchen counter for tonight's supper, a codfish stew. America!

He had been raised in a village that lacked electricity and running water during the dark time when the world was reeling from the Depression and war. As he grew, his older relatives passed on their gardening skills and their hopes for him. In America, they told him, a young man who worked hard could live his dreams.

In Massachusetts, he was a commercial fisherman, a carpenter, a cabbie, and a gardener. In 1990, a friend from New Bedford relocated to Florida and telephoned. "You'll like the climate," he advised. "It's good for growing things."

Serafim Da Conceicao moved south. In the industrial neighborhood he found the old dilapidated house and fixed the floor and the plumbing and the electrical system. He planted trees and established the chickens and the rabbits. He fed and clothed his three children. He acquired his first Chihuahua and now owns five: Taco, Chiquita, Nigi, Lita, and Netoball. They were in the good company when he ambled through the yard talking to the plants. He couldn't watch those tomato plants—we counted 74—by himself.

He and Arminda knew a bountiful spring was in store. They planned to peel and cook their vegetables and preserve them in glass jars. They would eat well through summer and fall until the next garden was ready. What was left they would share.

For years, they had given vegetables to neighbors in the mobile home village across the dirt road. But then the mobile home village closed. That's when he began stacking produce on the side of the fence nearest the pawn shop. America had been good to him, he explained carefully, and he wanted to give something back to Americans who had been less fortunate.

Sometimes in late afternoon they approached his fence and watched him through the mesh. Even after four decades, the English language challenged him, so he could not always understand what the poor people were saying to him. Perhaps "Thank you."

That night, he and Arminda ate a quiet meal. As she washed dishes, he watched the television news about the rich men who had stolen from other rich men and gotten the world into economic trouble.

Soon he was yawning. When the sun went down, he headed for bed, sometimes dreaming about his homeland or little dogs or tomatoes plants that spoke good English. But mostly he dreamt of the work he had to do in the morning, in his backyard, in America.

Winter 2009.

Bouzouki Man

They once were many, but now they were few—George Soffos and other men who knew how to play the stringed musical instrument known as the bouzouki and the melancholy tunes often described as Greek blues. In the old days the grizzled musicians sat in crowded cafés, bouzoukis on laps and cigarettes on lips, and played what they called rebetika music from dusk until dawn.

Sometimes a man listening to Soffos would feel compelled to dance— not as a performer who needed attention but as someone whose soul had just been touched. Perhaps the music reminded him of his homeland or his parents, long dead, or the girl who once had loved him, or the good job he had lost because he arrived at the dock one morning with retsina on his breath. The sharp, mournful notes played on the bouzouki somehow affirmed that life was a struggle and had been a struggle for all eternity.

So the dancer might stand, as if in a trance, and with arms outstretched and eyes half closed begin twirling. As the music took possession, he might snap his fingers and reach his hand to the floor and with knees bent and arms akimbo, twirl once more. Then without a trace of self-consciousness he might return with dignity to his seat and his glass of ouzo. Another would stand with eyes half closed to say that to suffer is to live.

In Tarpon Springs, where old Greek culture hung on despite the insistent and sometimes ghoulish march of the twenty-first century, George Soffos was the king of the bouzouki. He played many styles: classical Greek and the island music known as nisiotika. The old rebetika tunes especially came alive when the pick in his right hand assaulted the strings.

So here was the one he called "Conversations in Jail." Here was "The Junkie's Complaint." He played another about the man who tired of keeping his spoiled mistress happy and joined a monastery, became a monk, and took a vow of celibacy. Soffos had never served hard time. Nor did he self-medicate with a hash pipe. There had never been a spoiled mistress who brought misery to his life. Still, he was a human, which meant he was no stranger to the knowledge that we start dying the day we are born.

I couldn't help but notice the awful scar under his chin, the one that looked like a bad man had slit his throat. The bouzouki was the weapon of choice for Greek existentialists, rebetika the bullet.

In a community center a few blocks away from the sponge docks, Soffos, 57, struck a quivering, Middle Eastern–flavored note. "Bouzouki music must come out of your soul," Soffos reminded students who were wondering whether technique was enough.

They took group lessons from him on Sunday at the Tarpon Springs Heritage Museum. First they learned something about the instrument. The bouzouki, a distant cousin of the ancient lute, has a long neck and a half-watermelon-shaped bowl where the strings, usually in sets of three or four, are played with a pick. The bouzouki is more like a mandolin than a guitar, though not quite like a mandolin either. It's tuned differently and looks different and sounds different, especially when Soffos played the old music from the heart.

Of course he taught his students something about rebetika, about how it came along in the early part of the twentieth century, how it was often written and performed by poor and oppressed Greeks who some-times lived far away from home or in the ghettos of larger cities. Re-betika songs could be about love and sex and work and play. Rebetika songs might tell stories about old people with graveyard coughs or young mothers mourning babies who had died in infancy. Some were about prison life, encounters with prostitutes and relationships with bad men, mothers-in-law and swindlers, vamps and suckers. Sometimes the songs made you grin. "Rebetika," Soffos told his protégés, "is about life." They sat before him, some old and some young, some who spoke English with a Greek accent, and some American kids who knew more about rap than the rebetika of Greek men who were losing their hair.

The younger ones were there because their Greek parents had sent them for lessons "so you can play for your grandfather, your Pa-Pou, when you see him this summer in Cyprus." Clutching borrowed bouzou-kis, they sat before Soffos and tried in a small way to keep alive the cul-ture of Tarpon Springs for a little while longer.

George Soffos, master of the bouzouki. (Photo by Maurice Rivenbark.)

It wasn't easy in generic, fast-food, violent America, where culture often is what happened on reality television last night. Founded by Greek sponge divers about a century ago, famous today for Greek museums and Greek restaurants, Tarpon Springs battled to hold on to its small-town ethnic atmosphere. Six murders had been reported in the city the year I visited. Two-lane roads often were jammed with traffic while big-box stores on U.S. 19 threatened the old-timey family businesses in town.

"Try this," Soffos told an 11-year-old pupil. The boy's small fingers tried to cover the strings. Soffos reached over and helped. "Good," he said. "That's right, you got it."

When he talked, the words didn't come out of his mouth. Soffos spoke through a hole in his damaged throat. He added with a metallic rasp that "I do my real talking through the bouzouki."

He was born in 1953 in Warren, Ohio, where many Greeks moved to work in the steel mills after a sponge blight struck Tarpon Springs. His parents, from the Dodecanese islands, spoke Greek and lived like Greeks. He was only 5 years old when he first saw someone play a bouzouki. He remembered being smitten. It wasn't only the sound, he remembered, but the attitude of the musicians, how they held their instruments and even their cigarettes between ring fingers and pinkies. But mostly what got to him was how the music transfixed the audience.

At home the little boy tried making his own bouzouki out of string and cardboard. He pretended to play the instrument while sitting on the porch. He wore the kind of hat favored by bouzouki players and pretended to smoke like the bouzouki players did. Eventually his parents broke down and bought him a guitar, which he learned to play well enough to earn his first bouzouki. He learned to play by listening to old 78 rpm records. From time to time a Greek orchestra came through town and invited the precocious kid to join them.

He resented having to go to school. He resented having to do homework. He cared only about the bouzouki. Exasperated, his parents sent him to Washington to study with the most famous bouzouki teacher in the United States, John Tatasopoulous. For two years he lived with the master and played day and even night in the master's band. When his master fell ill, he became the bandleader known as "the boy wonder." He was offered gigs all over the country. The high school dropout was barely 17.

He saw a Led Zeppelin concert and liked the way Jimmy Page incorporated Middle Eastern sounds into the blues but remained true to the bouzouki. Over the decades Soffos was invited to play in the best Greek nightclubs in America and beyond. He played in Los Angeles, Las Vegas, Houston, Chicago, Detroit, Montreal, Toronto, Atlanta, Washington, New York, and Athens, Greece.

"There are people who believe he is the best American-born bouzouki player in the world," Dr. Tina Bucuvalas, the Tarpon Springs folklorist, told me. A few days later the secretary of state gave him a "Florida Cultural Award" for his cultural work in Tarpon Springs.

It was meant to be a celebration, so he didn't talk about his personal business, his own blues, his own rebetika.

Mother, my chest is hurting and I sigh.
This year, mother, I won't see it out.
When I die, mother, speak to the girl next door.
Tell her I'm dying for her and I'm on my way to hell.
Tell her to wash me, lay me out, light a candle for me.
Wash me, dry me, so my body can cease to be.
—A SONG RECORDED IN 1931

His own deep, rebetika blues started 13 years ago—with an earache. The doctor prescribed antibiotics. He had just moved to the Tarpon

Springs area. For four long years in Chicago he had owned a Greek club where every night he took the stage and played until dawn.

So yes, he was burned-out. And so, frankly, was his wife. After a dozen years of marriage, she wanted a husband who would be home at night, who would put down his bouzouki and instead read to his three beautiful daughters at bedtime. She wanted a husband who would take care of himself, eat better, and quit the two-pack-a-day habit that had turned his right hand yellow.

The antibiotics didn't work. The doctor ordered additional tests. It was a tumor. It was growing in his throat.

The radiation seemed to help at first. Anyway, the tumor shrank. But then it began growing again. Unless they started cutting, he was history at the age of 45. For his girls he imagined a life without a father. The doctor started cutting. Afterward he had to learn to breathe, eat, drink, and speak again.

His mother died.

His wife filed for divorce.

It was something out of a rebetika song.

He forgot about the feeding tube wrapped around his waist when he finally was strong enough to play the bouzouki again.

Soffos and his band, Ellada, played at Mythos, a Greek restaurant and nightclub in Clearwater, on the month's third Saturday. Their fans filed in early. When the show started at 8 p.m. every chair and every stool was taken.

The tall black-haired man with the scar on his throat dressed in black, wore black glasses and a black suit. The pick in his finger flew across the strings during an old tune, "Sabre Dance." As he played, he leaned toward the audience and made eye contact with fans who try to attend all of his shows.

He didn't sing, of course; Elias Poulos did. Dressed in white, Poulos walked between tables, leaned back and sang the old tunes in his hoarse, passionate voice. They were joined by Dino Theofilos, the keyboardist who had known Soffos since boyhood when "he didn't want to do anything but play the bouzouki."

Old pros, they seldom took breaks because they like to keep the dance floor crowded. One song led into another, often with a long and intricate bouzouki introduction that drew approving yells from the crowd. The band played one the older Greeks knew as "The Egyptian Girl"; the younger ones who remembered the film *Pulp Fiction* knew it as "Misir-lou." Dick Dale, say hello to the king of the bouzouki.

As the night went on, and the liquor took possession of some in the audience, Soffos leaned forward and began the intricate, well-known introduction to "To Vouno," or, in English, "The Mountain." Classic rebetika.

> I'm going to stay on the mountain,
> And far away from the world.
> I'm going to be crying by myself,
> I will be in pain,
> And I'm going to be heard throughout the mountain

A gray-haired man stepped onto the dance floor. As if in a trance, he extended his arms like wings and began to twirl. When he was through expressing himself—nobody knew the trouble he had seen—he returned to his table in the corner and wiped his dripping forehead with a napkin.

Spring 2011.

Moss Weaver

Dawn Klug loved Spanish moss more than anyone in Florida, if not the world. She lived in rural Citrus County, where Spanish moss hung from every oak tree like Jefferson Davis's beard. On moonlit nights, Spanish moss gave the oak-lined highway a Gothic feel.

Spanish moss—and we'll talk more about this a little later—saved Dawn's life during her darkest night of the soul. She lived alone in a humble mobile home surrounded by the inevitable moss-draped oaks. Her driveway, yard, deck, barn, and living room were graced by piles of moss, small and large.

She lacked many material possessions, but she felt rich when surrounded by moss. She would have rolled in it like a rambunctious child if she could have, but she is paralyzed from the waist down, the result of an auto accident long ago. She had no trouble gathering moss in her lap. She had no trouble working the moss with her gnarled fingers and spinning it into yarn. She weaved the Spanish moss yarn into beautiful blankets and saddle pads that throughout the South had become collectors' items.

In centuries past, Florida had dozens of people like her, Spanish moss weavers. Florida had become unpleasantly modern and she had become the last of her kind. Dawn was 52 at the time of my visit. She wore a purple bandanna, a long-sleeved shirt, and black trousers over her robust frame. She looked me in the eye, talked at a dizzying clip, and leaned a shotgun against the front door. Spanish moss tendrils lay upon her shoulders like little worms.

She was a visitor from another time. In Dawn's opinion, and she had many, Florida had too many cars on the roads, too few critters dwelling in our shrinking forests, and—pay attention—too many citified, fancy-pants people who knew nothing about Spanish moss.

"They ask if Spanish moss is going to kill the trees," she told me with a sniff. I got the impression she was testing me. "Okay. You do know that Spanish moss is not Spanish and it's not a moss, don't you?"

Uh . . .

"Spanish moss is an air plant, an epiphyte, you know that, right? It takes nourishment from the air and from the rain. Right? It isn't a parasite! Okay, sometimes in a storm, a clump of moss will get very wet and very heavy, and the weight will break off a branch. That happens, okay. But I hate to hear somebody say"—here she spoke in a high-pitched whine—"Spanish moss is a parasite!"

Unlike the rest of us, she had made understanding Spanish moss her life's work. When she wanted to impress, she might mention the genus and species, *Tillandsia usneoides*. She told me how Spanish moss became associated with Spaniards: in a southern folktale from the sixteenth century, a pioneer couple was waylaid by Cherokees unhappy to see white people on their land. Before releasing the couple, Dawn told me, the warriors cut the hair of the Spanish bride and threw it high into the branches of an old oak. Within a week the black hair was gray. That was the beginning of Spanish moss.

"Spanish moss was very important in the South and in Florida," Dawn went on. "It was used for everything. It stuffed mattresses and pillows and furniture. It was used for insulation. If you boil Spanish moss—let me warn you, it really stinks—you'll have this brew that makes this amazing fertilizer. And this is where I come in: in the Civil War, the Confederate soldiers all had Spanish moss blankets. And that's what I still make."

As Dawn talked, chaos broke out in her yard. Inches from her wheelchair, pet cats hissed while a bewildered dog slunk away. Chickens clucked and ran amok. A thoughtful neighbor borrowed her pitchfork—Dawn always had several pitchforks and neighbors around—and tossed Spanish moss from his truck onto her driveway. Dawn said, "My motto is 'Chaos—it's not a theory, it's my life.'"

She was born in South Carolina but considered herself a Floridian because her great-granddaddy had fought for the Confederacy out of Jacksonville and her dad served in the state during his Navy career.

Dawn had joined the Navy out of high school and served in Hawaii. At first she washed planes. Then she refueled jets. Her favorite job was aviation storekeeper. If you wanted a part, you came to see her. If she

Dawn Klug in her element. (Photo by Maurice Rivenbark.)

didn't have it, she'd find it for you, even if she had to barter for it with another aviation storekeeper. Strange, but the bartering prepared her for the next chapter of a life that was about to turn sad.

She got married in 1976 when she was 20. He was an Army guy, but the mixed marriage seemed to work. They had a son, Jason, and many good times. When their military careers ended, they moved to Floral City to be near relatives.

The accident happened on November 16, 1980. Dawn's husband was behind the wheel. She was riding shotgun. They backed out of the driveway onto the highway. Dawn looked out the window and saw a car bearing down. Later, she learned the other car was clocked at 70 mph. She had time for a curse word before impact. She was blown through the windshield just in time for the car to tumble and land on her. Her husband was roughed up; her spine was crushed. She spent seven months in the hospital.

Try to imagine: You are 24 years old. You have a good life, a husband, a son you enjoy chasing through the woods. You can climb a fence. You can stand on a chair to get a box of cornflakes off the top shelf. You can dance. You can make love. Then it's all over.

"Terrible depression. Awful suicidal thoughts. But of course I never acted on them, but they were there. It was bad." She and her husband and child tried to adjust to their new life, but after four years he told her he wanted a divorce. He was everything to her, her arms and legs. Now he was moving on.

Rage. Grief. Depression. Self-pity. She went to rehab, learned how to crawl in and out of a new van by herself. She learned how to drive using only her hands, how to sit herself on the toilet, how to get back into the wheelchair.

She found a new hobby: weaving. She bought a loom and had it customized for a person who couldn't use feet to press pedals. One night, reading, she discovered an article about the lost art of Spanish moss weaving. She became consumed by the idea of learning a lost art. Friends brought her moss, and she started weaving. It made her feel good about herself.

"Isn't that strange?" she said one day. "I had never had, what do you call it, good self-esteem." Now she wore a special T-shirt.

"FACE IT," it said in big letters across the front. "You know I'm right."

"I was born too late," she told me once. "I should have been born in the 19th century." It didn't sound like a cliché coming from her, though most likely she would have died from her injuries during Civil War time. "What I mean is I live simply."

She grew vegetables and fruits in pots, fertilizing them with Spanish moss brew. She canned the vegetables and fruit and traded for manual labor. She hated to pay for anything if she could barter.

She read no newspaper, owned no television. Sometimes a visitor brought her up to date. She had no furniture other than a bed, a lonely chair, and a desk for her only luxury, a computer. She had decided that a telephone was a luxury.

She survived on $800 a month from Social Security and her modest earnings from weaving. She had no problem selling wool or cotton tapestries, but the demand for Spanish moss weavings was limited to collectors and Civil War reenactors. They paid $600 for a saddle blanket. It took a year to do three. She had 17 on order.

Spanish moss, piled in her yard, took half a year to decay in the Florida heat and humidity. A 6-foot pile in January was 2 inches high in July and dark and wiry like a Brillo pad. Inside her living room, where the floor was plywood and covered with sand, she painstakingly removed debris from the Spanish moss Brillo.

Next she worked the tendrils into something resembling thread. On a small spinning wheel she fed the thread a little at a time. Within minutes she had a few feet of something that looked like yarn.

It took a week to position hundreds of strands of yarn properly onto her loom, a contraption as large as an upright piano. Alone in her mobile home, as she sat in her wheelchair, she slowly weaved her Spanish moss into something beautiful and utilitarian.

Often her only company turned out to be Lonesome George, a favorite chicken that had the run of her mobile home. Outside the open door, always trying to sneak in, was a prized hen, Scarlett. Scarlett was a widow; her mate, Rhett Butler, had been killed by a stray dog. Dawn heard the barking and the squawking, rolled her chair over to her shotgun and came up firing.

She missed, but the dog was scared away for good. "I can take care of myself," Dawn told me, and returned to the spinning wheel. In the afternoon sun, which poured through her front door, I could see dirt under her fingernails. She was not afraid of dirt, or, for that matter, much else.

Winter 2009.

58

Mother Hodges

The world has two kinds of people: those who iron their clothes and never misplace socks and those who always look rumpled and lose their socks. Ruth Hodges and her son, Keto, were the kind of people who ironed their clothes and never lost their socks. What's hard about ironing? What's difficult about keeping socks in pairs? Ruth Hodges made sure to enunciate properly when she told me: "NOTH-ING-A!" Eighty years old when I met her, mentally and physically vigorous, she valued discipline in every aspect of life, from pairing socks to scholarship.

Two decades ago, when she had first met Keto, he was near death, having been horribly burned in a campfire accident in Haiti. Ruth, a missionary, took the little boy to the United States for treatment. She adopted him when he was 9 and taught him to read and to write and to excel in everything he tried, even ironing.

Everybody in Tampa's Belmont Heights community seemed to call her Mother Hodges. She was barely 5 feet tall but somehow seemed taller. Part Mother Teresa and part Vince Lombardi, she was loving but strict. A devout Pentecostal, she sometimes spoke in tongues. She had two college degrees and the confidence to correct faulty grammar when she heard it.

At a time when many American parents seemed overwhelmed with doubt about how to do their jobs—who seemed as inclined to spoil their kids as to prepare them for life in the real world—Mother Hodges was an old-fashioned parent who never listened to Dr. Laura or Dr. Phil. She was the queen mother of high expectations.

Mother Hodges told me about the time her son disappointed her with a "C" in a finance course at the University of South Florida. "You're going to take that class AGAIN!" she declared. On second try, Keto earned an A. Graduating from USF with honors, he later earned a master's in business administration. He was 27 now, an analyst for Claris Law, the online publisher of legal information in Tampa. He also operated a part-time Internet business, The List by Keto, which networked young adults interested in culture and nightlife. He was in the process of figuring out how to add more irons to the fire of opportunity.

Keto lifted weights at the gym, jogged, mentored young people, played the piano, and performed charity work through his church. He read the Bible daily, and when he came to the last page he started over again. Every month he sent money to his relatives in Haiti.

Ruth Hodges was pleased when people praised her son. But she grimaced when he talked even modestly about himself. "God DESERVES the credit," she said to him. "Keto, PLEASE don't BRAG!" If Keto was five minutes late, she called him on his cell phone. If he was 10 minutes behind, she phoned him a second time and asked, "Where are you?"

Dawdlers sometimes arrived to find her waiting outside her apartment, seated next to her tomato plants, feet tapping with impatience.

Black men were more than twice as likely to be unemployed as white males, according to a report I read by the National Urban League. Young black men were more likely to be killed by firearms or AIDS. More black men sat in prison cells than in college classrooms, according to the Justice Policy Institute, a nonprofit organization in Washington, D.C.

Mother Hodges, employing her tough-love and high-expectations philosophy, was doing her best to reverse those trends. Keto was only one of her sterling pupils. She tutored mostly children, but adults, too, in subjects that included English, history, science, math, and life skills. "What are you DOING?" she asked an impudent boy we saw walking on her lawn.

"Nuttin'," he answered.

"No such word," she told him crisply. "It's N-O-T-H-I-N-G. NOTH-ING-A!"

A moment later, Jamari Johnson, 9, arrived for a lesson. "Where are YOUR supplies?" she asked. The solemn boy looked stricken. Listening from the couch, Keto tried to hide his empathy. After all, he had been in this situation before. "I expect you to BRING your OWN supplies," she scolded Jamari. "I will SELL you a pencil and I will SELL you some paper if you haven't thought to bring your OWN."

Years before, Mother Hodges had tutored Jamari's uncle, Garrett Johnson. He had been exactly like Jamari at that age, smart but scattered. She could see the talent deep within him and was determined to help drag it out.

Garrett eventually graduated magna cum laude from Florida State. Next he traveled to Oxford University in England as a Rhodes Scholar. Like Keto, like just about anyone who had crossed her path, Johnson had a Mother Hodges story he liked to tell of the sort told by ex-Marines who can laugh at boot camp memories.

One day years ago, proud of the way he had mastered Middle English pronunciations in college, Garrett Johnson decided to pay Mother Hodges a surprise visit. Sitting in her living room he announced he would treat her to a reading from a tome written just before the turn of the fifteenth century, *The Canterbury Tales*. He turned to his favorite chapter, "The Wife of Bath's Tale," and cleared his throat. He hadn't uttered a syllable before Mother Hodges, sitting on the couch, began reciting from memory:

> In th'olde dayes of the Kyng Arthour,
> Of which that Britons speken greet honour,
> All was this land fulfild of fayerye.
> The elf-queene, with hir joly compaignye,
> Daunced ful ofte in many a grene mede.

Garrett Johnson wasn't the only hotshot who knew Chaucer.

"My mother," Keto likes to tell people, often with a sigh, "is an unusual person." She had been born in New York City in 1926. She had five brothers and sisters. Her father, John Thomas, an apartment supervisor by day and a jazz musician at night, died when Ruth was 3. Her mother, Mary, fell into a deep depression. When Ruth was 6, her mother took the children on a walk. They marched to the middle of the Brooklyn Bridge. Her mother said, "Children, Daddy is calling me." She stuffed her purse under Ruth's arm, climbed onto the railing, and leaped to her death.

Ruth ended up with grandparents in Virginia. She remembered being hungry all the time. She remembered being a good student who could trade her tutoring services for an apple or a sandwich in the school cafeteria. Ruth moved to the District of Columbia when she was a teen. She graduated from high school, got married at 19, and had a daughter, Lanie.

Ruth's husband disapproved of women who wanted to go to college, putting a strain on a marriage already rocky from his drinking

Ruth Hodges, the queen of tough love. (Photo by Scott Keeler.)

and philandering. After the marriage failed, Ruth drank poison, but not enough to do serious harm. She took out razor blades and looked at them and then put the razor blades away. She supported herself and her child by cleaning houses, washing clothes, and tutoring children, all the while taking college night classes. She passed a civil service test and toiled as a file clerk on a naval base. In 1958 she developed cancer of the uterus. She told people, "God healed me."

In thanks she performed missionary work throughout the country, making ends meet by tutoring. She married again in 1963. James Hodges, she told me, was a good man who quit gambling when he found God. Ruth remembered standing in a church in Connecticut in 1969 and announcing her desire to do missionary work in Haiti. Her husband told her, "I won't be here when you get back," but he was. He started going to Haiti with her.

Ruth loved the traditions and the food. She especially loved the children, who were poor though joyful and curious. They considered the crayons and coloring books she handed out as a kind of miracle. Bitten by a mosquito, she developed dangerous dengue fever but survived. She continued going back to Haiti even after her husband died of cancer in 1974. She moved to Arkansas to work in a church. In 1984, she finished her college work at the University of Arkansas at Little Rock and got a degree in liberal arts. She liked to tell people: "It took me 40 years but I graduated."

Keto Nord was born in Cerca-Carvajal in northern Haiti in 1980. Following a Caribbean tradition, his grandparents were raising him. On his weekly visit to his mother in 1985, Keto dropped a toy next to the campfire where his mother was boiling rice. He lost his balance and fell against the pot. The red-hot cast iron cooked the left side of his face, destroying flesh and nerve endings.

For two months Keto barely hung on. Finally his Aunt Carona carried him by horseback to a little clinic five hours away. Keto's nostrils had melted; his lips were nearly welded shut. Nurses fed the boy by poking tiny pieces of pineapple through the little opening. Aunt Carona understood no English.

But the American missionary working at the clinic had taught herself Creole and explained what the doctors recommended. The doctors asked the missionary if she would take the little boy to America for treatment that might save his life.

Ruth Hodges, of course, booked a flight.

They flew to the Shriners Hospital in Cincinnati for the first of 14 surgeries to salvage his face. She taught the little boy to say "nurse" in English. She taught him to say "I brushed my teeth." Between surgeries he lived with her; she taught him reading and writing. He was ready for third grade within 18 months. Ruth then sent him to a real school. When other children taunted him about his appearance Ruth volunteered at the school so Keto would have someone to sit with at lunch. "You are burned, but you are a good person," she told him. "Work hard, behave, stay neat, and people will accept you."

She brought Keto along on missionary trips to Haiti. Keto's birth mother, who had eight other hungry children, agreed to let Ruth adopt her boy.

Ruth officially became Keto's mother on December 13, 1989.

As Keto grew, he studied the Bible. As Keto thrilled to *Robinson Crusoe*, Ruth read Thoreau and Martin Luther. She took Keto to museums and to the symphony. She taught herself how to play the piano so she could teach Keto. A natural, soon he was performing hymns at church and Beethoven at home.

Although she had reached retirement age, she taught him how to hit a baseball. She would race him across the lawn until her legs hurt too much to continue. They moved from Arkansas to Tampa because Ruth knew people in Tampa, including folks in the thriving Haitian community. She wanted Keto to stay in touch with his culture.

Returning to Tampa from Haiti after one missionary trip, Ruth learned that her landlord had sold the apartment building. During that bad patch, she and Keto spent a month in a homeless shelter, followed by a stint in a crack neighborhood apartment with a bullet hole in the window. When we drove around Tampa, Ruth liked to show me her old homes. "I know what it's like to be poor," she said. Ruth survived on Social Security, her late husband's VA benefits, and the modest fees she charged for tutoring and piano lessons.

After 10th grade, Keto passed the high school equivalency exam. His mother paid for his first semester at Hillsborough Community College with rent money. They somehow got by. After Keto's first high-achieving semester, he always had academic scholarships. At USF, he majored in business but took many electives. One classmate in his Haitian culture class was a diminutive woman who wore a neatly pressed blouse and skirt and sat in back.

"Keto," Mother Hodges promised, "I'll pretend I don't even know you."

At the time I was doing this story, Keto and Ruth were still spending time together. They attended events at USF and worked out at the same YMCA. They often took meals together at the tiny West Indies Cuisine restaurant on Floribraska in Tampa. Sometimes I went with them.

Mother Hodges liked to lean her head through the small server window and order in Creole. Mother Hodges peppered walk-in customers with questions in English, and if they didn't respond, tried Creole.

"Where are you from? What do you do?"

When a Haitian man in his 20s told her he was attending Jefferson High School, she beamed. "So many people do not take ADVANTAGE of the OPPORTUNITIES in this country," she announced to the room at large.

On Sundays, Keto attended Brown Memorial Church of God in Christ. It was more modern than Ruth's Pentecostal place of worship, Gospel

Kingdom Haitian Church, where services sometimes lasted all day. She told me she wanted Keto to worship with her, but professed to understand his desire to spend more time with people his own age.

When his friends planned a birthday party for him, Keto kept it a secret from his mother. As close as they were, Keto was working on having boundaries. If he had a girlfriend, he hadn't introduced her to Mother Hodges. Heaven help the girlfriend!

"We are both extremely focused," he told me the day we spent the afternoon together. "She's more a Type A person and I'm more Type B. That's a diplomatic way to put it, I think."

Like every mother in the history of the world, she was certain that her son needed to sleep more and socialize less. She disliked his business card that advertised his young adult networking company because the word "nightlife" was displayed prominently. To Mother Hodges, "nightlife" conjured images of half-naked women dancing provocatively. Dancing in front of her innocent son!

"I don't approve of nightlife, this entertainment thing of his," she told me once as Keto squirmed. "It does not bring glory to God."

Brought up to honor his elders, Keto didn't say as much as "Aw, Ma!" He told me, out of her earshot, that he hoped to attend a party tonight.

Keto was becoming his own person. He was in the process of moving his belongings—his ball caps and crisply ironed shirts and perfectly matched socks—out of their apartment. In the near future, he told me, he was going to move in with a friend from church.

Mother Hodges was unhappy about it; she was going to miss Keto. She was going to miss him so much she wasn't sure she could bear it. But she would try to keep busy and pray and God would answer.

One door was closing, but another was opening. Perhaps now she would have time to finish writing her book. She had finished 20 chapters of an autobiography. In the summer, she planned her 52nd missionary trip to Haiti. In the fall, when she turned 81, she expected to be the oldest person in an advanced French class at USF.

But she knew one thing. Her apartment was going to feel empty at night without Keto. She would remember taking her fragile little boy to museums and to symphonies—remember reading to him, traveling on buses with him, pointing out the sights to him. Being needed.

She told me she understood that a parent's role is to raise her child to be loving and self-reliant. But how would she stop being a mother when she had accomplished her task?

Mother Hodges relaxed in the big easy chair by the window and thought about that.

"It's the hardest thing to let your child grow up, to experiment with life, to make mistakes," she told me. "But you have to cut those apron strings."

She quoted the church adage about handing over your anxiety to God. "The problem is I want to help God," she said in a small voice.

Spring 2007.

59

Chesty Morgan

Today I offer a cautionary tale about jumping to conclusions, a tale about how we can go wrong when we judge a book by even the most eye-catching cover.

For example, what comes to mind when you hear the name "Chesty Morgan"? People of a certain age might think: "Wasn't she an exotic dancer in the 1970s? Famous for her measurements? She made a movie with Fellini, didn't she? She must have been some red-hot mama, right?"

Yes, that was Chesty Morgan, a woman objectified all over the planet for having what one nightclub promoter called "the world's largest natural breasts! She defies medical science!" Yes, Chesty Morgan—the woman with the alleged 73-inch bust. Have your laugh, but listen: the world is a complicated place. Even red-hot mamas have real lives. Often those lives are tragic. Sometimes they are beyond tragic.

Let's say you are shopping at a Publix supermarket. Shopping in the cake mix aisle, near the flour and the baking powder, you notice a striking older woman. She is tiny, probably a few inches short of 5 feet, but under a red windbreaker her sweatshirt is strained to the bursting point.

She makes polite small talk about baking. "I make lemon cake for all my friends," she says in a lilting Polish accent.

Her Florida driver's license, I will later find out, identifies her as Lillian Stello and says she is 72 years old. In person she seems younger. Maybe it's her lively blue eyes. Perhaps it's because she wears her hair in a blonde mullet.

Even longtime friends don't know Lillian's story. Sometimes it is easier to tell the whole, amazing story to a stranger.

She is a small child in 1937. Her father and mother are well-to-do Jews who live near Warsaw. In 1939, Germany invades Poland. Her parents lose their department store. They end up in the ghetto afraid for their lives.

Jeff Klinkenberg and former burlesque queen Chesty Morgan at her favorite Publix.

Her mother, Eva, leaves the apartment to find shoes for a niece. She is caught in a German sweep, hauled away in a boxcar, never to return. Little Lillian puts aside a little food every day—just in case her mother is hungry when she comes home.

Jews eventually fight back. Her father, Leon, is shot dead in a ghetto uprising.

Lillian ends up in Israel, where she lives in a series of orphanages, then in a kibbutz where she studies nursing. She has low self-esteem and worries about everything. Boys think she is beautiful. She doesn't understand why.

When she is about 20, she meets a man from America. Five days later they are married. She doesn't love him, but Joseph Wilczkowski is her ticket to the United States, to New York. "But guess what?" she asks me now. "He was a very good man, a very good provider. He had butcher shops. We have two children. He didn't see them much because he work so hard. I wanted to work with him, so I could have money of my own, but he wanted a wife who was at home. That was the only problem I had with him. I wanted to work and have a little money of my own."

Brooklyn, 1965.

A late-night phone call. Policeman says: "We need you to come down to the station." Lillian shrieks and bangs her head again and again against the wall. She has a bad feeling about what will come next.

The police tell her that armed robbers had herded her husband and two employees into a refrigerator and shot and stabbed them to death. Tabloids call the crime "the icebox murders."

Lillian, about 27, contemplates suicide. But she can't do it. One daughter is 4. The other is 4 months. She has to live for her kids. But what will become of them?

"Guess what?" she asks one day when we're sitting in front of Publix. "America is the greatest country on Earth. You know why? In America, you can do anything if you work hard. I am always willing to work hard."

In 2009, I tell her, it is difficult to find a good job no matter how hard you are willing to work. In 1965, she tells me, it was just as difficult. Especially if you are a Polish immigrant woman who speaks uncertain English and has limited job skills.

In 1965 she has a little money and a little property from the marriage, but New York is expensive. She worries about bankruptcy, being thrown out on the street. In her life she has lost two parents and a husband. It is her nature to expect the worst.

She is pretty. Voluptuous. Men knock on her door. A few even suggest marriage. She tells them, "I will never marry again. I'm too afraid." In her experience, love leads to death. How could she endure another tragedy?

She asks one suitor, Maury, to help find her a job. Maybe she would feel better about the prospect of marriage if she had a way of making a living and feeling in control. In 1972, Maury takes her to a smoky nightclub. On stage, a woman slowly removes her clothes while men hoot and holler. Maury says, "You're very attractive, Lillian. You know, you could do this. They'd pay you."

"Maury, I never want to see you again," Lillian says. "How dare you suggest it."

End of date.

At the Holocaust Museum in St. Petersburg, Lillian Stello, known as "Chesty Morgan" during her show business days, thinks about her life. (Photo by Scott Keeler.)

But she thinks about Maury's suggestion.

At first she calls herself Zsa Zsa; later, a nightclub owner sizes her up and suggests "Chesty Morgan." On her first engagement, she refuses to take off her bra. She soon gets over her shyness. She makes enough money to purchase custom bras and expensive costumes. She hires a choreographer, learns how to tell a joke and to sing.

Bookings all over the United States follow. In Boston, a writer describes Lillian as an exotic dancer "with a front as imposing as the Fenway wall," referring to the local baseball stadium's towering left field fence.

A B-movie director, Doris Wishman, hires Lillian for a couple of wonderfully awful R-rated films. The kitschy *Deadly Weapons* and *Double Agent 73* remain in circulation today. The famous Italian director Federico Fellini is in New York to promote his latest movie, *Amarcord*, and catches a glimpse of Chesty. He invites her to be in his upcoming film, *Fellini's Casanova*.

She dyes her hair black and flies to Rome. Casanova, played by Donald Sutherland, chases Barbarina, played by Chesty, around and around a table. Fellini cuts her part from the film, but the scene remains in a documentary that still circulates on the Internet.

Back in the States, she travels and performs and performs and travels, sometimes making $6,000 a week. "I was not stupid girl with a big chest," she once told me. "Nightclub owners, they want you to work for drugs or booze and I always wanted the money. Don't tell me you want me to come to San Francisco for a couple of shows, hon-ney. Pay me for a week. I have to fly across the country in an airplane, be away from my children, stay in a strange hotel, go without sleep. You have to pay me for all that trouble."

She tells nightclub owners, "I never show my bottom half. I never dance around pole or go in private room with customers."

She is among the last of the old-time burlesque queens who values the tease as much as the strip. In San Francisco, she christens a ship in a costume so tight the sailors have to carry her to the water. Now and again she is arrested, allegedly for letting men next to the stage touch the tops of her breasts. It's true: she wants the world to know they are real. Chesty Morgan does not need breast augmentation!

She marries again, in a lonely moment, and moves to Florida. Husband No. 2, a major league umpire named Richard Stello, is a nice man, fun to be around when home, but he is never home—he travels for a living. Of course, so does she. They divorce in 1979.

Still, they keep in touch. In 1984 he helps her through the death of her older daughter in a traffic accident in New York. She and her ex-husband remain close. He loves her chicken soup with matzo balls. In 1987 he is killed in an auto accident near Lakeland. They had planned to spend the Christmas holidays together. She was going to make him soup.

She continues dancing, crying, saving money, crying, investing in the stock market, buying real estate. In 1991 she dances in Houston for the last time. She remembers because it is the opening night of the Persian Gulf War. On stage she dances the hoochie koo. Backstage Chesty Morgan is glued to the television with the rest of America.

She now lives in an expensive house on Tampa Bay. In boxes she has old pictures, old posters, old costumes. She can no longer fit into her old size 5 costumes. But almost.

Every morning she walks to stay fit. One time, when I walked with her, she told me about her back. Her back, which struggled to support her chest for so many years, is an unforgiving antagonist. In a belt pouch she carries aspirin for chronic pain. Sometimes she wonders if she should finally get the breast reduction. Problem is, she distrusts doctors. They might try to cheat an older woman like her.

Some days she walks 2 miles, other days 8. When we walk together I get an earful of advice and warnings about dangers that may lurk around every corner. She worries about all the "For Sale" signs. She worries that her property is losing value. She worries about what is going on in Tallahassee and in Washington. Save us from Obama!

She distrusts politicians, especially Democrats, and listens almost exclusively to Fox News while baking lemon cakes or preparing chicken soup. "If I could," she says, "I would marry Glenn Beck, Sean Hannity, and Bill O'Reilly. I love them like they are my husbands."

After her walk she climbs into her 9-year-old pickup truck and backs out of the driveway. Tiny, she can hardly see above the steering wheel as she drives to the hardware store to buy supplies for the apartment buildings she owns.

In Home Depot, she is on a first-name basis with certain clerks. They don't know her show business background; they know her only as the older female fireball comfortable with manual labor. "They are kind to me there, so helpful. You say please in your story that 'Home Depot is a very good place.' Home Depot is one of the things I love about America."

From Home Depot she heads for a neat apartment building she owns near U.S. 19 in a working-class part of town. Sometimes she hires workmen to help, but often she takes care of upkeep herself. She climbs a ladder to the roof. I climb to the roof behind her. She tells me her last roofer forgot to seal the spot where the air conditioner rests. So now she has to do it. She knows plumbing, air conditioning, carpentry, and roofing.

She wears yellow rubber gloves, slacks, milk-white sneakers, and a tight sweatshirt. Soon her yellow gloves turn black with tar.

She is a long way from a nightclub stage in San Francisco. But I ask for a demonstration.

"My act? Hon-ney, I had better costumes than Liberace! First I walk through the crowd from the back so they can see me up close. I wear a long coat with a tail. I swing the tail this-a-way and that-a-way as I walk."

On the roof, she spices up her demonstration with body language.

"When I reach the stage I turn this way and that way and the coat opens, but just a little bit"—she pronounced it "leetle beet"—"just enough to give a peek. Then on stage I take off the coat and the gloves—

rhinestone gloves—one at a time, very slow, and then my top, except for the corset. After that I . . ."

Yes, Chesty Morgan was a stripper who bared her breasts without apology. She is in the Burlesque Hall of Fame in California, along with Gypsy Rose Lee, Josephine Baker, Sally Rand, Bettie Page, and Mae West. Yes, the pop singer Tom Waits mentions her in a song called "Pasties and a G-String." In Sweden, an avant-garde pop band calls itself Chesty Morgan.

In west-central Florida a tiny woman named Lillian fixes roofs, bakes lemon cakes, and makes matzo ball soup for friends. When she thinks of her murdered parents, a murdered husband, and a daughter killed in a traffic accident—when she visits the Holocaust Museum in St. Petersburg—she often breaks into tears.

But not right now, not while she works on the roof. On the roof, working with her hands, she can live in the present moment.

The tiny woman kneels, pours tar, massages it into an apartment roof with rubber gloves. She tells me, "Hon-ney, guess what? Sometimes if you want something done right, you got to do it yourself."

Fall 2009.

JEFF KLINKENBERG is the Florida culture writer with the *Tampa Bay Times*, previously the *St. Petersburg Times*. He is author of two previous books with the University Press of Florida, *Pilgrim in the Land of Alligators* and *Seasons of Real Florida*.

THE FLORIDA HISTORY AND CULTURE SERIES
Edited by Raymond Arsenault and Gary R. Mormino

Al Burt's Florida: Snowbirds, Sand Castles, and Self-Rising Crackers, by Al Burt (1997)

Black Miami in the Twentieth Century, by Marvin Dunn (1997)

Gladesmen: Gator Hunters, Moonshiners, and Skiffers, by Glen Simmons and Laura Ogden (1998)

"Come to My Sunland": Letters of Julia Daniels Moseley from the Florida Frontier, 1882-1886, edited by Julia Winifred Moseley and Betty Powers Crislip (1998)

The Enduring Seminoles: From Alligator Wrestling to Ecotourism, by Patsy West (1998)

Government in the Sunshine State: Florida since Statehood, by David R. Colburn and Lance de-Haven-Smith (1999)

The Everglades: An Environmental History, by David McCally (1999; first paperback edition, 2001)

Beechers, Stowes, and Yankee Strangers: The Transformation of Florida, by John T. Foster Jr. and Sarah Whitmer Foster (1999)

The Tropic of Cracker, by Al Burt (1999)

Balancing Evils Judiciously: The Proslavery Writings of Zephaniah Kingsley, edited and annotated by Daniel W. Stowell (1999)

Hitler's Soldiers in the Sunshine State: German POWs in Florida, by Robert D. Billinger Jr. (2000)

Cassadaga: The South's Oldest Spiritualist Community, edited by John J. Guthrie, Phillip Charles Lucas, and Gary Monroe (2000)

Claude Pepper and Ed Ball: Politics, Purpose, and Power, by Tracy E. Danese (2000)

Pensacola during the Civil War: A Thorn in the Side of the Confederacy, by George F. Pearce (2000; first paperback edition, 2008)

Castles in the Sand: The Life and Times of Carl Graham Fisher, by Mark S. Foster (2000)

Miami, U.S.A., by Helen Muir (2000)

Politics and Growth in Twentieth-Century Tampa, by Robert Kerstein (2001)

The Invisible Empire: The Ku Klux Klan in Florida, by Michael Newton (2001)

The Wide Brim: Early Poems and Ponderings of Marjory Stoneman Douglas, edited by Jack E. Davis (2002)

The Architecture of Leisure: The Florida Resort Hotels of Henry Flagler and Henry Plant, by Susan R. Braden (2002)

Florida's Space Coast: The Impact of NASA on the Sunshine State, by William Barnaby Faherty, S.J. (2002)

In the Eye of Hurricane Andrew, by Eugene F. Provenzo Jr. and Asterie Baker Provenzo (2002)

Florida's Farmworkers in the Twenty-first Century, text by Nano Riley and photographs by Davida Johns (2003)

Making Waves: Female Activists in Twentieth-Century Florida, edited by Jack E. Davis and Kari Frederickson (2003)

Orange Journalism: Voices from Florida Newspapers, by Julian M. Pleasants (2003)

The Stranahans of Ft. Lauderdale: A Pioneer Family of New River, by Harry A. Kersey Jr. (2003)

Death in the Everglades: The Murder of Guy Bradley, America's First Martyr to Environmentalism, by Stuart B. McIver (2003)

Jacksonville: The Consolidation Story, from Civil Rights to the Jaguars, by James B. Crooks (2004)

The Seminole Wars: America's Longest Indian Conflict, by John and Mary Lou Missall (2004)

The Mosquito Wars: A History of Mosquito Control in Florida, by Gordon Patterson (2004)

Seasons of Real Florida, by Jeff Klinkenberg (2004; first paperback edition, 2009)

Land of Sunshine, State of Dreams: A Social History of Modern Florida, by Gary R. Mormino (2005; first paperback edition, 2008)

Paradise Lost? The Environmental History of Florida, edited by Jack E. Davis and Raymond Arsenault (2005)

Frolicking Bears, Wet Vultures, and Other Oddities: A New York City Journalist in Nineteenth-Century Florida, edited by Jerald T. Milanich (2005)

Waters Less Traveled: Exploring Florida's Big Bend Coast, by Doug Alderson (2005)

Saving South Beach, by M. Barron Stofik (2005; first paperback edition, 2012)

Losing It All to Sprawl: How Progress Ate My Cracker Landscape, by Bill Belleville (2006; first paperback edition, 2010)

Voices of the Apalachicola, compiled and edited by Faith Eidse (2006)

Floridian of His Century: The Courage of Governor LeRoy Collins, by Martin A. Dyckman (2006)

America's Fortress: A History of Fort Jefferson, Dry Tortugas, Florida, by Thomas Reid (2006)

Weeki Wachee, City of Mermaids: A History of One of Florida's Oldest Roadside Attractions, by Lu Vickers (2007)

City of Intrigue, Nest of Revolution: A Documentary History of Key West in the Nineteenth Century, by Consuelo E. Stebbins (2007)

The New Deal in South Florida: Design, Policy, and Community Building, 1933–1940, edited by John A. Stuart and John F. Stack Jr. (2008)

The Enduring Seminoles: From Alligator Wrestling to Casino Gaming, Revised and Expanded Edition, by Patsy West (2008)

Pilgrim in the Land of Alligators: More Stories about Real Florida, by Jeff Klinkenberg (2008; first paperback edition, 2011)

A Most Disorderly Court: Scandal and Reform in the Florida Judiciary, by Martin A. Dyckman (2008)

A Journey into Florida Railroad History, by Gregg M. Turner (2008; first paperback edition, 2012)

Sandspurs: Notes from a Coastal Columnist, by Mark Lane (2008)

Paving Paradise: Florida's Vanishing Wetlands and the Failure of No Net Loss, by Craig Pittman and Matthew Waite (2009; first paperback edition, 2010)

Embry-Riddle at War: Aviation Training during World War II, by Stephen G. Craft (2009)

The Columbia Restaurant: Celebrating a Century of History, Culture, and Cuisine, by Andrew T. Huse, with recipes and memories from Richard Gonzmart and the Columbia restaurant family (2009)

Ditch of Dreams: The Cross Florida Barge Canal and the Struggle for Florida's Future, by Steven Noll and David Tegeder (2009)

Manatee Insanity: Inside the War over Florida's Most Famous Endangered Species, by Craig Pittman (2010)

Frank Lloyd Wright's Florida Southern College, by Dale Allen Gyure (2010)

Sunshine Paradise: A History of Florida Tourism, by Tracy J. Revels (2011)

Hidden Seminoles: Julian Dimock's Historic Florida Photographs, by Jerald T. Milanich and Nina J. Root (2011)

Treasures of the Panhandle: A Journey through West Florida, by Brian R. Rucker (2011)

Key West on the Edge: Inventing the Conch Republic, by Robert Kerstein (2012)

The Scent of Scandal: Greed, Betrayal, and the World's Most Beautiful Orchid, by Craig Pittman (2012)

Backcountry Lawman: True Stories from a Florida Game Warden, by Bob H. Lee (2013)

Alligators in B-Flat: Improbable Tales from the Files of Real Florida, by Jeff Klinkenberg (2013)